Consumed by Love

A Missionary Handbook
for Priestly and Lay Formation

Mary Elizabeth Kloska
Fiat.+

En Route Books and Media, LLC
Saint Louis, MO

⊕ENROUTE
Make the time

En Route Books and Media, LLC
5705 Rhodes Avenue
St. Louis, MO 63109

Cover credit: Mary Kloska

ISBN-13: 979-8-88870-065-5
Library of Congress Control Number: 2023942635

Copyright © 2023 Mary Kloska

© Dicastero per la Comunicazione - Libreria Editrice Vaticana

All rights reserved.

No part of this booklet may be reproduced, stored in a retrieval system, or transmitted in any form, or by any means, electronic, mechanical, photocopying, or otherwise, without the prior written permission of the author.

This book is consecrated to Our Lady, the greatest missionary of Jesus Christ that ever lived. May Her prayers enflame our hearts with the fire of the Holy Spirit's love so that we, too, may proclaim His Kingdom of Heaven on earth.

-Mary Kloska, July 16, 2023, Feast of Our Lady of Mt. Carmel

Table of Contents

Preface i

Chapter 1: What is a missionary? 1

Chapter 2: The Beginnings of Jesus Christ's Mission 7

Chapter 3: Jesus Christ, the Great Missionary 23

Chapter 4: Mary the Great Missionary and Her Children the Saints 47

Chapter 5: Characteristics of a Missionary 159

Photos 191

Chapter 6: Prayer, Mass, Eucharistic Adoration and the Rosary as the Center of Every Mission (and Missionary Life) 205

Chapter 7: The Missionary as Priest (Victim), Prophet (speaking God's word), and King (choosing God's will and the authority of love) 221

Chapter 8: Church Documents on Mission Life 237

Chapter 9: John Paul II's *Redemptoris Missio: The Mission of the Redeemer* (on the Permanent Validity of the Church's Missionary Mandate) 269

Chapter 10: Mission in My Own Life 333

Mary Kloska's Vocation 351

Preface

'Just Fiat.'

"Here I am, Lord, I have come to do your will." (Hebrews 10:7,9)

This should be the heartbeat of every missionary.

These words from the Old Testament are words that Jesus prayed throughout His entire life as a Jewish boy and man. They were spoken by Samuel in the Old Testament (1 Samuel 3:10) and prayed by the Psalmist in Psalm 40 (vs 8-9), but they were a prophesy foreshadowing Christ's living out of them in perfection with every breath He took. Jesus lived this life of 'Fiat' -and it is only by our own living of 'Fiat' along with Him that we will be able to accomplish God's will and become the saints He created us to be.

One is never a missionary for himself or because of himself. A true missionary is one called by God, formed by God, sent by God to do a work of God for God -a missionary only needs to be surrendered and docile before the Word of God.

God's Word spoke each of us into being. His Word is creative and life giving on its own accord. In Genesis God said, *'Let there be Light.'* (Genesis 1:3) And there was Light. And at the beginning of each of our lives within our mother's womb we were created by God's Word *'Let there be Mary.' 'Let there be John.'* God's word did not create us only once, but recreates us daily through the Holy Spirit -which is His Love. When God calls a person to a work, He infuses the grace into them that they need to accomplish it according to His will. When God sends a person on a mission -He goes before Him to prepare the way. The loving creative will of God is all around us -and all we must do is use our freewill to choose to surrender to His will -and then great miracles will happen.

This choosing of God's will is our 'Fiat' to Him.

I love the word 'Fiat.' My 80+ nieces and nephews used to call me 'Aunty Mary Fiat.' I write this word on all of my icons and pray this word with every beat of my heart. And I cannot tell you how many times people have asked me, *'Now what does your 'fiat' mean?'* This little four letter word has become the beat of my heart, the breath of my life, my strength, my peace, my joy, my protection and the source of deep union with sweet Jesus' Heart.

Fiat.

Its easy to say. Its hard to do at first, although it quickly picks up momentum if you are willing to follow Jesus in *'losing your life to save it.'* (Mt. 16:25)

Fiat is Latin, for *'Let it be done'*. It is a prayer of surrender to God. It is a prayer of letting go of our will -our control -our understanding of what is best for our little world -and handing all back over to the hands of Our Creator where we should have left it in the beginning. Fiat. We pray it in the Our Father when we say, *'Thy will be done'* or *'Fiat voluntas tua.'* And Our Blessed Mother spoke it when the Angel came and asked her to be the Mother of Jesus as she said, *'I am the handmaiden of the Lord, let it be done to me according to Your word,'* or *'Fiat mihi secundum verbum tuum.'* This simple 'Let it be done' - an act of deep surrender of one's life into the Hands of the Father - is something that Jesus lived His entire life (read the Gospel of John and count how many times He said, *'I have not come to do My Own will, but the Will of the One Who sent Me!'*) Jesus said that not all those say, *'Lord, Lord!'* will enter the Kingdom of Heaven -but only those who do the will of His Father." (Mt. 7:21) Jesus did not only live this in His ordinary life, but He especially lived 'Fiat' on the Cross. He said to His disciples, "I am troubled now. Yet what should I say? 'Father, save me from this hour'? But it was for this purpose that I came to this hour."(Jn 12:27)

Fiat.

It can mean so many things as you speak it throughout your day. Like Jesus on the Cross, it can mean:

'Father, I accept Your will.'

'Father, I trust in You.'

'Father, forgive them, they know not what they do.'

'Father, into Your Hands I entrust my spirit, my life, my family, my heart.'

'Father, I thirst for Your will to be done.'

'Father, give me peace.'

'Father, enflame me with Your Love.'

'Father, mercy.'

'Father, You are God and I am not.'

'Father, You know best.'

'Father, please fix this.'

'Father, I love you.'

Not only are we called to hand over the reigns of our lives to the Father in a surrender of 'Fiat,' but we are supposed to do that in joy, as a gift of praise. Jesus followed John 12:27 (above) with verse 28: *"Father, glorify Your Name."* He glorified the Father's Name by doing His will. And in turn, His Heart could share (even mysteriously in the midst of His suffering) in the Father's very joy -the joy of the Father's Presence and Love. Mary's Fiat was followed by the Magnificat -the perpetual song of praise ever being sung in the heart of Her tiny Son within Her Womb. *'My soul magnifies the Lord! -by doing His will!'* And Jesus' 'Fiat' on the Cross was anything but mumbled words offered in a begrudging way. He rejoiced in His surrender to the Father. Even in suffering. For Scripture tells us that *'rejoicing in the Lord must be your strength!'* (Nehemiah 8:10) Sometimes when something bad happens, the best thing we can do is break out in song praising and thanking Jesus for the present cross -making a joyful act of trust in His will -sometimes a chalice difficult to drink at the moment -but ultimately for our good.

The world is one of complaints. Nothing has changed much from the time of the Israelites when God brought them out of Egypt and gave them great gifts and all they did is walk around judging and complaining about the people around them and their new life. Even when God did miracles for them in the midst of tragedy and dire need, they refused to trust, to be thankful, to find the good and His abiding presence in the midst of their lives. The world is no better now. But the true Christian must be joyful and thankful and looking for the good in every person and situation. They must be kind and merciful, patient and full of passionate love for all their neighbors (whether rich or poor.) A true follower of Jesus must live as He did on the Cross -rejoicing in suffering, begging for strength when life seems a little too hard to bear -and trusting Him with the control of all things. Fiat... its amazing when you can turn your first reaction to all things in life to 'Fiat.' Not a begrudging 'Fiat,' -but a joyful 'Fiat.' Full of a joy and peace that comes when one truly decides to turn over their thoughts, words, actions, encounters and relationships every day to the will of the Father. How free we allow God to be in shedding His Love upon us when we simply throw up our arms and say (in rain or sun) *'Whatever YOU want, Father. For You know best.'* Then we allow Him to do great miracles in our lives. And the miracles we need in today's world -are the miracles of true, heroic virtue lived out in mundane, ordinary life. When your heart can complement a neighbor who lives differently than you would choose -simply because you've allowed the Holy Spirit to find the beauty of His presence in their hearts -that's a miracle. When you can rejoice at a hermitage full of dead ants that you have to hand pick out of the carpet -that's a miracle. When you laugh when your car breaks -simply seeing it as God's way of telling you to minister by smiling at the poor repair men at a car-fixing-shop -that's a miracle. When you truly don't care if the deer eat your tomato plants or not -since all is for the glory of God. That's a miracle. And when you can sing alleluia in the middle of the night when your baby wakes up for the 5th time -seeing that it must simply mean that God knows that child (or someone else) needs your prayers -that's a miracle.

You are always safe in imitating Mary and Jesus in their 'Fiat' -in the Cross and in the joy of God's Annunciations of great gifts in your lives. Think about the power of these words in the Our Father -*'Thy Will Be Done'*. If only God's will was done on earth as it is in heaven... what perfect healing and peace and joy would reign here. And we can help to make this happen -by surrendering the little space and time of our lives to the Hands of God -allowing (through 'Fiat') for Him to control and love us in our little piece of eternity within our souls.

Fiat gives peace -because it hands all problems, needs, hopes and desires over to the loving care of the most Perfect, Loving Being that exists. What a great sigh of relief to know that I'm not in charge of the universe. My loving Father is -and I can rest at night trusting Him to take care of everything, as long as I truly have let go of my own will and handed all things over to His care in faith.

Thank You, Jesus, for 'Fiat.' Help us live this in union with You.

Chapter 1

What is a missionary?

St. Mother Teresa said, **"God does not call us to be successful, but to be faithful."** This is very important for every missionary who is called by God to remember.

In 2000 I moved to Robstown, TX to spend a year volunteer teaching in a Jr. High School, along with going through spiritual formation with the founder of S.O.L.T. (The Society of Our Lady of the Most Holy Trinity) in preparation for the following year when I was supposed to travel to Eastern Siberia in Russia with a religious sister and priest to found a mission there. The daily formation that I received from Fr. Flanagan (S.O.L.T.'s founder) concerning what it means to be a missionary for Christ -with Christ -was spiritual food unlike any other I have ever encountered. This priest was a visionary -truly called by God to found an order of missionaries and to form them according to His Own Heart. And my daily conversations with him deeply imprinted a true missionary spirit upon my already mission-oriented vocation.

One thing that Fr. Flanagan really focused on was that a missionary carries out the work of the Lord **simply as a matter of faithfulness -because God has called him to do that.** It is an act of obedience in love offered to God as a sacrifice of praise. A true missionary must keep this focus as the center of his heart as he goes about his work. Many times, a missionary's work will look like Jesus' missionary work -feeding the hungry, teaching the ignorant, healing the sick, etc., -but all of these things find their meaning in Jesus Christ's greatest Missionary Work ever which was being the Savior of the world, redeeming all of humanity through His Passion, Death and Resurrection. Jesus' missionary work often did not seem 'successful'. People accused him of insanity, lawlessness, pride -and it ended with the seeming failure of His torture and death on a Cross. But Christ came *'to do the will of the Father and to accomplish His work'* (John 4:34). He left the fruitfulness of His 'work' (three years preaching and three hours on a Cross) in the hands of the Father. He was faithful and the Holy Spirit then bore fruit as He intended. Each missionary who comes after Christ must remember that his missionary endeavors will often look like Christ's -crucified -and we are called not to look successful to the world, but instead to be faithful to what was asked of us.

The word 'missionary' comes from the Latin word *'missio'* - meaning mission – to be 'sent'. In Scripture we read in John 3:16 that *"God so loved the world that He sent His only Son."* Jesus Himself was sent as the Second Person of the Trinity incarnate on a Mission to humanity to save them. In the Gospel, Jesus calls every soul to *'come after Him'* -to *'learn from Him'* and *'imitate Him.'* (Matthew 11:49) In John 20:21, Jesus said to his apostles, *"As the Father has sent me, so I send you,"* and He repeated something similar in Acts 1:8 saying, *"You will be my witnesses in Jerusalem, throughout Judea and Samaria, and to the ends of the earth."* Through this we see that the very mission of Jesus (Who was sent by the Father) to share His Love and proclaim the Kingdom of God to all people has been handed onto the Church through the Holy Spirit and through the Church to all individual believers in Baptism. In a Catholic context,

Chapter 1: What is a missionary?

it means that being a missionary means being sent by God through the Holy Spirit working in His Church to spread His Love and the Truth of the Gospel and the Catholic Faith to all peoples.

At Baptism every Catholic is given a mission apostolate. It is because through Baptism all Christians are brought into union with Christ as their Head and His Life begins to live through them. Each Baptized soul is called to be a missionary because Christ's way was missionary. All Baptized Catholics are sent to make the name of Jesus known and loved in the world around them and to share the specific gifts that God has given to them to build up the Body of Christ. Through this the soul continues Jesus' mission of *"bringing good news to the poor, liberty to captives, recovery of sight to the blind, freedom for those who are oppressed and to proclaim a year acceptable to the Lord"* as stated in Luke 4:18-19.

The Church is missionary in four different ways. First, the Church has a mission to continually enrich and build up all of Her members. This is done by making the Sacraments available, offering proper preparation and continual education in various aspects of the faith, and in providing opportunities for the faithful to share their individual gifts.

Second, there is the Mission to the ends of the earth where the Gospel of Jesus is shared. This can mean travelling to remote and troubled areas to bring the Good News of Christ.

Third, there is the mission field of transforming the world, which means contributing towards bringing about God's kingdom in our modern time.

Finally, there is the mission of the new evangelization. This is the attempt to reach out to those who may have fallen from the Church or become separated for any number of reasons.

Baptism calls the entire Church into Christ's mission and there are many ways and opportunities for believers to engage in mission according to individual gifts. Believers can discern those gifts and interests through study, experience and prayer and being open to the Holy Spirit. Some are given a special vocation to leave their home and travel to a new and foreign land to bring Christ. Others engage in shorter trips and carry their experiences into their daily lives. The missionary is one who crosses many borders to carry the Word of the Lord to those still waiting to hear it, as well as to those needing encouragement to continue to grow in their faith.

Fr. Flanagan used to teach the S.O.L.T. missionaries in formation that Christ is the Good Shepherd Who incarnates Himself into our humanity and fully identifies with us as 'His sheep.' He would tell us that we are called to do the same thing with the 'sheep' that the Good Shepherd entrusts to us. Father would say that wherever a missionary is sent they must connect with the people – *'eat what they eat, live like they live and die like they die.'* St. Paul similarly preached that as a missionary he had to be *'all things to all people'*:

> "Although I am free in regard to all, I have made myself a slave to all so as to win over as many as possible. To the Jews I became like a Jew to win over Jews; to those under the law I became like one under the law—though I myself am not under the law—to win over those under the law. To those outside the law I became like one outside the law—though I am not

Chapter 1: What is a missionary?

outside God's law but within the law of Christ—to win over those outside the law. To the weak I became weak, to win over the weak. I have become all things to all, to save at least some." (1 Cor 9:19-22)

A missionary is not called to bring a new culture to a people, but instead to enter the culture of the people they serve and to show where Christ is already present among them.

I remember being so overwhelmed when I arrived in Eastern Siberia by the vastness of suffering and needs of the Russian people - they seemed to be crucified in every way, but had suffered mostly from Christ being stolen from their Cross by atheism. Suffering without God is hell. I remember really meditating on Fr. Flanagan's teachings to us and realizing that I could not come and 'fix' every problem in Russia. I could not even 'give God' to them. Instead, I had to come and become like them -to eat what they ate, to live like they lived, to suffer what they suffered -but I was to bring Christ to their Cross. I was simply supposed to allow Jesus Crucified to hang upon my heart in the midst of these people and to show them where He already was present with them in their suffering. I had to simply 'be a resting place for the Holy Spirit' to land and work among the darkness that consumed them from Communism.

If I ever expected to see the fruit of my work in Russia, I would have left within the first few months. A missionary is not supposed to see fruit -many of the greatest saints who were missionaries did not see the vastness of how God used them to spread the Gospel. Instead, I had to be very close to Jesus on the Cross and be content with suffering that darkness (a blindness to what fruit God was bearing) -knowing that my prayer, my sacrifice, my faith and trust and hope and love in the midst of these people was not only 'enough' -it was 'plenty' for God to work with to bring about great miracles in the hearts of those around me.

Often today in 2023 people lose sight of this very important fact: *'We are not called to be 'successful', but instead we are called to be 'faithful."* Often within the Church people equate holiness with success -the people who are most popular, who have the biggest ministries, who are 'out there' on TV and the Internet, those who sell the most books or preach to the most people are considered 'great missionaries.' But God does not judge that way. And most often God will call souls to be saintly missionaries the way He called Mary and Joseph -hidden, silent, simply carrying the presence to Jesus to their families (like to Elizabeth in the Visitation) or to foreigners (like they did in Egypt). It was the prayer and love of Mary and Joseph for Jesus in Bethlehem that allowed the Light of Christ to shine so brightly that poor shepherds and pagan kings were able to find Him and do homage. Often the 'best missionaries' will be like St. Therese of Lisieux (the patron saint of missions) by hiding away and offering prayer and sacrifice from a cloister. In an age where social media and noise gets the most attention, God needs real missionaries of the heart -people who bring the Gospel to others in an incarnated way simply by living holy lives among them. Popularity will not win souls for Christ -instead doing God's will with pure, humble love will conquer hearts. And so that needs to be the central focus of any soul seeking to live a missionary life in their homes, vocations, work or abroad.

Chapter 2

The Beginnings of Jesus Christ's Mission

The Incarnation

"In the beginning was the Word, and the Word was with God, and the Word was God. He was in the beginning with God. All things came to be through him, and without him nothing came to be. What came to be through him was life, and this life was the light of the human race; the light shines in the darkness, and the darkness has not overcome it... The true light, which enlightens everyone, was coming into the world. He was in the world, and the world came to be through him, but the world did not know him. He came to what was his own, but his own people did not accept him. But to those who did accept him he gave power to become children of God, to those who believe in his name, who were born not by natural generation nor by human choice nor by a man's decision but of God. And the Word became flesh and made his dwelling among us, and we saw his glory, the glory as of the Father's only Son, full of grace and truth." (John 1:1-5, 9-14)

Jesus Himself was the first and greatest Missionary that there has ever been. Jesus was the Word, the Second Person of the Trinity, sent in the Incarnation to earth for the work of the Redemption of all Mankind. His entire purpose in coming into the world was to reconcile poor sinners who had been separated from God with God. This mission work of Jesus was not easy -it was the work of redemptive suffering. Here we read at the very beginning of the Gospel of John that *'He came to what was his own, but his own people did not accept him.'* Jesus' selfless love and sacrifice is admirable, and yet it is His rejected, crucified Love that still remained faithful that radiates as a magnificent light to the world. It is normal for a person to sacrifice for the one they love -a mother for her child, a husband for his wife, a friend or a brother or a sister… but it took the example of God Himself made man to teach humanity what heroic love, total selfless love looked like. Jesus' love was his greatest missionary tool -it was a brilliant light that came into a darkness to free those imprisoned by sin, and yet *"this is the verdict, that the light came into the world, but people preferred darkness to light, because their works were evil. For everyone who does wicked things hates the light and does not come toward the light, so that his works might not be exposed. But whoever lives the truth comes to the light, so that his works may be clearly seen as done in God."* (John 3:19-21)

The first seed of Christ's missionary activity was in the action itself of the Incarnation. Simply by taking on flesh -becoming *'like man in all things but sin'* (Hebrews 4:15) -by coming to *'dwell among us'* (John 1:14) -His very existence proclaimed a new path -a great road of hope -for all people. Just Jesus' simple presence within the womb of His Mother Mary -simply His Heartbeat hidden deep inside of her (a Heartbeat that proclaimed *'Fiat- I have come to do your will'* to the Father in every pulsation) -sent forth waves of peace, healing, reconciliation, comfort, joy, hope and grace to all in the world.

Chapter 2: The Beginnings of Jesus Christ's Mission

From the very moment that the Word touched the flesh of man we were given the possibility of eternal life again.

I think it is very appropriate for all missionaries to take some time to meditate on this first missionary activity of Jesus from within His Mother's womb. Because every missionary is going to take their identity from His example. The greatest mission work that any soul can do to proclaim God in the world is to live according to His will, to live in love union with Him -and in this way simply the *presence* of a missionary in any place is a conduit of God's grace to those around him. Our mission as missionaries is to -like baby Jesus - simply create a resting place (by offering to God our hearts) for the Holy Spirit to come and reign on earth. Adam and Eve's 'no' to God was reversed by Our Lady's 'yes' to the angel and Christ's 'yes' to the Father in all things -even unto death on a Cross. And yet we as Christians are able to also undo the 'no' of those who choose sin by offering our hearts and souls to God with unqualified absolute 'fiats' ('yes!') and through this allowing Him to live fully in us and to pour out grace on others through us. Keeping one's heart centered in God brings His presence to those who one encounters. Simply being a presence of love, prayer, sacrifice and holiness in the world is a great missionary work.

There is a story about the Cure of Ars (St. John Vianney). One day the devil told him, *"If there were three such priests as you, my kingdom would be ruined."* See what power the simple existence of one holy soul has to conquer evil, satan, death and sin? Jesus' greatest missionary tools were His 'Fiat' to the Father in all things, His 'meek and humble heart', His Love -especially crucified on the Cross. And these need to be the tools all missionaries take up when they are sent into the world to imitate Him. These are the tools that bring light, grace, healing, peace, joy, conversion and love to others.

The Visitation

Jesus began His mission work from within His Mother's womb - and this is an example to missionaries that one doesn't have to be big, popular, powerful, rich, well-educated or strong in order to be sent by God. Baby Jesus was a little embryo simply growing within His Mother's womb when He first manifested His missionary call by baptizing St. John the Baptist within the womb of St. Elizabeth. *"When Elizabeth heard Mary's greeting, the infant leaped in her womb, and Elizabeth, filled with the holy Spirit, cried out in a loud voice and said, "Most blessed are you among women, and blessed is the fruit of your womb. And how does this happen to me, that the mother of my Lord should come to me? For at the moment the sound of your greeting reached my ears, the infant in my womb leaped for joy. Blessed are you who believed that what was spoken to you by the Lord would be fulfilled."* (Luke 1:41-45)

This passage is followed by a great hymn of praise (the Magnificat) that sprang from Jesus' Heart to His Mother and through Her is proclaimed to the world. It is incredible to see here how from the very beginning of His coming to earth, Jesus wanted to use others to be instruments of His voice. His Mother's voice brought grace from the Infant Jesus to St. Elizabeth and St. John the Baptist, and His Mother's voice proclaimed great glory to the Father -a song that was properly Christ's song praying through Mary.

Chapter 2: The Beginnings of Jesus Christ's Mission

My soul proclaims the greatness of the Lord,
my spirit rejoices in God my Savior,
for he has looked with favor on his lowly servant.
From this day all generations will call me blessed:
the Almighty has done great things for me,
and holy is his Name.
He has mercy on those who fear him
in every generation.
He has shown the strength of his arm,
he has scattered the proud in their conceit.
He has cast down the mighty from their thrones,
and has lifted up the lowly.
He has filled the hungry with good things,
and the rich he has sent away empty.
He has come to the help of his servant Israel
for he has remembered his promise of mercy,
the promise he made to our fathers,
to Abraham and his children forever.
Glory to the Father and to the Son and to the Holy Spirit,
as it was in the beginning, is now, and will be forever. Amen.

After this great manifestation of Christ's power as Savior, the Gospels grow silent about Him until His birth. And yet we can be sure that Jesus -the Great Missionary -continued to actively redeem the world from within His Mother's womb those nine months. But He did this primarily through *His Presence* -His silent life of prayer, surrender, sacrifice and praise.

Missionaries must take this background of Christ's example as their ideal in their own missionary life. Primary to any 'work' one might do for the Lord is the day in and day out life of prayer, surrender, sacrifice and praise that one offers to Him. In that way one's very presence in a mission is redemptive for the people one serves -and it provides the seeds 'planted' through mission work the atmosphere of grace to help them germinate and bear fruit within souls. A missionary's faithful striving towards holiness -even at times just through a silent presence -is fundamental to all mission work.

The Birth of Jesus

As we continue to meditate on the mission work of Jesus even as a baby, we come to the time of His Birth. Yet this is still an example of Him working passively with the Father to proclaim the Kingdom of Heaven. Christ speaks no words -and He performs no signs and wonders on His Own. His first call from the Father at the humble beginning in Bethlehem was that of *being*. The Father arranged the circumstances of His birth -He chose His parents, the place, those who would be His first followers and worshipers (the shepherds and pagan-secular wise men). Jesus simply trusted -passively as a baby does -accepting the will of His Heavenly Father in all things. This is a very important example for missionaries.

God calls each missionary to a specific time and place and people and circumstance. No matter how much a missionary can try to research where they are going or who they will be serving, there is a familiarity with those one is called to serve that only comes through grace and experience. A missionary must allow the Father to call and

Chapter 2: The Beginnings of Jesus Christ's Mission 13

then to place him or her where He desires -and the first days and months of a mission (whether it be a new parish assignment or a new country) must be spent in openness -in prayer -in listening to the Holy Spirit -in accepting where one has been placed. This will help a missionary become incarnate to those he is sent to serve just as Jesus was made incarnate in human flesh in order to serve (and save) us. Often the Lord will ask sacrifices of a missionary just as He asked it of His Son from the very beginning. Jesus was displaced even at His birth -I am sure He did not feel 'at home' in a cave. The housing was less than ideal. And yet He accepted the plan of the Father that was greater than human comforts. In fact, we see how *'He came to his own people and his people did not accept Him.'* (John 1:11) There was concretely *'no room for them in the inn.'* (Lk 2:7) Eventually the rejection of Christ grew to such hatred (even early on) that Herod (the Jewish King) tried to have Jesus killed. (see Matthew 2:16)

All of this does not mean that Jesus' early missionary life was fruitless -in fact the opposite. From the beginning Jesus was showing us the power of sacrifice, of suffering offered in love. It is this Christmas story that generations have meditated on year after year and often that draws souls fallen away from God or steeped in sin back to a life of grace. There is a brilliant radiance of God's pure love seen in this little Child -accepting His Father's will -hated, but Who continues to surrender, trust and Love.

God shows a snippet of this first missionary grace of Christ in the stories of the Gospels of the angels appearing to the poor shepherds announcing His birth and filling the heavens with the song of Gloria. It is seen in a bright star appearing in the sky over the stable and in the moving of the hearts of three wise men from the East who set forth to find the source of all Light. It is seen in Mary and Joseph's own prayerful love -peaceful acceptance of painful circumstances - courageous obedience in fleeing at night to a foreign land to save the Baby Christ Child. Jesus left heaven to give all to mankind on earth. The shepherds left their flocks to find Him. The wisemen left their homes and gave the gifts of great riches to Him. Mary and Joseph obediently left their own people to save Him in their flight into Egypt. And all missionaries are called to imitate these examples in the same way -to give all to the mission of God put before us, to be so distracted by His Love and Calling that the rest of this world simply fades away. This is what Jesus later praised in the temple when he witnessed the poor widow offer to God *'her whole livelihood'* (Mark 12:44). It is also from our places of brokenness, poverty, even seeming failure that we can offer everything to the Lord and then He can use it as the *"grain of wheat that falls to the ground and dies, and produces much fruit"*. (John 12:24)

The Presentation in the Temple

We cannot leave our meditation on the mission work of Christ in His childhood without reflecting on the Presentation in the Temple. At first glance, Jesus seems to be the receiver in this passage of Scripture -He is the one offered and He is the one prophesized about. But in reality -because He is God -He is the source of self-offering and He is the conduit of the Holy Spirit (Trinitarily one with Him) Who prophesizes to the world about His Mission. Mary and Joseph come poor to the temple in obedience to the law. And as a missionary we follow in obedience to where God calls us -poor in ourselves and

Chapter 2: The Beginnings of Jesus Christ's Mission

trusting in Him. They offer a sacrifice of thanksgiving to the Father and that is what a missionary's entire life is to be -a *'sacrifice of praise'*. (Hebrews 13:15) It is through the Holy Family's obedience and heroic offering of all of themselves to the Father in the Presentation that the Holy Spirit finds a portal to fly with grace upon Simeon and Anna enlightening them as to who Baby Jesus was and His future Mission. They speak of His greatness as Savior and yet *from the very beginning* acknowledge that *"Behold, this child is destined for the fall and rise of many in Israel, and to be a sign that will be contradicted"*. And turning to His Mother added, *"And you yourself a sword will pierce) so that the thoughts of many hearts may be revealed."* (Luke 2:34-35) No missionary will be free from a life of suffering with Christ to help save those to whom he is sent. Mary was to suffer not on a physical cross, but **by love, through love** and Joseph hearing these words spoken about His son and wife also felt pierced through by the sword of sorrow. One suffers to the degree one loves and to the degree one love on earth they suffer. Only in heaven is love separate from suffering. And so, to the degree that a missionary loves Christ and is united with Him in His Mission, is the degree that a missionary will be called to **suffer with Christ** for the Salvation of souls. Christ as a sign of contradiction was not far off in time -for only a very short time later Herod would try to kill Him and the Holy Family would have to flee into Egypt.

The Flight into Egypt

God is in control of everything. And the Father could have prevented King Herod from trying to kill His Son. Just as years later He could have prevented Pilate from crucifying Him. But God created humanity free and this freedom is necessary in order for a person to love. Each soul is given a chance to use their freedom to accept God's grace and love into their minds, hearts and lives. And each soul must be given a chance to reject it. Only love chosen freely is truly love. And so, the Father had to allow Herod's heart -hardened by sin -to reject the gift of His Son come to earth as the redeemer. And this rejection of grace affected not only Herod (breaking his relationship with God), but also the Holy Family who had to flee to a pagan country, as well as all of the babies killed and families who suffered under his reign.

This is a good place to be reminded once again that as missionaries chosen, called and sent by God to do a work does not mean that the work will be successful. In fact, when we meditate on Christ's mission work, we see the opposite. Oftentimes those who Christ came to teach, heal and forgive were the very ones who rejected and persecuted Him. But as we quoted Mother Teresa at the beginning of this book *"God does not call us to be successful, but to be faithful."* Baby Jesus came as Love Incarnate to save the world from Hell -and from the very beginning of His Life on earth His Love was rejected. Yet, *"Where sin abounds, grace superabounds."* (Romans 5:20). Through Herod's persecution of the Christ Child, the Holy Family was driven into the pagan country of Egypt to bring the Light of Salvation to them as well. *"See, the LORD is riding on a swift cloud on his way to Egypt; The idols of Egypt tremble before him, the hearts of the Egyptians melt within them."* (Isaiah 19:1) The Holy Family had no visible 'mission work' in Egypt except of living as poor refugees among these pagans, and yet their idols fell -the Gospel was preached

-by every breath the Christ Child took in that foreign land. After King Herod died God sent an angel in a dream to St. Joseph instructing the Holy Family to return to Nazareth. Jesus was God, but the Father did not tell Him directly His will. He used St. Joseph as the proper authority to guide the Holy Family back to safety. So, too, sometimes the Lord will use one's lawful superiors to guide one's mission work, even if it might seem humanly less prudent than one figuring out himself God's will for a mission.

The Finding in the Temple

The Finding in the Temple is the first record we have of Jesus' exterior mission work being revealed. At the time He was still a child -12 years of age -and yet He knew to Whom He belonged. He knew that the Father in Heaven was calling Him to His Temple and sending Him to teach (both the priests as well as his earthly parents a lesson). In this Scripture passage that we read in Luke we see how Jesus knew His identity both as a child of God (when He states He must be in His Father's House) as well as a child of man (as he went home and was obedient to his parents once they found Him). *"Now his parents went to Jerusalem every year at the feast of the Passover. And when he was twelve years old, they went up according to custom; and when the feast was ended, as they were returning, the boy Jesus stayed behind in Jerusalem. His parents did not know it ...After three days they found him in the temple, sitting among the teachers, listening to them and asking them questions; and all who heard him were amazed at his understanding and his answers"* (Lk 2:41-47).

The Catechism of the Catholic Church explains about this text: *"The finding of Jesus in the temple is the only event that breaks the silence of the Gospels about the hidden years of Jesus. Here Jesus lets us catch a glimpse of the mystery of his total consecration to a mission that flows from his divine sonship: 'Did you not know that I must be about my Father's work?' (Lk 2:49)"* (CCC, 534).

Jesus knew that He was 'sent' on a mission and He was faithful in fulfilling it even when it cost misunderstanding and pain to His earthly parents. He remained in the temple opening the Scriptures to the priests and astounding them by His answers. This in itself is not surprising -He was the living Scriptures, as the Word of God Incarnate. As God, He was in His right place. And yet even though He knew the Father had sent Him to earth with a mission, He bowed before the human authority placed before Him in Mary and Joseph and returned home with them to await the perfect timing of the Father for Him to reveal Himself. When one is called to a mission work -there is the call from God, the work itself, as well as the details that have to be according to God's will -these include the place, culture, timing and structure of that work. Jesus was faithful to the Holy Spirit in remaining in His Father's House to give a little preview of His great Mission to the priests (some of whom would remember Him years later when He revealed Himself in the public life) and He was faithful in humbling Himself in following His parents home. Jesus knew that not only His words would teach the Jews (as He did in the Temple), but that His own example would also be an important tool in teaching the Kingdom of Heaven. He lived what He taught. And He not only was teaching the priests on that day when His parents found Him, the entire experience was a pruning of Mary and

Chapter 2: The Beginnings of Jesus Christ's Mission

Joseph's hearts. Jesus' response was not immediately understood - they had to *'ponder it in their hearts.'* (Luke 2:51) Their losing of Jesus for three days was preparation for the three days Jesus would be in the tomb and Mary would be left alone without Him. The loss of Jesus for three days was the very Passion Joseph lived ahead of time, perfecting his Love in the crucible of faith, hope and love.

The Hidden Years

After Jesus' teaching in the temple at the age of 12 the Scriptures grow quiet about His life until His manifestation at His Baptism with St. John the Baptist. These hidden years are years that often will resonate powerfully with one called to give one's entire life as a missionary. When one is called to a mission there is excitement and the initial shock and grace of following the call carries a soul with great enthusiasm. But the greatest missionary work that has been done in the world over the past 2000 years is hidden from the eyes -from the written reports or in more modern times photos of what is being accomplished. The greatest missionary work comes in a missionary's faithfulness to the task God sets before him long after the hullabaloo of his original call. It is in the hidden hours of the night alone in his bedroom where he waters his day's work with prayer and tears -it is in the sore feet from walking to minister to a lost soul or in the growling stomach having missed another meal to hear a repentant sinner's confession. It is in the long afternoons of silence and in the empty response of new parishioners that a missionary is tilling the ground (just through his own faith, hope, trust, patience) for the next planting of spiritual crops. It is in his daily routine that sometimes includes a boredom or disappointment -yet is filled by his faithfulness -that fills up much of the time between one's original call by God and the end of his days of fulfilling it. Jesus was silent and faithful and ordinary for 30 years before His public ministry and He will call a missionary to rest with Him or wait with Him in a hidden life from time to time. In this season of a missionary's life, the gift is in the waiting -as long as one recognizes Who he is waiting with and for. When Jesus is one's companion during the hidden years of ordinary, mundane mission, those years often turn out to bear more fruit than the sensational ones of initial excitement and crowds. There's a lot of ordinary work and tiredness in mission life that calls a soul to ordinary trust and faithfulness. And Jesus gives us an example of how to live this during the hidden years He humbly lived at home. His hidden conversations with His Mother while they ate filled the universe with great graces of salvation, even if no other human would ever know them verbatim. Simply their life of love together fed the world God -light, love, and peace. And sometimes a missionary will be called to have his own hidden conversations with God do the same thing.

    The presence of prayer provides a resting place for God. Often, we hear of violent areas of big cities where a convent of sisters establishes a monastery or a parish begins perpetual adoration. Always the results are that violence slowly leaves that area of the city -peace comes to it. We as missionaries are called to have a profound interior life of prayer with the Lord, so that we can be instruments of peace where we serve -not necessarily through what we do or say, but through our silence, our acceptance of God's will (our 'Fiat'), our faithful love of Him lived out in a daily, humdrum routine. A missionary should never underestimate the power of witness in his work. And even when he thinks his witness is going unnoticed, if he is following the will of God for his life, he can be sure he is leaving the fingerprints of God everywhere he goes.

Chapter 3

Jesus Christ, the Great Missionary

A Call to the Desert

Before anyone is called to a mission, there is a time of discernment leading up to that call. The human heart has to give God room to speak -and so in some way before every missionary is called, there is a time of retreat from which this call springs forth. For some it is a literal retreat they go on to discern what God is asking of their lives. For others the call from God can be traced back to a time where He began taking more and more time of their lives in prayer. But God needs an atmosphere of listening within a soul before He can call a soul to His work. There is a stripping away of this world, a 'desert experience' that one almost always undergoes before God enters in to direct him anew. And we see this in Jesus' life as well. Scripture says:

> "John [the] Baptist appeared in the desert proclaiming a baptism of repentance for the forgiveness of sins. People of the whole Judean countryside and all the inhabitants of Jerusalem were going out to him and were being baptized by him in the Jordan River as they acknowledged their sins.... And it happened in those days that Jesus came from Nazareth of Galilee and was baptized in the Jordan by John. On coming up out of the water he saw the heavens being torn open and the Spirit,

like a dove, descending upon him. And a voice came from the heavens, "You are my beloved Son; with you I am well pleased." (Mark 1:4-5, 9-11)

"Then Jesus came from Galilee to John at the Jordan to be baptized by him. John tried to prevent him, saying, "I need to be baptized by you, and yet you are coming to me?" Jesus said to him in reply, "Allow it now, for thus it is fitting for us to fulfill all righteousness." Then he allowed him. After Jesus was baptized, he came up from the water and behold, the heavens were opened [for him], and he saw the Spirit of God descending like a dove [and] coming upon him. And a voice came from the heavens, saying, "This is my beloved Son, with whom I am well pleased." (Matthew 3:13-17)

Here -at the beginning of Jesus' Great Mission -the first place that He goes is into the desert. As I said, in order to prepare for a mission a soul must enter a sort of desert time with the Lord -he must leave what is ordinary in the world with all of the distractions and enter in a time of barrenness -where he can pray and allow God to manifest His will to him. Each mission is different and each brand of sheep one is called to guide is different. This is true whether one is called to serve in a foreign country or is simply being called to change from parish to parish within one's own diocese or even simply to a new ministry within one's present locale -each change in one's place of vocation and the people he is called to serve is unique involving unique souls with a specific need and so to prepare one needs to take a step back into the desert with God to listen to Him.

Chapter 3: Jesus Christ, the Great Missionary

A missionary is a shepherd -and often people assume that when you are a shepherd the 'work' is the same wherever you go. But when you begin to learn about shepherds you come to see that being a shepherd in Israel is very different than in Ireland -the terrain is different, the dangers are different, and the needs of the sheep are different. In fact, worldwide there are over 1000 distinct breeds of sheep. Each breed looks differently, behaves differently and has different needs. Some breeds are better for meat, some are better for wool, some are very strong and durable in arid places, some are more friendly as pets, some are more social and some are better alone. Each breed has its own gifts and weaknesses and their shepherds need to know these particular things in order to shepherd them well. The same is true for souls. Christ is the Good Shepherd and missionaries are called to imitate Him in this Goodness -yet not all of His sheep are the same. I see this clearly in my own life -the sheep I tend in Africa are very different than Pakistan or Russia -and they differ greatly than the souls I tend in my family or from the wealthy elite in big cities. As a shepherd after the heart of Christ, a missionary must know the breed of sheep assigned to him -and this happens by taking time away with the Lord in the desert before his work even begins in order to listen to Him teach about the mission that is being laid before him.

Jesus Himself did this by going into the desert. And when he reached the desert, He found John the Baptist baptizing in the River Jordan and preparing souls through a call of repentance for the coming of the Messiah. Jesus came into the world as the Great Shepherd but He also always was the humble Lamb of His Father. We see this in the meeting He had with St. John the Baptist. Jesus was greater than John -He was God Himself. And yet, He respected the work that the Father had assigned to John to prepare souls for Christ and Jesus wanted to lead souls through this process determined by the Father (of meeting John, being baptized and converted and then receiving the words of Christ) through His own example. And so, Jesus came to be baptized not because He needed to repent but because He had to lead souls to repentance. And after humbling Himself and going into the water He came out and the Holy Spirit announced to the people present through His Presence as a Dove and in a loud Voice from the Father the message: *"You are my beloved Son; with you I am well pleased."* In this the Spirit and the Father conferred upon Jesus His mission and confirmed to those around Him that He indeed was sent from heaven. This, in turn, opened their hearts to learn from Him.

The work that a missionary does is never from himself. It always has to have its root and center in the Trinity. In fact, I would argue that the more one puts himself into the work, the less power it has to change hearts. A missionary is called by God and sent by God to be an instrument of God. The work is God's. The missionary is the instrument. A missionary is called to be humble like Christ, and to baptize his work into Christ by following Him in lowering himself into the waters and then following Him out -allowing the Holy Spirit to go before him to lead and guide him and to then go behind him to finish the work he began -to make the seeds of the Kingdom of Heaven sprout forth. The Holy Spirit will sometimes be visible to those he serves (as He was in the dove) to make them believe in the supernaturality of his message. He will also sometimes move invisibly around the missionary -ever so delicately calling souls to follow in his footsteps which follow the footsteps of Christ.

Prayer and Spiritual Warfare

Immediately after the Baptism of Jesus in Matthew, Chapter 3 we read about His time of Fasting, Prayer and Temptation in the Desert in Chapter 4. The same Holy Spirit that led Jesus into the desert to humble Himself in Baptism and Who manifested His Identity through the Dove and the Father's booming voice, then led Jesus to the desert to prepare for His mission through intense prayer, fasting and even temptation. Imagine the power of God able to work in the ministries of missionaries all over the world if they -before embarking on any mission -first allowed the Holy Spirit to lead them to a desert retreat to pray, fast and even fight satan through temptations. In doing this Jesus was preparing Himself for His future mission - but also, He was tilling the soil of the souls He would encounter -He was fighting satan for them (fighting off demons that would tempt them to walk away aloof of His message of repentance and love). He was preparing the world through being an instrument of suffering prayer to earn grace for the future mission.

This reminds me of how Fr. Jim Flanagan -the founder of SOLT (the Society of Our Lady of the Most Holy Trinity) always imitated Jesus in going forth to start new missions. And since I was involved in founding the Russian mission, I will share my experience of this there. I was told that before SOLT ever embarked on a mission to Russia, Fr. Flanagan visited Russia. He spent the time of his visit there sitting in a chapel praying -from early morning until late at night. Those he was visiting asked him if he wanted to travel around to see the problems of the area or to experience the people and culture in order to discern the greatest needs of the people. But he refused. He was with God. I forget if he spent days or weeks in Russia (I believe it was in Moscow), but upon the end of his time there he exited the chapel and gave a total explanation of the spiritual situation of Russia that flabbergasted those he was visiting. He knew everything about the people, their wounds and the problems of Russia - but he had learned it from the Lord in Adoration. And he knew the solution was above all, prayer. He told me before I left for Russia that the greatest work I would do for Russia -in Russia -was being a presence of prayer.

I also saw the power of prayer in a mission the first time I visited Moscow in 1994 when I was only a Junior in high school. Walking down the street one day I had a handful of miraculous medals and when I approached a few gossiping babushkas in the park offering them they fell on their knees kissing my hands saying 'spaceeba - thank you' and asking for more. Their reaction seemed worth much more than the small gesture of prayerful kindness I had offered them. But at that time I reflected on how for many years following the apparitions of Our Lady of Fatima the world has followed Her instruction praying for 'the conversion of Russia' and this filled the country with great grace -as if a spiritual gasoline -so that many years later when I offered one little spark of God's Love, a great fire exploded in the hearts of these people who had been prepared by many years of people's prayers for them.

And so, we see Jesus setting this example from the onset. Before He embarked on His public ministry, He went to the desert to pray

Chapter 3: Jesus Christ, the Great Missionary

and fast -and ultimately to fight satan away from souls so that His words could take root. We read in Matthew 4 how satan approached Him and tried to dissuade Him from the humble path of redemption that the Father had sent Him on – and we read how Jesus answered each temptation courageously and powerfully through the Holy Spirit's words of Scripture:

> *"Then Jesus was led by the Spirit into the desert to be tempted by the devil. He fasted for forty days and forty nights, and afterwards he was hungry. The tempter approached and said to him, "If you are the Son of God, command that these stones become loaves of bread." He said in reply, "It is written: 'One does not live by bread alone, but by every word that comes forth from the mouth of God.'" Then the devil took him to the holy city, and made him stand on the parapet of the temple, and said to him, "If you are the Son of God, throw yourself down. For it is written: 'He will command his angels concerning you' and 'with their hands they will support you, lest you dash your foot against a stone.'" Jesus answered him, "Again it is written, 'You shall not put the Lord, your God, to the test.'" Then the devil took him up to a very high mountain, and showed him all the kingdoms of the world in their magnificence, and he said to him, "All these I shall give to you, if you will prostrate yourself and worship me." At this, Jesus said to him, "Get away, Satan! It is written: 'The Lord, your God, shall you worship and him alone shall you serve.'" Then the devil left him and, behold, angels came and ministered to him."* (1-11)

Jesus is Sent to Begin His Work

It is important to note that in the following verses of Matthew 4, Jesus again is following the promptings of the Holy Spirit. Absolutely everything in His mission is led by the Holy Spirit -everything is a matter of Jesus being *sent* by God to do His will. His location is chosen by God. And those who will help Him are also chosen by God. And in this, everything in Jesus Christ's life is a fulfillment of Scripture and God's eternal plan for mankind.

> (Matthew 4: 13-17) *"He left Nazareth and went to live in Capernaum by the sea, in the region of Zebulun and Naphtali, that what had been said through Isaiah the prophet might be fulfilled: "Land of Zebulun and land of Naphtali, the way to the sea, beyond the Jordan, Galilee of the Greligious entiles, the people who sit in darkness have seen a great light, on those dwelling in a land overshadowed by death light has arisen." From that time on, Jesus began to preach and say, "Repent, for the kingdom of heaven is at hand."*

After Christ's time in the desert, He went forth and chose twelve men to join His mission work as Apostles -they would learn from Him and carry on His work after His death, passing it on to those who came after them and on down the Apostolic line until today. Jesus realized even though the Father sent Him alone to be the Redeemer of the world, He needed a team formed by His teaching, example, prayer and love in order to reach the masses. Regardless of how solitary one feels called to live in his own vocation and mission,

Chapter 3: Jesus Christ, the Great Missionary

others are needed in order to fulfill the fullness of the will of God. St. Anthony of Egypt the great Hermit of the desert needed a few brothers to stay near him, bring him food and to minister to the people who flocked to the desert to see him. St. Damian of Molokai exiled alone to the Hawaiian island of lepers needed brothers to send materials and even one to come near on a ship to hear his Confession yelled across the waters. Founders of great missions needed to form others in their spirituality and to help them with their work just as Christ the Great Missionary and Shepherd did. St. Vincent de Paul had a mission to the poor, but he needed a whole band of priests to help him -as well as a religious sister with a similar spiritual heart to form women to care for the girls. It was Jesus Christ Himself who modeled for all missionaries the communal nature of being sent by God on a mission. People are needed to help with work (preaching, caring for the poor, etc.), people are needed to fund missions (money has to be sent to help with financial needs), people are needed to support missions in prayer (prayers for protection, wisdom of discernment, prayers for strength and for fruitfulness). There are many ways a community can surround a missionary to work with him as a team -but we see in Christ calling Apostles and enrolling disciples (both men and women) to aid in His work, He is showing an example of humility and generosity that all missionaries are to follow in calling forth others to partake of the work with them.

Three Years Teaching, Calling to Repentance, Forgiving Sins and Healing

After His Baptism, 40-day retreat in the desert (where He conquered satan's temptations) and choosing His Apostles, Jesus embarked on His 'Mission' to teach the world that the 'Kingdom of God is at hand.' The first public miracle that Jesus performed was at the Wedding at Cana. Immediately Christ launched into the ordinary life of the Israelite people. Weddings are ordinary situations and the married couple found themselves in a very difficult temporal predicament (they had no wine). Jesus came to redeem man from sin, save him from hell and offer to him eternal life. And yet He did not begin His public ministry simply throwing away all that was earthly and imposing a divine reality on the people. Instead, He began in their ordinary, earthly reality (something familiar to them) -He took concern over their temporal problems -and He helped them. But there was a mysterious Divine Thread woven through all that He said and did. He entered time to raise their eyes and hearts to heaven. The people at the Wedding at Cana could not have understood the deep spiritual implications of what was being done and foreshadowed around them. They had no wine -they filled empty jars with water - and then they had wine. But 2000 years later we can look back at this first miracle of Christ's Mission and see what the Holy Spirit was doing and how He was preparing the world through this miracle for salvation. Here in Cana -where they watched Jesus give them wine - they actually were receiving much deeper gifts. Jesus was giving His Mother to us as an intercessor through the example of their conversation. He was revealing Her role as the New Eve as He called Her

Chapter 3: Jesus Christ, the Great Missionary

Woman (the same word used in Genesis as well as the name He called Her under the Cross). He was also foreshadowing the Mass - where He would then take wine and turn it into His Precious Blood. The Holy Spirit was weaving all of Salvation History through the words and gestures of Jesus in this one incident -and yet Jesus started with the ordinary. *"On the third day there was a wedding in Cana in Galilee, and the mother of Jesus was there. Jesus and his disciples were also invited to the wedding. When the wine ran short, the mother of Jesus said to him, "They have no wine.""* (John 2:1-3) And He entered the ordinary and brought it to the Divine. Here at the beginning of His public ministry, He is already speaking about 'His Hour' when wine would be changed to Blood *'which will be shed on behalf of many for the forgiveness of sins.'* (Mt 26:28)

> *"[And] Jesus said to her, "Woman, how does your concern affect me? My hour has not yet come." His mother said to the servers, "Do whatever he tells you." Now there were six stone water jars there for Jewish ceremonial washings, each holding twenty to thirty gallons. Jesus told them, "Fill the jars with water." So they filled them to the brim. Then he told them, "Draw some out now and take it to the headwaiter." So they took it. And when the headwaiter tasted the water that had become wine, without knowing where it came from (although the servers who had drawn the water knew), the headwaiter called the bridegroom and said to him, "Everyone serves good wine first, and then when people have drunk freely, an inferior one; but you have kept the good wine until now." Jesus did this as the*

beginning of his signs in Cana in Galilee and so revealed his glory, and his disciples began to believe in him." (John 2:4-11)

Jesus followed this miracle with three years of a powerful ministry that eventually would lead to His death. He served the people that the Father drew to Him through three primary ways of teaching, forgiving their sins and healing them. Jesus was ultimately sent to earth to plant the Kingdom of Heaven on earth -to reconcile man to God not only by offering eternal life to those who died, but by teaching them a divine, heavenly way of living while still here on earth. The first way that Jesus prepared the hearts of those around Him was by teaching anew the ways and laws of God's kingdom. He did it in a brilliant way that inspired love of God and true sorrow for sins, as opposed to terror of punishment. He called people to repent of their sins by inspiring them to desire to live righteously. We see examples of this all throughout the Gospels. In Matthew 19:16-22 a rich, young man is drawn to Jesus and asks 'What must I do to inherit eternal life.' A desire had been planted in his heart -and Jesus first called him to follow the commandments -but when the Holy Spirit stretched the young man to search deeper saying, 'I have done all of this -what else' Jesus called him to a higher plane of closeness to Himself by saying, *'If you wish to be perfect, go sell what you have and give it to the poor and then come follow me...'* Jesus inspired Zacchaeus in Luke 19:1-10 to climb a tree to see Him and by coming to his house for a meal inspired him to say that he would change his dishonest ways and repay those he had cheated. Jesus in Luke 7:36-50 inspired a sinful woman to repent of her sins so fully that she washed His feet with her tears. Numberless times in Scripture Jesus said the powerful

Chapter 3: Jesus Christ, the Great Missionary

words, 'Your sins are forgiven you.' Jesus first rooted out sin before bestowing physical healing on people -putting an emphasis on spiritual healing over the importance of physical healing.

The healing miracles of Jesus -as well as His other miracles such as multiplying bread and fish -were meant to inspire confidence in the people around him in the power of God's love for them. He had to establish His authority over life and death -health and sickness -heaven and earth -in order for hearts to be opened to receive the gift of His teaching and then ultimately, the gift of salvation. When Jesus taught it was to show the people the right way of living and to inspire love in their hearts -a love that humbled them and a love that drove them to imitate Him.

In the Sermon on the Mount we see Jesus' powerful gifting of Heavenly Wisdom to the world. He is clear in teaching the importance of not judging, of forgiving, of not being angry or lustful, in not being attached to this world or money -but He also stretches His listeners to contemplate and trust in the heavenly wisdom of God's providence, love and often supernatural grace. Most profoundly we see this in His teachings of the Beatitudes and being salt and light in Matthew 5:3-16, as well as His teaching on Dependence on God in Matthew 6: 25-34:

> *"Blessed are the poor in spirit, for theirs is the kingdom of heaven.*
> *Blessed are they who mourn, for they will be comforted.*
> *Blessed are the meek, for they will inherit the land.*
> *Blessed are they who hunger and thirst for righteousness, for they will be satisfied.*

Blessed are the merciful, for they will be shown mercy.

Blessed are the clean of heart, for they will see God.

Blessed are the peacemakers, for they will be called children of God.

Blessed are they who are persecuted for the sake of righteousness, for theirs is the kingdom of heaven. Blessed are you when they insult you and persecute you and utter every kind of evil against you [falsely] because of me. Rejoice and be glad, for your reward will be great in heaven. Thus they persecuted the prophets who were before you."

"You are the salt of the earth. But if salt loses its taste, with what can it be seasoned? It is no longer good for anything but to be thrown out and trampled underfoot. You are the light of the world. A city set on a mountain cannot be hidden. Nor do they light a lamp and then put it under a bushel basket; it is set on a lampstand, where it gives light to all in the house. Just so, your light must shine before others, that they may see your good deeds and glorify your heavenly Father."

"Therefore I tell you, do not worry about your life, what you will eat [or drink], or about your body, what you will wear. Is not life more than food and the body more than clothing? Look at the birds in the sky; they do not sow or reap, they gather nothing into barns, yet your heavenly Father feeds them. Are not you more important than they? Can any of you by worrying add a single moment to your life-span? Why are you

anxious about clothes? Learn from the way the wild flowers grow. They do not work or spin. But I tell you that not even Solomon in all his splendor was clothed like one of them. If God so clothes the grass of the field, which grows today and is thrown into the oven tomorrow, will he not much more provide for you, O you of little faith? So do not worry and say, 'What are we to eat?' or 'What are we to drink?' or 'What are we to wear?' All these things the pagans seek. Your heavenly Father knows that you need them all. But seek first the kingdom [of God] and his righteousness, and all these things will be given you besides. Do not worry about tomorrow; tomorrow will take care of itself. Sufficient for a day is its own evil."

Christ sets a powerful example for all missionaries in the order in which He established His Mission of Salvation, forming the Catholic Church and planting the Kingdom of Heaven in hearts on earth. He begins by calling people to turn away from evil -to repent of what they have done wrong and to seek reconciliation with God (and those men they may have wronged). He is very just in His definition of right and wrong -but Jesus is also very generous with His mercy to repentant hearts. Missionaries must be this way as well. We must proclaim truth -both 'in and out of season.' We must never bend right to wrong for the sake of making people comfortable or happy in earthly terms. We must present sin as sin -but do it in a way that inspires a desire to change evil ways to good and clear of anything that would intimate or scare a soul from accepting the mercy of God for his sins. When one is walking through a swampy area of nature, it is very important to find solid footholds made of rock where one can safely step without sinking. In our journey to heaven while on earth, it is similarly important for a soul to find solid footholds of truth where they can step as they travel through this wishy-washy world of sin. A missionary must present truth as truth in a very clear way -and yet with a strength that equally offers the gentle peace of mercy to those who may have fallen on an erroneous path and desire to step back into a right relationship with God and man.

As a missionary teaches about God's ways and the sinful ways of satan and fallen man, he must provide a way for those he is addressing to turn back to God. If the missionary is a priest -he must make sacramental confession very available for his people so that the obstacle of sin can be quickly wiped from those who are repentant -making room in their souls for more grace to be at work within them. Teaching right and wrong is something parents should do from the youngest ages of their children -but to those who weren't raised with a solid grasp of right living -this is the first work of a missionary: to teach the commandments of God -basic right and wrong. We do this with children and sometimes we must do it with adults: "*We don't lie. We don't steal. We don't cheat. We don't hurt people. We don't gossip. We don't act selfish. We don't participate in impure things. We pray every day. We go to Mass on Sunday. We apologize. We forgive. Etc.,*" By a missionary helping a soul be free of sin, they are freeing that soul from the grasp and influence of satan -making room for the great waterfall of grace that a soul is offered in Baptism to flourish freely in and through them.

After Jesus taught about sin, called people to conversion, forgave them, healed their hearts -He offered an alternative to sin -mainly a way of living according to the Wisdom of the Holy Spirit. This is what we see in His Sermon on the Mount and in all of the parables He told. He is speaking mysteriously to the human heart teaching as if to children -in simple ways -so that heaven can take root in souls. He not only teaches about the right way to live, but He teaches those who gather around Him the right way to pray… humbly, generously, intimately with His Father in Heaven. He teaches about Himself trying to instill confidence in all souls in His mission of Salvation. He says, "I am the Good Shepherd," (John 10:11) "I am the Light of the World," (John 8:12) "I am the Way, the Truth and the Life," (John 14:6) "I am the Bread of Life," (John 6:35) etc., -He wants those He serves to see Him as a human Brother and yet, also as their God Who is all-powerful and all-loving.

A missionary -regardless if he is working among pagans or working among Catholics in a normal parish -must imitate Christ in His order of work. A missionary must first help those he serves rid themselves of sin -he must be an instrument of healing -he must be a teacher of truth -he must inspire those he serves to prayer and through all of this, he will lead those sheep entrusted to him to God.

Jesus' Mission of the Cross

The Passion and Death of Jesus -as well as the power of His Life-giving Resurrection -cast its shadow from all of Jesus' life and ministry on earth. As a baby He suffered from mankind and for mankind. In the temple at age 12 He already was offering glimpses of the resurrected light of heaven on those who were receiving His words to their hearts. And yet, the apex of Jesus' mission on earth was in the actual gift of Himself in the Eucharist lived out fully in His

Passion, Death and Resurrection. Jesus' mission of the Cross was the meaning behind all of the words and actions He lived the years leading up to Calvary. Jesus' example of forgiveness, trust in His Father, obedience, surrender, offering and prayer in His Passion and Death was a perfect culmination of His life -it was a completion of His healings and forgiveness -and it was an incarnation of the message He taught. The greatest 'Mission' Christ had was Redemption won for us -beginning in Gethsemane and completed by His last breath on Golgotha. The Spring of Life that came from His pierced side visible in Blood and Water spoke louder than any word the Word had spoken on earth. The Resurrection silenced the world -because it was God's last word to satan and his kingdom of ruin. It was an open invitation to all souls in all times to turn from evil and to 'taste and see the goodness of the Lord' eternally by accepting Jesus Christ's gift of Salvation.

Missionaries themselves are not saviors. Jesus is the only Savior and any missionary called into the work of salvation with Christ is called simply to help create a path for souls to travel into the Heart of Jesus -Who is the Savior. A missionary brings souls to God -Who then provides all that is needed for salvation. And yet, because missionaries are part of the Church and make up the 'Body of Christ', as they teach Jesus' words and do His work, they must also live by His example -and that example is one of crucified love. To be a Christian means to be grafted onto the Body of Christ (*"I am the Vine, you are the branches..." (John 15:5)* and to the degree one becomes one with Christ is the degree He will suffer with Him for His sheep. Jesus said, *"I came not to be served but to serve, and to give My life as a ransom for many."* (Matthew 20:28) and this total emptying of self is something every missionary is called to live with Christ. The more a missionary empties himself before God for his people, the greater work the Holy Spirit can do with Christ through him. In essence, a missionary is called to be the very Face of Jesus to all those around him. Jesus commanded us: *"Remain in me, as I remain in you. Just as a branch cannot bear fruit on its own unless it remains on the vine, so neither can you unless you remain in me. I am the vine, you are the branches. Whoever remains in me and I in him will bear much fruit, because without me you can do nothing."* (Jn 15:4-5) Jesus does not say, 'Without me you cannot do very much…' He says, **"Without me you can do <u>nothing</u>."** For this reason, it is critical that every missionary draws personally close to Christ and tries to imitate Him in all things. In fact, He must *become another Christ*. St. Teresa of Avila knew this very well as she prayed:

> *Christ has no body but yours,*
> *No hands, no feet on earth but yours,*
> *Yours are the eyes with which He looks*
> *Compassion on this world,*
> *Yours are the feet with which He walks to do good,*
> *Yours are the hands, with which He blesses all the world.*
> *Yours are the hands, yours are the feet,*
> *Yours are the eyes, you are His body.*
> *Christ has no body now but yours,*
> *No hands, no feet on earth but yours,*
> *Yours are the eyes with which he looks*
> *compassion on this world.*

Christ has no body now on earth but yours.
— St. Teresa of Ávila

Christ Sends the Apostles and Disciples

The last thing the Jesus does before returning to heaven after His passion, death and resurrection is to send others to continue His work. We see this immediately in the Resurrection accounts with the women disciples -as He sends them (and specifically Mary Magdalene) to proclaim His resurrection to the others. He then appears to the incredulous apostles to confirm their faith and then to send them to the world. *"As the Father sent me so I send you…"* (Jn 20:21)

> *"Then Jesus approached and said to them, "All power in heaven and on earth has been given to me. Go, therefore, and make disciples of all nations, baptizing them in the name of the Father, and of the Son, and of the holy Spirit, teaching them to observe all that I have commanded you. And behold, I am with you always, until the end of the age."* (Mt 28:18-20)

He speaks to Peter about the primacy of love and the great responsibility of those sent by His Love to imitate Him in a life of crucified Love.

> *"When they had finished breakfast, Jesus said to Simon Peter, "Simon, son of John, do you love me more than these?" He said to him, "Yes, Lord, you know that I love you." He said to him, "Feed my lambs." He then said to him a second time, "Simon,*

Chapter 3: Jesus Christ, the Great Missionary

son of John, do you love me?" He said to him, "Yes, Lord, you know that I love you." He said to him, "Tend my sheep." He said to him the third time, "Simon, son of John, do you love me?" Peter was distressed that he had said to him a third time, "Do you love me?" and he said to him, "Lord, you know everything; you know that I love you." [Jesus] said to him, "Feed my sheep. Amen, amen, I say to you, when you were younger, you used to dress yourself and go where you wanted; but when you grow old, you will stretch out your hands, and someone else will dress you and lead you where you do not want to go." He said this signifying by what kind of death he would glorify God. And when he had said this, he said to him, "Follow me." (Jn 21:15-19)

After conferring His Mission upon His disciples, He instructed them to return to the city, gather together, wait and pray. Their hearts needed this time of preparation in order to receive the Holy Spirit and then do all that He instructed them. God is outside of time, but man lives according to time while on earth and God respects the slow, natural growth process of man. Jesus had said to them:

"I have much more to tell you, but you cannot bear it now. But when he comes, the Spirit of truth, he will guide you to all truth. He will not speak on his own, but he will speak what he hears, and will declare to you the things that are coming. He will glorify me, because he will take from what is mine and declare it to you. Everything that the Father has is mine; for this reason

I told you that he will take from what is mine and declare it to you." (John 16:12-15)

"*He presented himself alive to them by many proofs after he had suffered, appearing to them during forty days and speaking about the kingdom of God. While meeting with them, he enjoined them not to depart from Jerusalem, but to wait for "the promise of the Father about which you have heard me speak; for John baptized with water, but in a few days you will be baptized with the holy Spirit."* (Acts 1:3-5)

"*When they entered the city they went to the upper room where they were staying, Peter and John and James and Andrew, Philip and Thomas, Bartholomew and Matthew, James son of Alphaeus, Simon the Zealot, and Judas son of James. All these devoted themselves with one accord to prayer, together with some women, and Mary the mother of Jesus, and his brothers."* (Acts 1:13-14)

In this, He instructs them to gather and pray before going out (go into Jerusalem and pray, waiting for the gift of the Spirit) -and in this teaching all missionaries who would go forth to the end of time to do as He did -retreat, pray and then obey the Father's Mission -even unto death.

He promises them help -not only in the gift of His Mother's help (as He offers Her to John under cross in John 19:25-27[1]), the Holy Spirit's help *("I will ask the Father, and he will give you another Advocate to be with you always, the Spirit of truth."* -Jn 14:16-17), but also His own presence (in the Eucharist and mystically in His Church – *"I will not leave you orphans; I will come to you. In a little while the world will no longer see me, but you will see me, because I live and you will live."* Jn 14:18-19 And *'I am with you always until the end of the world.'* Mt 28:20) and then He entrusts them into the hands of the Father's will.

---

[1] "Standing by the cross of Jesus were his mother and his mother's sister, Mary the wife of Clopas, and Mary of Magdala. When Jesus saw his mother and the disciple there whom he loved, he said to his mother, "Woman, behold, your son." Then he said to the disciple, "Behold, your mother." And from that hour the disciple took her into his home."

Chapter 4

Mary the Great Missionary and Her Children the Saints

The Blessed Mother

"During those days Mary set out and traveled to the hill country in haste to a town of Judah, where she entered the house of Zechariah and greeted Elizabeth. When Elizabeth heard Mary's greeting, the infant leaped in her womb, and Elizabeth, filled with the Holy Spirit, cried out in a loud voice and said, "Most blessed are you among women, and blessed is the fruit of your womb. And how does this happen to me, that the mother of my Lord should come to me? For at the moment the sound of your greeting reached my ears, the infant in my womb leaped for joy. Blessed are you who believed that what was spoken to you by the Lord would be fulfilled." (Luke 1:39-45)

From the moment that Our Lady gave Her 'Fiat' and became the Mother of God, She also became a missionary with Him. Immediately after we read about the Annunciation in the first chapter of Luke's Gospel, we read about Our Lady being sent to Her cousin Elizabeth. Mary became a Tabernacle of Christ as He became incarnate within Her womb, and then She carried Him as a Monstrance to the family of Her cousin Elizabeth. Mary was so full of God that simply at the sound of Her voice the Holy Spirit sprang from the Heart of the Infant Christ within her to St. John the Baptist in the womb of Elizabeth. And when Mary was honored by Elizabeth's proclamation *'Blessed are you who believed that what was spoken to you by the Lord would be fulfilled,'* She immediately prophesized the greatness of God by singing Her Prayer of the Magnificat.

> *"And Mary said: "My soul proclaims the greatness of the Lord; my spirit rejoices in God my savior. For he has looked upon his handmaid's lowliness; behold, from now on will all ages call me blessed. The Mighty One has done great things for me, and holy is his name. His mercy is from age to age to those who fear him. He has shown might with his arm, dispersed the arrogant of mind and heart. He has thrown down the rulers from their thrones but lifted up the lowly. The hungry he has filled with good things; the rich he has sent away empty. He has helped Israel his servant, remembering his mercy, according to his promise to our fathers, to Abraham and to his descendants forever." Mary remained with her about three months and then returned to her home."* (Luke 1:46-56)

Mary not only proclaimed the greatness of the Lord, but she followed it up by the action of showing His great love for Elizabeth, Zachariah and little John by remaining among them -as a presence of prayer and service -to show them His Love through action.

The next time we see Our Lady in Scripture is in the birth of Jesus in Bethlehem. Once again, She and Joseph are **sent** by God to the town of David. They are not received by the townspeople and have

Chapter 4: Mary the Great Missionary and Her Children the Saints

to give birth to Jesus in a cave, and yet they graciously receive the shepherds and the wise men sharing the gift of God in the little Savior with them. After this Mary and Joseph together are **sent** to present Jesus in the temple and as they bring Him in the Holy Spirit takes hold of Simeon the Priest and Anna the Prophetess -the mission of Mary and Joseph to share Christ with them moves into their mission to proclaim to 'all who came to the temple' the greatness of God in sending Jesus into the world. Simeon sang his canticle of praise to God for allowing him to see the promised Messiah and Anna *'gave thanks to God and spoke about the child to all who were awaiting the redemption of Jerusalem...'* (Luke 2:38)

When Baby Jesus' life is threatened by King Herod, the Holy Family is sent on a mission into Egypt. Yes, this was in order to save the Christ Child from death -but also to proclaim the kingdom of heaven even in the land of pagans.

Mary is again sent on mission at the Wedding at Cana -this time prompted by the Holy Spirit to bring the wedding couple and their problems to Jesus and to teach them that if they entrust everything to Him and obey Him in all things, He will take care of their needs. Mary continues Her mission as the helpmate of Christ throughout His public life and unto the Cross -faithfully standing beneath Him on Calvary and taking John into Her Heart as Jesus asks Her to be the disciple's Mother. As Simeon prophesized at the Presentation, Our Lady's Mission included a *'sword piercing Her Heart'* (Luke 2:35), for one suffers as much as one loves and no one loved Christ Crucified more than His Immaculate Mother. Mary surely witnesses the Resurrection and then is left on earth to continue Her mission work of reconciling man with God simply by teaching them in a motherly way (and by example) what it means to be His perfect disciple. It is a great miracle that Mary remained on earth after the Ascension -for She who is one flesh and one heart with Jesus would naturally be drawn into Heaven with Him. But He leaves Her to complete Her Mission with the early Church -to pray with the Apostles for the coming of the Spirit and to be present to them as they begin the work of evangelizing the world.

The Blessed Mother's missionary work did not end as She was assumed into heaven body and soul. For the last 2000 years She has appeared to holy men and women in the Church continuing to try to reconcile sinners with their Redeemer and God. She has appeared on every continent and Her name has been called upon in every language by Her spiritual children on earth striving to find their way back to Jesus after losing Him. Millions have prayed, *"Holy Mary, Mother of God, pray for us sinners now and at the hour of our death."* Mary is a missionary both as a model of how each soul is called to imitate Christ in virtue, as well as a Mother who wins grace for sinners to be reconciled to God by Her own faithful Fiat to His will and through Her prayer for all of us.

St. John Paul II explains Mary's Role as Missionary, Mother and Intercessor in His encyclical Redemptoris Mater (paragraph 6):

> *"...The Council emphasizes that the Mother of God is already the eschatological fulfillment of the Church: "In the most holy Virgin the Church has already reached that perfection whereby she exists without spot or wrinkle (cf. Eph. 5:27)"; and at the same time the Council says that "the followers of Christ still strive to increase in holiness by conquering sin, and so they*

> *raise their eyes to Mary, who shines forth to the whole community of the elect as a model of the virtues." The pilgrimage of faith no longer belongs to the Mother of the Son of God: glorified at the side of her Son in heaven, Mary has already crossed the threshold between faith and that vision which is "face to face" (1 Cor. 13:12). At the same time, however, in this eschatological fulfillment, Mary does not cease to be the "Star of the Sea" (Maris Stella) for all those who are still on the journey of faith. If they lift their eyes to her from their earthly existence, they do so because "the Son whom she brought forth is he whom God placed as the first-born among many brethren (Rom. 8:29)," and also because "in the birth and development" of these brothers and sisters "she cooperates with a maternal love."*

To be a missionary means to be called and sent by Christ -and so all missionaries can find their identity in St. John entrusted to Mary under the Cross. We need Her -the perfect Disciple and Missionary of Jesus -in order to succeed in the mission Christ entrusts to us. We need both Her example and Her Prayer to fulfill God's call in our lives. The saints always recognized this -as we see from these four quotes below:

> "The greatest saints, those richest in grace and virtue will be the most assiduous in praying to the most Blessed Virgin, looking up to her as the perfect model to imitate and as a powerful helper to assist them." --Saint Louis Marie de Montfort

"Mary having co-operated in our redemption with so much glory to God and so much love for us, Our Lord ordained that no one shall obtain salvation except through her intercession."
--St. Alphonsus Maria de Liguori

"The Immaculate alone has from God the promise of victory over Satan. She seeks souls that will consecrate themselves entirely to her, that will become in her hands forceful instruments for the defeat of Satan and the spread of God's kingdom." --St. Maximilian Kolbe

"In dangers, in doubts, in difficulties, think of Mary, call upon Mary. Let not her name depart from your lips, never suffer it to leave your heart. And that you may obtain the assistance of her prayer, neglect not to walk in her footsteps. With her for guide, you shall never go astray; while invoking her, you shall never lose heart; so long as she is in your mind, you are safe from deception; while she holds your hand, you cannot fall; under her protection you have nothing to fear; if she walks before you, you shall not grow weary; if she shows you favor, you shall reach the goal." --Saint Bernard of Clairvaux, Father and Doctor of the Church

St. Joseph

St. Joseph is the silent missionary in Scripture -and yet no one after Mary does more to reconcile humanity with Jesus their Savior. The first way we see that Joseph is sent to bring us to Jesus is by His

Chapter 4: Mary the Great Missionary and Her Children the Saints

example of perfect obedience to God, as well as by His care for the gift of Christ entrusted to Him. St. Joseph spent his entire life being the savior of the Savior -fleeing to Egypt to keep Him safe, working long days to earn Him food and a home, teaching Him prayer and to read and write, praying with Him for the salvation of the world. Joseph loved Jesus' Mother -a most precious gift for a spiritual father to give his children (love for their Spiritual Mother) and Joseph modeled for all missionaries the virtues one needs to embrace in order to be a disciple of Jesus. He was the epidemy of humility, meekness, gentleness, purity, courage, obedience, trust and faithfulness.

"To give life to someone is the greatest of all gifts. To save a life is the next. Who gave life to Jesus? It was Mary. Who saved his life? It was Joseph. Ask St. Paul who persecuted him. Ask St. Peter who denied him. Ask all the saints who put him to death. But if we ask, 'Who saved his life?' Be silent, patriarchs, be silent, prophets, be silent, apostles, confessors, and martyrs. Let St. Joseph speak, for this honor is his alone; he along is the savior of his Savior." -Blessed William Joseph Chaminade

"The Almighty has concentrated in St. Joseph, as in a Sun of unrivalled lustre, the combined light and splendor of all the other saints." -St. Gregory of Nanzianzen

"St. Joseph did not do extraordinary things, but rather by the constant practice of ordinary and common virtues, he attained that sanctity which elevates him above all the other saints." -St. Joseph Marello

St. John the Baptist

"John wore clothing made of camel's hair and had a leather belt around his waist. His food was locusts and wild honey. At that time Jerusalem, all Judea, and the whole region around the Jordan were going out to him and were being baptized by him in the Jordan River as they acknowledged their sins." (Matthew 3:4-6)

"...The word of God came to John the son of Zechariah in the desert. He went throughout [the] whole region of the Jordan, proclaiming a baptism of repentance for the forgiveness of sins, as it is written in the book of the words of the prophet Isaiah: "A voice of one crying out in the desert: 'Prepare the way of the Lord, make straight his paths. Every valley shall be filled and every mountain and hill shall be made low. The winding roads shall be made straight, and the rough ways made smooth, and all flesh shall see the salvation of God.'"

He said to the crowds who came out to be baptized by him, "You brood of vipers! Who warned you to flee from the coming wrath? Produce good fruits as evidence of your repentance; and do not begin to say to yourselves, 'We have Abraham as our father,' for I tell you, God can raise up children to Abraham from these stones. Even now the ax lies at the root of the trees. Therefore every tree that does not produce good fruit will be cut down and thrown into the fire." And the crowds asked him, "What then should we do?" He said to them in reply, "Whoever

Chapter 4: Mary the Great Missionary and Her Children the Saints

has two tunics should share with the person who has none. And whoever has food should do likewise." Even tax collectors came to be baptized and they said to him, "Teacher, what should we do?" He answered them, "Stop collecting more than what is prescribed." Soldiers also asked him, "And what is it that we should do?" He told them, "Do not practice extortion, do not falsely accuse anyone, and be satisfied with your wages."

Now the people were filled with expectation, and all were asking in their hearts whether John might be the Messiah. John answered them all, saying, "I am baptizing you with water, but one mightier than I is coming. I am not worthy to loosen the thongs of his sandals. He will baptize you with the holy Spirit and fire. His winnowing fan is in his hand to clear his threshing floor and to gather the wheat into his barn, but the chaff he will burn with unquenchable fire." Exhorting them in many other ways, he preached good news to the people." (Luke 3:2-18)

"A man named John was sent from God. He came for testimony, to testify to the light, so that all might believe through him. He was not the light, but came to testify to the light. The true light, which enlightens everyone, was coming into the world." (John 1:6-9)

"John testified to him and cried out, saying, "This was he of whom I said, 'The one who is coming after me ranks ahead of me because he existed before me.'" (John 1:15)

"And this is the testimony of John. When the Jews from Jerusalem sent priests and Levites [to him] to ask him, "Who are you?" he admitted and did not deny it, but admitted, "I am not the Messiah." So they asked him, "What are you then? Are you Elijah?" And he said, "I am not." "Are you the Prophet?" He answered, "No." So they said to him, "Who are you, so we can give an answer to those who sent us? What do you have to say for yourself?" He said: "I am 'the voice of one crying out in the desert, "Make straight the way of the Lord,"' as Isaiah the prophet said." Some Pharisees were also sent. They asked him, "Why then do you baptize if you are not the Messiah or Elijah or the Prophet?" John answered them, "I baptize with water; but there is one among you whom you do not recognize, the one who is coming after me, whose sandal strap I am not worthy to untie." This happened in Bethany across the Jordan, where John was baptizing. John the Baptist's Testimony to Jesus. The next day he saw Jesus coming toward him and said, "Behold, the Lamb of God, who takes away the sin of the world. He is the one of whom I said, 'A man is coming after me who ranks ahead of me because he existed before me.' I did not know him, but the reason why I came baptizing with water was that he might be made known to Israel." John testified further, saying, "I saw the Spirit come down like a dove from the sky and remain upon him. I did not know him, but the one who sent me to baptize with water told me, 'On whomever you see the Spirit come down and remain, he is the one who will baptize *with the holy Spirit.' Now I have seen and testified that he is the Son of God."* (John 1:19-34)

St. John the Baptist is truly the bridge between the Old and the New Testament. He is the last great prophet preparing the way in the hearts of the Jewish people for the coming of Christ, the Messiah. And he is the first man called by God to be a missionary disciple - one to go forth and proclaim Jesus Christ as the Savior of the world -even before the 12 apostles are called by Christ. St. John the Baptist prepared the way for Jesus not only by his teaching, example and words, but also by a life of penance -fasting -and prayer, living in the desert for many years offering this to God as the last needed 'fuel' of grace to prepare hearts for Jesus. And immediately upon seeing Him St. John announced to those present the Gospel: *"Behold the Lamb of God Who takes away the sins of the world..." "He will baptize you with fire and the Holy Spirit..."* At this, St. John humbles himself so greatly that he -who spoke so powerfully and eloquently to all who came to listen about the identity of Christ that he was named 'the voice' -suddenly faded quickly into silence and the background. He is a great example for all missionaries.

A missionary is called to prepare hearts for the coming of Jesus. A missionary does this not only through his words and his life as an example, but also through intense prayer, sacrifice and fasting offered to win grace for the souls entrusted to him to be ready to receive Jesus. St. John the Baptist never looked at what those around him would think or how they would judge him for speaking radical truth about Jesus and the Kingdom of Heaven. Eventually this cost him his life. St. John shows us that a missionary is called to be like

Christ in all things -first and foremost in humility, fading to the background 'decreasing' in his own identity so that Christ can increase, so that Jesus Christ can live in him. There is much we can learn from St. John the Baptist -and all missionaries should spend time not only meditating on his example but also praying for his intercession and help in their own missions given by Jesus to prepare hearts and spread His teachings throughout the world.

Apostles, Paul and the Women Disciples

To be a missionary is to be 'sent' -and so as Jesus chose His first Apostles and disciples, He did so to form them according to His Father's ways and then to send them to the world to bring other lost sheep into the heavenly fold.

> *"And Jesus came and said to them, "All authority in heaven and on earth has been given to me. Go therefore and make disciples of all nations, baptizing them in the name of the Father and of the Son and of the Holy Spirit, teaching them to observe all that I have commanded you. And behold, I am with you always, to the end of the age."* (Matthew 28:18-20)

> *"And he called the twelve and began to send them out two by two, and gave them authority over the unclean spirits."* (Mark 6:7)

> *"After this the Lord appointed seventy-two others and sent them on ahead of him, two by two, into every town and place*

where he himself was about to go. And he said to them, The harvest is plentiful, but the laborers are few. Therefore pray earnestly to the Lord of the harvest to send out laborers into his harvest." (Luke 10:1-2)

"You did not choose me, but I chose you and appointed you that you should go and bear fruit and that your fruit should abide, so that whatever you ask the Father in my name, he may give it to you." (John 15:16)

"But you will receive power when the Holy Spirit has come upon you, and you will be my witnesses in Jerusalem and in all Judea and Samaria, and to the end of the earth." (Acts 1:8)

"As you sent me into the world, so I have sent them into the world. And for their sake I consecrate myself, that they also may be sanctified in truth. I do not ask for these only, but also for those who will believe in me through their word, that they may all be one, just as you, Father, are in me, and I in you, that they also may be in us, so that the world may believe that you have sent me." (John 17:18-21)

"The King will reply, 'Truly I tell you, whatever you did for one of the least of these brothers and sisters of mine, you did for me." (Matthew 25:40)

"While they were worshiping the Lord and fasting, the Holy Spirit said, "Set apart for me Barnabas and Saul for the work to which I have called them." So after they had fasted and prayed, they placed their hands on them and sent them off." (Acts 13:2-3)

"For this is what the Lord has commanded us: "'I have made you a light for the Gentiles, that you may bring salvation to the ends of the earth.' " (Acts 13:47)

"For 'everyone who calls on the name of the Lord will be saved.' How then will they call on him in whom they have not believed? And how are they to believe in him of whom they have never heard? And how are they to hear without someone preaching? And how are they to preach unless they are sent? As it is written, 'How beautiful are the feet of those who preach the good news!'" (Romans 10:13-15)

It is so beautiful to see here Jesus' missionary call to these first Apostles and disciples. Jesus looks at them with love. He sees them. He knows them. And then He chooses them. And in choosing them He is conferring on them the power they need to fulfill the mission He lays on their backs -in their hearts. Jesus arranges everything for them -this we do not always see with our human eyes, but instead it is something visible to our hearts if we ponder God's call (to these first chosen ones -as well as to all missionaries of all ages). God calls a missionary and sends them -but He also arranges graces in the hearts of those to whom he is sent to preach. God arranges the

Chapter 4: Mary the Great Missionary and Her Children the Saints

circumstances of how and where he will live, what he will do -all of their lives are laid forth in a great pre-determined plan of God, allowing for deviations caused by man's freewill to accept or reject grace, and yet even these changes are accounted for in the great plan of God. If the Lord calls a soul to a work, He at the same time enables him to be able to do it. He provides for what the soul needs in order to fulfill the will and plan of God. And so, we see Jesus clearly calling these first Apostles and disciples -and we trust that as He called them, He also arranged so many little details (surrounding their work as well as within their own minds and hearts) so that this work would be successful and bear fruit that would last for heaven.

Because it was our Almighty God who called each one of them - they were strengthened with heroic virtue to carry out this missionary task in a noble and awe-inspiring way. In 2 Corinthians St. Paul lists the sufferings he endured well in order to spread the Gospel:

"Are they ministers of Christ? (I am talking like an insane person.) I am still more, with far greater labors, far more imprisonments, far worse beatings, and numerous brushes with death. Five times at the hands of the Jews I received forty lashes minus one. Three times I was beaten with rods, once I was stoned, three times I was shipwrecked, I passed a night and a day on the deep; on frequent journeys, in dangers from rivers, dangers from robbers, dangers from my own race, dangers from Gentiles, dangers in the city, dangers in the wilderness, dangers at sea, dangers among false brothers; in toil and hardship, through many sleepless nights, through hunger and thirst, through frequent fastings, through cold and exposure. And

> *apart from these things, there is the daily pressure upon me of my anxiety for all the churches. Who is weak, and I am not weak? Who is led to sin, and I am not indignant? Paul's Boast: His Weakness. If I must boast, I will boast of the things that show my weakness."* (2 Corinthians 11:23-30)

This same great Apostle -while suffering all of this and knowing the great hardships one faces as a follower and preacher of Christ - did not use it as an excuse to be lackadaisical in the expectations he placed on himself and others as to the degree of virtue a missionary is expected to live. He continuously encourages his readers to 'consider his weakness' instead of his great feats. And he places a lofty goal of perfection for all who desire to follow his footsteps as a missionary disciple of Christ.

> *"For if I preach the gospel, that gives me no ground for boasting. For necessity is laid upon me. Woe to me if I do not preach the gospel!"* (1 Corinthians 6:19)

> *"Consider your own calling, brothers. Not many of you were wise by human standards, not many were powerful, not many were of noble birth. Rather, God chose the foolish of the world to shame the wise, and God chose the weak of the world to shame the strong, and God chose the lowly and despised of the world, those who count for nothing, to reduce to nothing those who are something, so that no human being might boast before God."* (1 Corinthians 1:26-29)

Chapter 4: Mary the Great Missionary and Her Children the Saints

> *"Love must be sincere. Hate what is evil; cling to what is good. Be devoted to one another in love. Honor one another above yourselves. Never be lacking in zeal, but keep your spiritual fervor, serving the Lord. Be joyful in hope, patient in affliction, faithful in prayer. Share with the Lord's people who are in need. Practice hospitality."* (Romans 12:9-13)

> *"What then shall we say to these things? If God is for us, who is against us? He who did not spare His own Son, but delivered Him over for us all, how will He not also with Him freely give us all things? Who will bring a charge against God's elect? God is the one who justifies; who is the one who condemns? Christ Jesus is He who died, yes, rather who was raised, who is at the right hand of God, who also intercedes for us. Who will separate us from the love of Christ? Will tribulation, or distress, or persecution, or famine, or nakedness, or peril, or sword?"* (Romans 8:31-35)

St. Paul had the courage to preach such inspiring words in the midst of great suffering simply because He was well grounded in who God was -especially from His Revelation for thousands of years to the Jews. St. Paul knew that God would protect His missionaries and so exhorted all those following the way of Christ to trust in His saving Love. Jewish salvation history was full of examples of the Lord miraculously coming to the aid of the people He had chosen as His own. Look at these prayers from the Old Testament:

> "Be strong and courageous. Do not fear or be in dread of them, for it is the LORD your God who goes with you. He will not leave you or forsake you." (Deuteronomy 31:6)

> "My God is my rock, in whom I take refuge, my shield and the horn of my salvation. He is my stronghold, my refuge and my savior— from violent people you save me. I called to the LORD, who is worthy of praise, and have been saved from my enemies. The waves of death swirled about me; the torrents of destruction overwhelmed me. The cords of the grave coiled around me; the snares of death confronted me. 'In my distress I called to the LORD; I called out to my God. From his temple he heard my voice; my cry came to his ears." (2 Samuel 22:3-7)

> "The righteous person may have many troubles, but the LORD delivers him from them all." (Psalm 34:19)

> I raise my eyes toward the mountains. From whence shall come my help? My help comes from the LORD, the maker of heaven and earth. He will not allow your foot to slip; or your guardian to sleep. Behold, the guardian of Israel never slumbers nor sleeps. The LORD is your guardian; the LORD is your shade at your right hand. By day the sun will not strike you, nor the moon by night. The LORD will guard you from all evil; he will

guard your soul. The LORD will guard your coming and going both now and forever." (Psalm 121:1-8)

Women from Scripture

In addition to Jesus calling the first Apostles to His mission work, Jesus also called disciples -many of whom were women. We read in Scripture about these special 'chosen, called and sent' by Christ to help spread His message of the Kingdom of Heaven:

"Afterward he journeyed from one town and village to another, preaching and proclaiming the good news of the kingdom of God. Accompanying him were the Twelve and some women who had been cured of evil spirits and infirmities, Mary, called Magdalene, from whom seven demons had gone out, Joanna, the wife of Herod's steward Chuza, Susanna, and many others who provided for them out of their resources." (Luke 8:1-3)

"As they continued their journey he entered a village where a woman whose name was Martha welcomed him. She had a sister named Mary [who] sat beside the Lord at his feet listening to him speak. Martha, burdened with much serving, came to him and said, "Lord, do you not care that my sister has left me by myself to do the serving? Tell her to help me." The Lord said to her in reply, "Martha, Martha, you are anxious and worried about many things. There is need of only one thing. Mary has chosen the better part and it will not be taken from her." (Luke 10:38-42)

We see specifically in this story of Mary and Martha that being a missionary is first a work of listening to Christ (in prayer) and of being united to Him in Love -and secondly comes the place of actual service work for Him. Jesus in this story did not say Martha's service was bad -because it was necessary and helpful to accomplishing His bigger mission in the world. What He corrected was the state of her heart in the midst of her service -she was preoccupied with worry about getting everything done and she was looking at Mary comparing herself to her instead of looking at Christ and allowing Him to provide for all she needed. Mary was the perfect missionary in first sitting at the feet of Jesus and praying, listening in love, before she joined Martha in physical service of Christ. Let this be a lesson to all missionaries that first place of importance in any mission is the 'work' of prayer, of listing to Christ, of keeping one's eyes focused on Him (and not the problems nor the people around him), of loving Him -and second place is given to actual duties performed.

Part of being a missionary in those first years with Christ meant loving Him enough to suffer with Him. At the time of Jesus' death, it was the women who were mentioned as surrounding Him at the foot of the Cross on Calvary:

> *"Standing by the cross of Jesus were his mother and his mother's sister, Mary the wife of Clopas, and Mary of Magdala."* (John 19:25)

And it was to these women that Christ first entrusted the Easter message of His Resurrection -sending them to share the news with others. Mary Magdalene is often called the 'Apostle to the Apostles' as she met Christ in the garden and He instructed her to 'go to the brothers' to tell them the good news. Her fiery love drew Jesus to reveal Himself to her weeping in the garden, and her fiery love drove her to proclaim His resurrection even when those who she told did not believe her.

> *"But Mary stayed outside the tomb weeping. And as she wept, she bent over into the tomb and saw two angels in white sitting there, one at the head and one at the feet where the body of Jesus had been. And they said to her, "Woman, why are you weeping?" She said to them, "They have taken my Lord, and I don't know where they laid him." When she had said this, she turned around and saw Jesus there, but did not know it was Jesus. Jesus said to her, "Woman, why are you weeping? Whom are you looking for?" She thought it was the gardener and said to him, "Sir, if you carried him away, tell me where you laid him, and I will take him." Jesus said to her, "Mary!" She turned and said to him in Hebrew, "Rabbouni," which means Teacher. Jesus said to her, "Stop holding on to me, for I have not yet ascended to the Father. But go to my brothers and tell them, 'I am going to my Father and your Father, to my God and your God.'" Mary of Magdala went and announced to the disciples, "I have seen the Lord," and what he told her.* (John 20:11-18)

These women who surrounded Christ during the years of His public ministry were missionaries to the early Church. They supported Jesus in prayer, in providing hospitality in housing, preparing food, in sharing the Gospel message (think of the woman at the well in John 4 who told her entire village all about her encounter with Jesus), through financial help and through simply being a motherly presence bringing souls to Him. And in the early years of the Church (after the Ascension) Paul several times mentioned women who supported his ministry -both financially as well as by serving side by side with him.

> *"On the sabbath we went outside the city gate along the river where we thought there would be a place of prayer. We sat and spoke with the women who had gathered there. One of them, **a woman named Lydia**, a dealer in purple cloth, from the city of Thyatira, a worshiper of God, listened, and the Lord opened her heart to pay attention to what Paul was saying. After she and her household had been baptized, she offered us an invitation, "If you consider me a believer in the Lord, come and stay at my home," and she prevailed on us."* (Acts 16:13-15)

> *"I commend to you **Phoebe our sister**, who is [also] a minister of the church at Cenchreae, that you may receive her in the Lord in a manner worthy of the holy ones, and help her in whatever she may need from you, for she has been a benefactor to many and to me as well."* (Romans 16:1-2)

> *"Greet **Prisca and Aquila**, my co-workers in Christ Jesus, who risked their necks for my life, to whom not only I am grateful but also all the churches of the Gentiles; greet also the church*

Chapter 4: Mary the Great Missionary and Her Children the Saints

at their house. Greet my beloved Epaenetus, who was the firstfruits in Asia for Christ. Greet **Mary**, who has worked hard for you. Greet Andronicus and **Junia**, my relatives and my fellow prisoners; they are prominent among the apostles and they were in Christ before me. Greet Ampliatus, my beloved in the Lord. Greet Urbanus, our co-worker in Christ, and my beloved Stachys. Greet Apelles, who is approved in Christ. Greet those who belong to the family of Aristobulus. Greet my relative Herodion. Greet those in the Lord who belong to the family of Narcissus. Greet those workers in the Lord, **Tryphaena and Tryphosa**. Greet the beloved **Persis**, who has worked hard in the Lord. Greet Rufus, chosen in the Lord, and **his mother and mine**. Greet Asyncritus, Phlegon, Hermes, Patrobas, Hermas, and the brothers who are with them. Greet Philologus, **Julia**, Nereus and **his sister**, and Olympas, and all the holy ones who are with them." (Rom 16:3-1i5)

"The churches of Asia send you greetings. **Aquila and Prisca** together with the church at their house send you many greetings in the Lord." (1 Cor 16:19)

"Give greetings to the brothers in Laodicea and to **Nympha** and to the church in her house." (Col 4:15)

"Paul, a prisoner for Christ Jesus, and Timothy our brother, to Philemon, our beloved and our co-worker, to **Apphia our** *sister*, *to Archippus our fellow soldier, and to the church at your house.*" (Philemon 1:1-2)

"*Greet* **Prisca** *and Aquila and the family of Onesiphorus. Erastus remained in Corinth, while I left Trophimus sick at Miletus. Try to get here before winter. Eubulus, Pudens, Linus,* **Claudia**, *and all the brothers send greetings.*" (2 Tim 4:19-21)

Missionary Saints

This leads us to the examples of all the missionary saints that God has given us as examples of missionary zeal over the past 2000 years. There are so many different ways of being a missionary. One can preach the Gospel, one can feed the hungry, one can pray ardently for conversions, one can donate money -all of these aspects of serving as missionaries are necessary in order to get the message of Christ out to souls. But the heart of every way of being a missionary in the world is being madly in love with God and allowing His love to transform one's own soul so completely that simply by being in the world one sets it on fire around himself.

"**The well-being of souls is only in Christ. Therefore, let the love of Jesus be our perfection and our profession. Let us light our hearts from the eternal flames of love that radiate from the Sacred Heart of Jesus.**" -Bl. Paolo Manna

"**Be who you were created to be, and you will set the world on fire.**" –St. Catherine of Siena

Chapter 4: Mary the Great Missionary and Her Children the Saints

There are so many examples of the saints –both male and female, active and contemplative, rich and poor, well-educated and with no education at all, famous and obscure, adults and children -that it is difficult to pick just a few to highlight here as examples for our own missionary zeal. At yet, it is by reading all of these different ways that the people of God were called, formed and sent by His Love to bring the Gospel to many nations that we are inspired to imitate them by imitating the fiery love Jesus ignites us with through the Sacraments.

St. Francis Xavier

There are some missionary saints who immediately come to mind when someone hears the word 'missionary.' The first is St. Francis Xavier. He is the patron saint of all missionaries and all missions. This is because his apostolic zeal was most outstanding. Born in Spain to an influential family, raised in a castle and sent to study in Paris, he was greatly influenced by St. Ignatius of Loyola and joined him becoming a Jesuit. St. Ignatius of Loyola taught a practical insight into being a missionary saying, *"If you want to make progress in love, speak about love; for holy conversation, like a breeze, fans the flame of charity."* St. Francis Xavier caught the missionary flame of love from the heart of his founder, who also insisted that all should be done "*ad majorem dei gloriam,*" or "for the greater glory of God." St. Francis Xavier taught philosophy at the University of Paris and he wanted to travel to the Holy Land to convert non-believers. He said, "*I want to be where there are out and out pagans.*" While he was studying for the priesthood, Portugal was colonizing India and many of the Portuguese were being influenced by pagan ways and abandoning their Catholic faith. The Pope who had made St. Ignatius' band of men an official order in the Church asked them to send missionaries to India, and St. Francis Xavier was chosen to be one of these. The Pope also made him the Papal Nuncio to the region. Francis worked not only among the Portuguese in India but converted the locals as well. He eventually traveled to Japan and it was on his way to China that he caught a fever and died. They say that St. Francis Xavier personally baptized 700,000 Catholics.

St. Francis Xavier understood the flexibility that a missionary must have (both interiorly and exteriorly) in order to reach those he is sent to -embracing change while remaining stouthearted in all of the teachings of the Church. In Japan poverty was deeply looked down upon, and so he would have to dress in fine clothes -leaving his poor habit with the missionaries outside the building -when he went in to speak with local leaders. By looking respectable to them, they were willing to embrace the faith.

St. Francis Xavier suffered a great thirst for souls when he saw so many sheep without shepherds. His life was an echo and reflection of his founder and dear friend St. Ignatius' prayer:

> *"Lord Jesus, teach me to be generous. Teach me to serve as you deserve, To give and not to count the cost, To fight and not to heed the wounds, To labor and not to seek to rest, To give of myself and not ask for a reward, Except the reward of knowing that I am doing your will."* St. Ignatius of Loyola

St. Francis Xavier's heart bled for souls to be saved and He was one heart with Christ in Matthew 9:36-38:

Chapter 4: Mary the Great Missionary and Her Children the Saints

> "At the sight of the crowds, his heart was moved with pity for them because they were troubled and abandoned, like sheep without a shepherd. Then he said to his disciples, "The harvest is abundant but the laborers are few; so ask the master of the harvest to send out laborers for his harvest."

In fact, St. Francis Xavier wrote letters home to the priests sitting comfortably in Paris teaching at Universities exhorting them to follow his footsteps along Calvary and to join him in the East. He wrote:

> "Tell the students to give up their small ambitions and come eastward to preach the gospel of Christ."
>
> "Many, many people hereabouts are not becoming Christians for one reason only: there is nobody to make them Christians. Again and again I have thought of going round the universities of Europe, especially Paris, and everywhere crying out like a madman, riveting the attention of those with more learning than charity. What a tragedy: how many souls are being shut out of heaven and falling into hell, thanks to you! I wish they would work as hard at this as they do at their books, and so settle their account with God for their learning and the talents entrusted to them. This thought would certainly stir most of them to meditate on spiritual realities, to listen actively to what God is saying to them. They would forget their own desires, their human affairs, and give themselves over entirely to God's will and his choice. They would cry out with all their heart: Lord, I am here! What do you want me to do?"

St. Francis Xavier, Missionary to Asia, pray for us!

St. Patrick

St. Patrick is another awe-inspiring missionary. He was born in Britain and lived there until he was kidnapped at the age of 14 and sent to Ireland as a slave -where he was put in charge of herding sheep. The country was full of pagans and druids, but Patrick kept the faith and during this time of slavery wrote his *Confessions*. In this book he wrote:

> *"The love of God and his fear grew in me more and more, as did the faith, and my soul was roused, so that, in a single day, I have said as many as a hundred prayers and in the night, nearly the same. I prayed in the woods and on the mountain, even before dawn. I felt no hurt from the snow or ice or rain."*

At age 20 he had a dream that he was to escape back home to the East, which he did and where he was reunited with his family. Yet a few years later he had a dream that inspired him to study for the priesthood. In his memoirs he wrote:

> *"I saw a man coming, as it were from Ireland. His name was Victoricus, and he carried many letters, and he gave me one of them. I read the heading: 'The Voice of the Irish.' As I began the letter, I imagined in that moment that I heard the voice of those very people who were near the wood of Foclut, which is beside*

the western sea-and they cried out, as with one voice: 'We appeal to you, holy servant boy, to come and walk among us.'"

After being ordained a priest and eventually a Bishop he was sent back to Ireland to convert the Irish. With nothing but forgiveness and Christian love in his heart for his former captors St. Patrick courageously arrived in Ireland and found nothing but difficulty in his attempts to convert the people. The chieftain of one of the druid tribes even tried to kill him. After 8 years of struggle, St. Patrick climbed a mountain and entered a cave on Ash Wednesday and remained there fasting and praying for 40 days. When he emerged, he was able to convert the entire Island. St. Patrick used the local vegetation of clover shamrocks to teach the people about the Trinity. And he is a witness to all missionaries of the importance of prayer, fasting and sacrifice as the foundation of any missionary endeavor. Patrick wrote the beautiful Breastplate Prayer which he prayed for protection before he embarked on his dangerous mission -and many people even today find powerful spiritual protection from evil in praying this prayer daily. St. Patrick worked in Ireland for 40 years before his death. About his experience as a missionary in Ireland St. Patrick wrote:

> *"I know for certain, that before I was humbled, I was like a stone lying in deep mire, and he that is mighty came and, in his mercy, raised me up and, indeed, lifted me high up and placed me on top of the wall. And from there I ought to shout out in gratitude to the Lord for his great favors in this world and forever, that the mind of man cannot measure."*

"I came to the people of Ireland to preach the gospel, and to suffer insult from the unbelievers, bearing the reproach of my going abroad and many persecutions even unto bonds, and to give my free birth for the benefit of others."

"I pray to God to give me perseverance and to deign that I be a faithful witness to him to the end of my life for my God."

"For daily I expect to be murdered or betrayed or reduced to slavery if the occasion arises. But I fear nothing, because of the promises of Heaven; for I have cast myself into the hands of Almighty God, who reigns everywhere. As the prophet says: 'Cast your burden on the Lord and he will sustain you.'"

"[God] watched over me before I knew him, and before I learned sense or even distinguished between good and evil, and he protected me, and consoled me as a father would his son."

"Christ with me,
Christ before me,
Christ behind me,
Christ in me,
Christ beneath me,
Christ above me,
Christ on my right,
Christ on my left,
Christ when I lie down,
Christ when I sit down,
Christ when I arise,
Christ in the heart of every man who thinks of me,
Christ in the mouth of everyone who speaks of me,

Chapter 4: Mary the Great Missionary and Her Children the Saints

> *Christ in every eye that sees me,*
> *Christ in every ear that hears me."* -(A portion if St. Patrick's Breastplate Prayer)

St. Patrick, Missionary to Ireland, pray for us!

St. Anthony Maria Claret

Another powerful missionary, archbishop and founder is St. Anthony Maria Claret. Born in Spain he, too, desired to join the Jesuits -but ill health prevented him and he became a secular priest. He eventually founded the Claretian Missionary Sons of the Immaculate Heart of Mary, Apostolic Training Institute of the Immaculate Conception and the Claretian nuns. From 1850-1857 he served as the Archbishop of Cuba and later returned to be the Confessor to the Queen -going with her into exile. When he was ordained a Bishop he added 'Maria' to his name as a form of consecrating his life to our Heavenly Mother. He attended the First Vatican Council in 1870 and eventually died in a Monastery in France.

St. Anthony Claret was literally on fire with love for Jesus -and he was known to have the Blessed Sacrament's Presence continually in his heart (which is visible in icons and paintings of him). He taught his spiritual sons about the process of being put into the fire with Christ to be shaped as His tool and then sent into the world. St. Anthony Claret was opposed by many in this world -liberals in the Church as well as enemies of religion and several attempts were made at his life. He wrote 144 books and preached an estimated 25,000 sermons -once preaching 12 sermons in one day! In Cuba he reorganized the seminary, tightened priestly discipline and validated 9000 marriages. He had made a vow to himself to never waste one moment of time.

During his mission work, he accepted no money and walked everywhere -- from town to town through rugged terrain. He had only one pair of shoes, one set of clothes and a few books. He neither ate meat nor drank wine, and slept only 3 - 5 hours per night. After one remarkable mission, Father Claret's bishop wrote: *"this town has never seen the likes of this. Enemies are at peace. Scandals have been ended. Broken marriages are repaired. Restitutions have been made. No one can withstand the fire of his preaching, the kindness of his manner. Everyone, even the proudest, fall at his feet."*

The secret of his success was the FIRE of Jesus' LOVE. He himself explained:

> *"Love is the most necessary of all virtues. Love in the person who preaches the word of God is like fire in a musket. If a person were to throw a bullet with his hands, he would hardly make a dent in anything; but if the person takes the same bullet and ignites some gunpowder behind it, it can kill. It is much the same with the word of God. If it is spoken by someone who is filled with the fire of charity- the fire of love of God and neighbor- it will work wonders."* (Autobiography #438-439)

He was also known as a powerful confessor, often having the gift of reading and discerning hearts. He was truly a fire of love. He not only lived this fire of love himself, but taught it to his Claretian sons and brothers:

Chapter 4: Mary the Great Missionary and Her Children the Saints

"The man who truly loves God also loves his neighbor. The truly zealous man is also one who loves, but he stands on a higher plane of love so that the more he is inflamed by love, the more urgently zeal drives him on. But if anyone lacks this zeal, then it is evident that love and charity have been extinguished in his heart. The zealous man desires and achieves all great things and he labors strenuously so that God may always be better known, loved and served in this world and in the life to come, for this holy love is without end."

"Christian perfection consists in three things: praying heroically, working heroically, and suffering heroically."

"An apostolic missionary must have both heart and tongue ablaze with charity. Lord, by the words of consecration the substance of the bread and wine is converted into the substance of your Body and Blood. All powerful Lord, say over me the word which will change me into You."

"When I see the need for Divine teaching and how hungry people are to hear it, I am atremble to be off and running throughout the world, preaching the word of God. I have no rest, my soul finds no other relief, than to rush about and preach."

Driven by the fire of the Holy Spirit, the holy apostles traveled throughout the earth. Inflamed with the same fire, apostolic missionaries have reached, are now reaching, and will continue to reach the ends of the earth, from one pole to the other, in order to proclaim the word of God. They are *deservedly able to apply to themselves those words of the apostle Paul: "The love of Christ drives us on."*

The love of Christ arouses us, urges us to run, and to fly, lifted on the wings of holy zeal. The zealous man desires and achieves all great things and he labors strenuously so that God may always be better known, loved and served in this world and in the life to come, for this holy love is without end.

Because he is concerned also for his neighbor, the man of zeal works to fulfill his desire that all men be content on this earth and happy and blessed in their heavenly homeland, that all may be saved, and that no one may perish forever, or offend God, or remain even for a moment in sin. Such are the concerns we observe in the holy apostles and in all who are driven by the apostolic spirit.

For myself, I say this to you: The man who burns with the fire of divine love is a son of the Immaculate Heart of Mary, and wherever he goes, he enkindles that flame; he deserves and works with all this strength to inflame all men with the fire of God's love. Nothing deters him: he rejoices in poverty; he labors strenuously; he welcomes hardships; he laughs off false accusations; he rejoices in anguish. He thinks only of how he might follow Jesus Christ and imitate him by his prayers, his labors, his sufferings, and by caring always and only for the glory of God and the salvation of souls."

St. Anthony Maria Claret, Missionary Son of Mary, pray for us!

Chapter 4: Mary the Great Missionary and Her Children the Saints

St. Maximilian Kolbe

If we are comparing great missionary saints to a fire of God's love in the midst of His people, we immediately must turn to St. Maximillian Kolbe to add him to this list. St. Maximilian Kolbe was born as Raymund Kolbe on January 8, 1894 in Poland. He was a Polish Conventual Franciscan friar who spent his life before being martyred in Auschwitz spreading devotion, love and consecration to the Immaculate Heart of Mary. Much of his life was strongly influenced by a vision he had of the Virgin Mary when he was 12. He explained:

"That night I asked the Mother of God what was to become of me. Then she came to me holding two crowns, one white, the other red. She asked me if I was willing to accept either of these crowns. The white one meant that I should persevere in purity, and the red that I should become a martyr. I said that I would accept them both."

Following the footsteps of his older brother he joined the Conventual Franciscans and was given the name Maximillian. He organized the Militia Immaculata (Army of the Immaculate One) after witnessing demonstrations against the Pope. His goal was to work through intercession of Mary for the conversion of sinners and enemies of the Church, specifically, the Freemasons.

In 1918, he was ordained a priest and continued his work of promoting Mary throughout Poland. Over the next several years, Kolbe took on publishing. He founded a monthly periodical titled, "*Rycerz Niepokalanej*" (Knight of the Immaculate) printing 5000 copies the first edition. He insisted that there be no price for the paper and that it would be made available for free for the poor. A hundred years later, his magazine is still in print.

Fr. Kolbe also operated a religious publishing press and founded a new Conventual Franciscan monastery 40km west of Warsaw called Niepokalanow, (meaning, 'City of the Immaculate Virgin') which became a major religious publishing center.

Kolbe also founded monasteries in both Japan and India. In 1936, Kolbe's poor health forced him to return home to Poland, and once the WWII invasion by Germany began, he became one of the only brothers to remain in the monastery. He opened up a temporary hospital to aid those in need and was arrested once, but released after three months. When he returned to the monastery Kolbe refused to sign a document that would recognize him as a German citizen with his German ancestry and continued to work in his monastery, providing shelter for refugees - including hiding 2,000 Jews from German persecution. After receiving permission to continue his religious publishing, Kolbe's monastery acted as a publishing house again and issued many anti-Nazi German publications. On February 17, 1941, the monastery was shut down; Kolbe was arrested by the German Gestapo and taken to the Pawiak prison, three months later being transferred to Auschwitz.

While in Auschwitz a prisoner escaped and the soldiers chose 10 prisoners to be killed by starvation in retribution. When a man cried out that he had a wife and children and begged to be spared the death sentence, Fr. Kolbe stepped forward offering to take his place.

During the last days of his life Fr. Maximillian Kolbe led prayers to Our Lady with the prisoners and remained calm. He was the last of the group to remain alive, after two weeks of dehydration and starvation. The guards gave him a lethal injection of carbolic acid. The stories tell that he raised his left arm and calmly awaited death. In the midst of great suffering in prison, Fr. Kolbe said: *"For Jesus Christ I am prepared to suffer still more."* For he truly believed: *"Let us not forget that Jesus not only suffered, but also rose in glory; so, too, we go to the glory of the Resurrection by way of suffering and the Cross."*

Fr. Kolbe was a great missionary of the Immaculata. He proclaimed the Gospel through his writing, publishing, missionary travels and ultimately by the silent witness of his martyrdom. In fact, he saw his arrest as missionary work -saying to his brothers the first time he was arrested: *"Courage, my sons. Don't you see that we are leaving on a mission? They pay our fare in the bargain. What a piece of good luck! The thing to do now is to pray well in order to win as many souls as possible."*

Fr. Kolbe understood that love was the impetus behind all missionary activity -and for him it was not only love for Jesus Christ, but also a deep love for His Mother that inspired his work. Such love was impossible without much sacrifice. Fr. Kolbe explained:

> *"Let us remember that love lives through sacrifice and is nourished by giving. Let's remember that not everything which is good and beautiful pertains to genuine, essential love, because even without those other things love can be present, indeed a perfected love. Without sacrifice there is no love."*

St. Maximilian Kolbe did not preach that we should only love God with such sacrifice, but that we should extend our love for God to all people, even to one's enemies. He said, *"A single act of love makes the soul return to life."* And he firmly believed that *"The Cross is the school of love."* This was the power that drove his missionary zeal -that kept the flame of his love alive even in the mire of the concentration camp. As he died in Auschwitz, his example of love for the soldiers who killed him was a missionary work greater than all the rest he did or said. He once explained this:

> *"We need to love our neighbor not just because he is pleasant or helpful or rich and influential or even because he shows us gratitude. These motives are too self-serving, unworthy of our Lady's Knights. Genuine love rises above creatures and soars up to God. In him, by him, and through him it loves all men, both good and wicked, friends and enemies. To all it stretches out a hand filled with love; it prays for all, suffers for all, wishes what is best for all, desires happiness for all—because that is what God wants."*

Where did he get the strength to love like this -from his Mother, who he affectionately called 'the Immaculata'. He said:

> *"It is not enough to become the Immaculata's within some defined limit. In every respect, we must desire to radiate her, so as to draw to her the souls of all others who are, will be, and might be—without restriction. In a word, we are to become*

hers, more and more ready to sacrifice self entirely for her, to the last drop of blood in the conquest of the whole world and every soul in particular—as soon as possible, as soon as possible, as soon as possible."

"Let us let ourselves be led, then; let us not attempt to do more than that which [Mary] wills or more quickly. Let us let ourselves be carried by her;

She will think of everything and take care of all our needs, of the soul and of the body.

Let us give every difficulty, every sorrow to her, and have confidence that she will take care of it better than we could.

Peace then, peace, much peace in an unlimited confidence in her.

Above all, never let yourselves be troubled, never be frightened, never fear anything.

The Immaculate, in fact, is she perhaps not aware of everything?

If this were not the case, it would really be a problem."

St. Maximillian Kolbe truly believed that as a missionary it was only by working, praying -even breathing -through and with the Heart of Mary, that one was able to reach God. He teaches us that missionary genius is knowing that you are a child of Our Lady and living accordingly. He said:

"In her womb the soul must be regenerated according to the form of Jesus Christ."

"A man cannot rise any higher than this. The Immaculate is the highest degree of perfection and sanctity of a creature. No man will ever attain this celestial summit of grace, for the Mother of God is unique. However, he who gives himself without limits to the Immaculate will in a short time attain a very high degree of perfection and procure for God a very great glory."

"The most holy Mother is Mediatrix of all graces without exception… Therefore the life of grace of a soul depends on the degree of its closeness to her. The closer a soul approaches her, the more pure it becomes, the more lively becomes its faith. Its love becomes more beautiful, and all virtues, being the work of grace, are strengthened and vivified. We cannot seek grace anywhere else because she is its Mediatrix."

"Our dependence on Mary is greater than we can imagine. We receive all graces, absolutely all of them, from God through the Immaculate, who is our universal mediatrix with Jesus."

"The Immaculata will conquer, through us, the whole world and every single soul."

"You are hers: Let yourself be led by the Immaculate"

St. Maximillian Kolbe, Missionary of Auszwitz, Knight of the Immaculata, pray for us!

St. Damian of Molokai

Another great missionary model for our times is St. Damian of Molokai. He was born Jozef De Veuster in rural Belgium, on January

3, 1840. He grew up in a large family on a farm where he was expected to help with the heavy work. Eventually he followed his brother in joining the Congregation of the Sacred Hearts of Jesus and Mary and he took the name Damian. His brother was supposed to travel to a mission in Hawaii, but upon becoming ill and unable to go Damian offered to take his brother's place. The brothers worried that Br. Damien was too uneducated to become a priest, although he was not considered unintelligent. Br. Damien demonstrated his ability by quickly learning Latin from his brother. He was also devoted in prayer. Br. Damien prayed each day before an icon of Saint Francis Xavier to be sent on a mission. Eventually, his religious brothers agreed to send him and have him ordained. And so, Brother Damian arrived in Hawaii in 1864 and he was ordained two months later. In 1866 Hawaii established a leper colony as a place of quarantine for those diagnosed with leprosy. These people desperately needed both physical and spiritual care and so in 1873 Fr. Damian offered to go to live among them as a missionary.

When Fr. Damian arrived, he found the conditions of the island deplorable. Anarchy reigned there -patients were not provided with adequate care, many turned to drink and became alcoholics and all sorts of lawlessness and immorality was on display among the island's inhabitants. Fr. Damian discerned that the people needed leadership -so he organized the building of houses, schools and eventually a church. He cared for the sick and buried the dead. He most importantly treated the lepers with dignity and respect, kindness and love -and eventually this won their souls for Christ. He said:

> *"I feel no disgust when I hear the confessions of those near their end, whose wounds are full of maggots...This may give you some idea of my daily work. Picture to yourself a collection of huts with 800 Lepers. No doctor; in fact, as there is no cure, there seems no place for a doctor's skill."*

At first Fr. Damian was only supposed to be on the island for a short time -eventually being replaced by another volunteer priest. But he grew attached to the people and found Christ in his difficult daily work and he petitioned to remain as a missionary on the island and his request was granted. In 1885 he himself contracted the disease and slowly it ate away at his body -while only strengthening his soul as he was united to Jesus Crucified.

> *"I make myself a leper with the lepers to gain all to Jesus Christ."*
>
> *"I would not be cured if the price of the cure was that I must leave the island and give up my work I am perfectly resigned to my lot. Do not feel sorry for me."*

He saw his suffering as part of his missionary work -the sacrificial price needed to be paid in order to save the souls entrusted to him. He knew that by suffering with Christ, he was being conformed to Christ -and this witness of Christ living in him among the lepers would be the greatest gift he could offer them. He said, *"May God strengthen me and give me the strength of perseverance and of a happy*

Chapter 4: Mary the Great Missionary and Her Children the Saints

death.... I try to make slowly my way of the Cross and hope soon to be on top of my Golgotha."

Fr. Damien continued his work, despite his illness, which slowly took over his body. He derived strength from Our Lady in praying the Rosary, as well as from prayer before the Blessed Sacrament. He said, *"It is at the foot of the altar that we find the strength we need in our isolation."*

> *"I find my consolation in the one and only companion who will never leave me, that is, our Divine Savior in the Holy Eucharist. The Eucharist is the bread that gives strength... It is at once the most eloquent proof of His love and the most powerful means of fostering His love in us. He gives Himself every day so that our hearts as burning coals may set afire the hearts of the faithful."*
>
> "Without the Blessed Sacrament a position like mine would be intolerable."
>
> "The Blessed Sacrament is indeed the stimulus for us all, for me as it should be for you, to forsake all worldly ambitions. Without the constant presence of our Divine Master upon the altar in my poor chapels, I never could have persevered casting my lot with the lepers of Molokai; the foreseen consequence of which begins now to appear on my skin, and is felt throughout the body. Holy Communion being the daily bread of a priest, I feel myself happy, well pleased, and resigned in the rather exceptional circumstances in which it has pleased Divine Providence to put me."

Fr. Damian died of leprosy on the leper's island in Hawaii in 1889. He is a great saintly example for all missionaries to find the center of their missions -and their source of strength -in prayer before Jesus in the Blessed Sacrament. Especially being in a mission alone -without the support of other priestly brothers or sisters -St. Damian of Molokai had to depend on Jesus in the Eucharist as His Crutch, His Lantern and His Rest. The courage of St. Damian of Molokai came from his union with Jesus in the Tabernacle -and from daily calling upon the help of the Blessed Mother through the Rosary.

St. Damian of Molokai, Missionary to the Leapers, pray for us!

St. Francis of Assisi

"All the darkness in the world cannot extinguish the light of a single candle." St. Francis of Assisi

St. Francis of Assisi was another type of great missionary -he was a missionary to the Church Herself, who had grown lukewarm and fallen from following the Gospel of Christ without compromise. St. Francis changed the Church from within -by forming missionary disciples who preached the Word of God through the example of their lives of radical poverty and prayer. Saint Francis of Assisi said, *"All the darkness in the world cannot extinguish the light of a single candle."* And he fought the darkness of the world by simply becoming consumed with the Light of Christ and in forming thousands of men through the ages in a life of such radical poverty that the Light of Christ could show through them in complete translucence.

Chapter 4: Mary the Great Missionary and Her Children the Saints

St. Francis was born to a wealthy cloth merchant. He was a soldier for a time and lived a life of comfort and sin. One day on the way to the Fourth Crusade he heard God telling him to return home and he did. His conversion happened slowly -but he eventually withdrew to a cave to pray and one day heard God say to him **'Rebuild my Church.'** Francis thought God was speaking about a dilapidated church building and he began to repair it -but what the Lord had in mind was much greater than a building project. When Francis met a leper one day, he fought his repugnance and kissed the man -in return receiving a Kiss of Peace form the Lord. Eventually St. Francis repudiated his inheritance and took to a life of radical poverty and prayer. He also took to preaching -to call those around him back to core Gospel values. Slowly companions came to Francis, people who wanted to follow his life of sleeping in the open, begging for garbage to eat and loving God. With companions, Francis knew he now had to have some kind of direction to this life so he opened the Bible in three places. He read the command to the rich young man to sell all his goods and give to the poor, the order to the apostles to take nothing on their journey, and the demand to take up the cross daily. *"Here is our rule,"* Francis said as simple, and as seemingly impossible, as that. He wanted to do what the world said was impossible: to live by the Gospel.

Francis did not try to abolish poverty, he tried to make it holy. When his friars met someone poorer than they, they would eagerly rip off the sleeve of their habit to give to the person. Francis taught: *"Remember that when you leave this earth, you can take with you nothing that you have received–only what you have given."* St. Francis also said: *"My dear and beloved Brother, the treasure of blessed poverty is so very precious and divine that we are not worthy to possess it in our vile bodies. For poverty is that heavenly virtue by which all earthy and transitory things are trodden under foot, and by which every obstacle is removed from the soul so that it may freely enter into union with the eternal Lord God. It is also the virtue which makes the soul, while still here on earth, converse with the angels in Heaven. It is she who accompanied Christ on the Cross, was buried with Christ in the Tomb, and with Christ was raised and ascended into Heaven, for even in this life she gives to souls who love her the ability to fly to Heaven, and she alone guards the armor of true humility and charity."* (The Little Flowers of St. Francis of Assisi)

He and his brothers worked for all necessities and only begged if they had to. But Francis would not let them accept any money. He told them to treat coins as if they were pebbles in the road. When the bishop showed horror at the friars' hard life, Francis said, *"If we had any possessions, we should need weapons and laws to defend them."* Possessing something was the death of love for Francis. Also, Francis reasoned, what could you do to a man who owns nothing? You can't starve a fasting man, you can't steal from someone who has no money, you can't ruin someone who hates prestige. They were truly free.

St. Francis not only encouraged his religious brothers to embrace physical poverty, but strongly emphasized the importance of interior poverty of spirit -the gift of humility. This was something that he taught first of all by his life -and then by his words. He both taught and lived these sayings:

> *"I have been all things unholy. If God can work through me, He can work through anyone."*
>
> *"Preach the Gospel at all times. Use words if necessary."*
>
> *"The deeds you do may be the only sermon some persons will hear today."*

And he often held up Jesus Himself -especially in Bethlehem, on the Cross and in the Eucharist -as the greatest example of Humility that all are called to follow. *"Every day He humbles Himself just as He did when from His heavenly throne into the Virgin's womb; every day He comes to us and lets us see Him in lowliness, when He descends from the bosom of the Father into the hands of the priest at the altar."*

After a life of deprivation and much suffering (the brothers once kicked him out of his own religious order for being too strict with the rules), St. Francis was totally conformed to Christ through the gift of the stigmata. These wounds emanated from a vision of a seraph in the form of a cross, and consisted of nail marks on his hands and feet, and a gash in the side of his chest. The stigmata remained until his death two years later.

St. Francis of Assisi has remained a missionary within the Church even up unto the present time. How could a poor, little beggar for Christ change the entire world? He himself said: *"Start by doing what is necessary, then what is possible, and suddenly you are doing the impossible."* St. Francis' genius was his total dedication to living the Gospel verbatim as Jesus Christ presented it. We pray that all missionaries can follow his great example and mission as laid forth in his most famous prayer:

"Lord, make me an instrument of thy peace.
Where there is hatred, let me sow love,
Where there is injury, pardon;
Where there is doubt, faith;
Where there is despair, hope;
Where there is darkness, light;
And where there is sadness, joy.

O Divine Master, grant that I may not so much seek
to be consoled as to console,
to be understood as to understand,
to be loved, as to love.

For it is in giving that we receive,
It is in pardoning that we are pardoned,
and it is in dying that we are born to eternal life."

St. Francis Poor Missionary of Assisi, pray for us!

St. Charles de Foucauld

Charles Eugène de Foucauld was born on 15 September 1858 in Strasbourg, France and died as a martyr on 1 December 1916 in Tamanrasset (Algeria) while living as a hermit. St. Charles de Foucauld was a cavalry officer in the French Army, then an explorer and geographer before he finally went as a Catholic priest and hermit to live among the Tuareg in the Sahara in Algeria. Upon arriving he wrote home: *"Islam shook me deeply. Seeing such faith, seeing people living in the continual presence of God, I came to glimpse something greater and more real than worldly occupations."* It was because of his great respect for the Muslims he lived among that he was able to make such inroads showing them the Gospel of Christ. And yet, this did not prevent him from being betrayed by the man who brought him his mail and because of the betrayal he was assassinated in 1916. Because he was killed for his faith, he is considered by the Church to be a martyr. St. Charles de Foucauld was such a great missionary that he went alone to live as a hermit priest among the Muslims -simply using his prayer and life of witness as his way of preaching the Gospel to these souls who did not know Christ nor recognize Him as their Savior. He was known to say that all Christians should *"cry the Gospel with your whole life."* His missionary strategy is laid forth in his letters home. He wrote:

> *"The moment I realized that God existed, I knew that I could not do otherwise than to live for him alone… Faith strips the mask from the world and reveals God in everything. It makes nothing impossible and renders meaningless such words as anxiety, danger, and fear, so that the believer goes through life calmly and peacefully, with profound joy- like a child, hand in hand with his mother."*
>
> *"It is not necessary to teach others, to cure them or to improve them; it is only necessary to live among them, sharing the human condition and being present to them in love."*
>
> *"You have only one model, Jesus. Follow, follow, follow him, step by step, imitating him, sharing his life in every way."*

"We should never forget the two axioms: 'Jesus is with me' and whatever happens, happens by the will of God."

"Whether our life be that of Nazareth, the Public Life or the Desert… it should cry the Gospel…"

"The evangelization that I am called to live is not through the word but through the presence of the Blessed Sacrament, the offering of the sacrifice of the Mass. It is through prayer and penance and the practice of the Gospel virtues – love, fraternal and universal love, sharing even my last mouthful of bread with every poor person, with every visitor, every stranger, and welcoming each person as a beloved brother or sister."

"I want all the people here, Christians, Muslims, Jews, non-believers, to look on me as their brother, the universal brother. They begin to call my house 'the fraternity' and this makes me happy."

"Above all, always see Jesus in every person, and consequently treat each one not only as an equal and as a brother or sister, but also with great humility, respect and selfless generosity."

"Be loving, gentle, humble, with all human beings. This is what we have learned from Jesus, not to be aggressive towards anyone. Jesus taught us to go out like lambs among wolves."

"We are all children of the Most High. All of us: the poorest, the most outcast, a newborn child, a decrepit old person, the least intelligent human being, the most abject, an idiot, a fool, a sometimes sinner, the greatest sinner, the most ignorant, the last of the last, the one most physically and morally repugnant

Chapter 4: Mary the Great Missionary and Her Children the Saints

– all children of God and sons and daughters of the Most High. We should hold all human beings in high esteem. We should love all humankind, for they are all children of God."

"Have that tender care that expresses itself in the little things that are like a balm for the heart... With our neighbors go into the smallest details, whether it is a question of health, of consolation, of prayerfulness, or of need. Console and ease the pain of others through the tiniest of attentions. Be as tender and attentive towards those whom God puts on our path, as a brother towards brother or as a mother for her child. As much as possible be an element of consolation for those around us, as soothing balm, as our Lord was towards all those who drew near to him."

"Set up home as Jesus of Nazareth, obscurely, poorly, humbly with hard work. Imitate as closely as possible the humble and hidden existence of the Divine Worker of Nazareth, living solely from the work of your hands."

"We must stand up for the rights of our neighbor who is suffering from injustice; we must defend them all the more vigorously because we see Jesus present in them. Surely this is our duty because of our love for others for his sake. We have no right to be 'sleeping watchmen' or dumb watch-dogs. Whenever we see evil we must sound the alarm."

"There is one case when we must resist evil forcefully. It is when it is not a case of defending ourselves but of protecting others. It takes forcefulness to defend the weak and the innocent

> when their oppressors wrong them. The spirit of peace is not a spirit of weakness but a spirit of strength."
>
> "It pleased God to make it easy for us to be saved. He didn't attach salvation to knowledge or intelligence or wealth, nor to long experience or rare gifts that are not given to all. He attached it to something within the reach of everyone, absolutely everyone. Jesus attaches salvation to humility, to the act of making yourself little. That is all it takes to win heaven."
>
> "What great faith our Lord Jesus Christ asks of us – and how just that is. Do we not owe him such faith? It looks impossible to us, but Jesus is Master of the impossible."

What gave St. Charles de Foucauld the courage to leave France, to leave his religious community and to go to the desert land of Muslims where he would be alone and surely face dangers and death? It was his absolute abandon and trust in the loving Providence of God. He said:

> "Father of mine, I abandon myself to you, make of me that which is pleasing to you. Whatever you might do to me, I thank you."
>
> "The one thing we owe absolutely to God is never to be afraid of anything." ...
>
> "Crosses release us from this world, and by doing so, bind us to God."
>
> "What is impossible for humans is possible for God: 'Caritas omnia sperat' – 'Love hopes for everything'. God loves and

can do anything. God respects the freedom God gave to humankind but God does not hold back when freely giving graces. God's grace can be such that it overturns all obstacles and brings the calm after the storm. Let us know how to obtain powerful graces from the one who said: 'Ask and you shall receive' and 'When two or more of you are gathered in prayer, I am among you.'"

"Forgive us our debts. One cannot ask for forgiveness if one has not forgiven. Forgiveness like grace is something one does not ask for oneself alone, but for all people."

"Real faith causes every impossibility to disappear. It makes a nonsense of those words, anxiety, danger and fear. It makes us walk through life with calm peace and deep joy, like a child holding its mother's hand."

St. Charles de Foucauld -missionary to the Muslims, pray for us!

St. Peter Claver

Each missionary is called to a specific place and people. While St. Francis was called to a work in the Church calling it back to her Gospel roots and St. Charles de Foucauld to a work among Muslims, St. Peter Claver was called to a mission life serving slaves -fighting for their just treatment and bringing them to the freedom of Salvation in Christ through Baptism. He in fact worked so tirelessly at this work assigned to him by God that he was known in his own time as the 'slave of the slaves.'

St. Peter Claver was born at Verdu, Catalonia, Spain in 1580. He entered the Jesuit college of Barcelona, after completing the Jesuit novitiate he took his final vows on Aug 8, 1604. During his years of study, the young religious was influenced by St. Alphonsus Rodriguez (a holy door keeper at the school) to go to the Indies and save "millions of perishing souls." St. Alphonsus adhered to a few simple spiritual guidelines that navigated him through his troubles and trials and he taught these to St. Peter Clever. For example, St. Alphonsus explained a method for finding joy in hardship:

> *"Another exercise is very valuable for the imitation of Christ—for love of him, taking the sweet for the bitter and the bitter for sweet. So, I put myself in spirit before our crucified Lord, looking at him full of sorrow, shedding his blood and bearing great bodily hardships for me.*
>
> *As love is paid for in love, I must imitate him, sharing in spirit all his sufferings. I must consider how much I owe him and what he has done for me. Putting these sufferings between God and my soul, I must say, "What does it matter, my God, that I should endure for your love these small hardships? For you, Lord, endured so many great hardships for me." Amid the hardship and trial itself, I stimulate my heart with this exercise. Thus, I encourage myself to endure for love of the Lord who is before me, until I make what is bitter sweet. In this way learning from Christ our Lord, I take and convert the sweet into bitter, renouncing myself and all earthly and carnal pleasures,*

delights and honors of this life, so that my whole heart is centered solely on God."

(In his old age, Alphonsus experienced no relief from his trials. The more he mortified himself, the more he seemed to be subject to spiritual dryness, vigorous temptations, and even diabolical assaults. In 1617 his body was ravaged with disease and he died at midnight, October 30.)

A few years later, St. Peter Clever took the spiritual advice and missionary flame shared with him by St. Alphonsus and left his homeland to become a missionary in the colonies of the new world. In 1610, he landed at Cartagena (modern Colombia), the principal slave market of the New World, where a thousand slaves were landed every month. After his ordination in 1616, he dedicated himself by special vow to the service of the Negro slaves-a work that was to last for thirty-three years. He labored unceasingly for the salvation of the African slaves and the abolition of the Negro slave trade, and the love he lavished on them was something that transcended the natural order.

St. Peter Claver believed that *"We must speak to them with our hands by giving, before we try to speak to them with our lips."* And so, boarding the slave ships as they entered the harbor, he would hurry to the revolting inferno of the hold, and offer whatever poor refreshments he could afford; he would care for the sick and dying, and instruct the slaves through Negro catechists before administering the Sacraments. Through his efforts by 1651 300,000 souls entered the Church. St. Peter Claver himself described his work in a letter. He wrote:

"Yesterday, May 30, 1627, on the feast of the Most Holy Trinity, numerous blacks, brought from the rivers of Africa, disembarked from a large ship. Carrying two baskets of oranges, lemons, sweet biscuits, and I know not what else, we hurried toward them.

When we approached their quarters, we thought we were entering another Guinea. We had to force our way through the crowd until we reached the sick. Large numbers of the sick were lying on the wet ground or rather in puddles of mud. To prevent excessive dampness, someone had thought of building up a mound with a mixture of tiles and broken pieces of bricks. This, then, was their couch, a very uncomfortable one not only for that reason, but especially because they were naked, without any clothing to protect them. We laid aside our cloaks, therefore, and brought from a warehouse whatever was handy to build a platform. In that way we covered a space to which we at last transferred the sick, by forcing a passage through bands of slaves.

Then we divided the sick into two groups: one group my companion approached with an interpreter, while I addressed the other group. There were two blacks, nearer death than life, already cold, whose pulse could scarcely be detected. With the help of a tile we pulled some live coals together and placed them in the middle near the dying men. Into this fire we tossed aromatics. Of these we had two wallets full, and we used them all up on this occasion. Then, using our own cloaks, for they had

Chapter 4: Mary the Great Missionary and Her Children the Saints

nothing of this sort, and to ask the owners for others would have been a waste of words, we provided for them a smoke treatment, by which they seemed to recover their warmth and the breath of life. The joy in their eyes as they looked at us was something to see.

This was how we spoke to them, not with words but with our hands and our actions. And in fact, convinced as they were that they had been brought here to be eaten, any other language would have proved utterly useless. Then we sat, or rather knelt, beside them and bathed their faces and bodies with wine. We made every effort to encourage them with friendly gestures and displayed in their presence the emotions which somehow naturally tend to hearten the sick.

After this we began an elementary instruction about baptism, that is, the wonderful effects of the sacrament on body and soul. When by their answers to our questions they showed they had sufficiently understood this, we went on to a more extensive instruction, namely, about the one God, who rewards and punishes each one according to his merit, and the rest.

We asked them to make an act of contrition and to manifest their detestation of their sins. Finally, when they appeared sufficiently prepared, we declared to them the mysteries of the Trinity, the Incarnation and the Passion. Showing them Christ fastened to the cross, as he is depicted on the baptismal font on which streams of blood flow down from his wounds, we led them in reciting an act of contrition in their own language."

Furthermore, St. Peter Claver did not lose sight of his converts when they left the ships, but followed them to the plantations to which they were sent, encouraged them to live as Christians, and prevailed on their masters to treat them humanely. While he was not able to abolish slavery, he did fight for laws that allowed for Christian marriage for slaves and that forbade the separation of families. St. Peter Claver declared himself to be the "slave of the Negroes forever." He shared the same characteristic that all other missionary saints had -being a fiery love of God and docile adherence (trust) in His will and designs which together made him a powerful missionary instrument in the Divine Hands. St. Peter Claver said:

> "To love God as He ought to be loved, we must be detached from all temporal love. We must love nothing but Him, or if we love anything else, we must love it only for His sake."
>
> "Seek God in all things and you shall find God by your side."
>
> "Let us learn of Him, that holy preference, which shows most love, to those who suffer most."
>
> "Let us go in simplicity, where merciful Providence leads us, content to see the stone on which we should step, without wanting to discover, all at once and completely, the windings of the road."

Finally after suffering from illness for four years, St. Peter Claver died on Sept. 8, 1654.

St. Peter Claver, dedicated slave of the slaves, pray for us!

St. Louis de Montfort

St. Louis de Montfort was a missionary of another kind -he was a missionary of the Blessed Mother's Heart, whose teachings still inspire and form souls many hundreds of years after his death. He firmly believed that *"It is through the most Blessed Virgin Mary that Jesus Christ came into the world, and it is also through her that he will reign in the world."* And he felt it his life's mission to share this truth with everybody. He taught:

> *"Our entire perfection consists in being conformed, united and consecrated to Jesus Christ. Hence the most perfect of all devotions is undoubtedly that which conforms, unites and consecrates us most perfectly to Jesus Christ. Now, since Mary is of all creatures the one most conformed to Jesus Christ, it follows that among all devotions that which most consecrates and conforms a soul to our Lord is devotion to Mary, his Holy Mother, and that the more a soul is consecrated to her the more will it be consecrated to Jesus Christ."*

He was born Louis Marie Grignon in Montfort, France, in 1673, the oldest living child of a large farm family. He was ordained in 1700, becoming a chaplain in a hospital in Poitiers. His prayer was, *"I am continually asking in my prayers for a poor and small company of good Priests to preach missions and retreats under the standard and protection of the Blessed Virgin"*. This led to the formation of a new congregation called the Missionaries of the Company of Mary. He also founded a congregation for women called the Daughters of

Divine Wisdom. St. Louis de Montfort spent much time preaching missions -and his missions and sermons raised complaints. He became frustrated with the local Bishops and made a pilgrimage to Rome to ask Pope Clement XI what he should do. The Pope recognized his real vocation, and sent him back to France under the title of "Apostolic Missionary". For several years he preached in missions from Brittany to Nantes, and his reputation as a Missionary Preacher grew. He then left Nantes, and the next several years were spent in preaching missions, always traveling on foot. He wore himself out with his work and endured many hardships. Someone even poisoned him for his heated style of preaching, but it was not fatal. During his years preaching he also found time to write, "True Devotion to Mary", "The Secret of Mary", "The Secret of the Rosary", and rules for the Company of Mary. Just before writing True Devotion he became a Dominican Tertiary. He later died from illness and exhaustion at the early age of 43.

The greatest witness as to how St. Louis de Montfort spent his Marian Missionary life is simply by reading some quotes from his writings left behind -which are still sources of conversions in our modern-day world. His love for Mary was his strength, inspiration, protection and hope. And nothing shows us an example of a missionary's closeness with his Heavenly Mother as being the source of the fecundity of his work like St. Louis de Montfort. I would suggest that every missionary should read his three books mentioned here and make a consecration to Our Lady according to his formula. This would ensure a continual growth in virtue and quick advancement on the path of God's will for each missionary soul and work. St. Louis de Montfort's words should be taken to heart by every missionary in the world today. His is not a spirituality only for a few -but one that is most necessary to accomplish God's plan in the modern world. St. Louis de Montfort wrote:

> "It would hardly be possible for me to put into words how much Our Lady thinks of the Holy Rosary and of how she vastly prefers it to all other devotions. Neither can I sufficiently express how highly she rewards those who work to preach the devotion, to establish it and spread it, nor on the other hand how firmly she punishes those who work against it."
>
> "If priests and religious have an obligation to meditate on the great truths of our holy religion in order to live up to their vocation worthily, the same obligation, then, is just as much incumbent upon the laity — because of the fact that every day they meet with spiritual dangers which might make them lose their souls. Therefore they should arm themselves with the frequent meditation on the life, virtues and sufferings of Our Blessed Lord — which are so beautifully contained in the 15 mysteries of the Holy Rosary."
>
> "If I were asked by someone seeking to honor our Lady, 'What does genuine devotion to her involve?' I would answer briefly that it consists in a full appreciation of the privileges and dignity of our Lady; in expressing our gratitude for her goodness to us; in zealously promoting devotion to her; in constantly appealing for her help; in being completely dependent on her; and in placing firm reliance and loving confidence in her motherly goodness."

"The Rosary is the most powerful weapon to touch the Heart of Jesus, Our Redeemer, who loves His Mother."

"If you say the Rosary faithfully until death, I do assure you that, in spite of the gravity of your sins you shall receive a never-fading crown of glory. Even if you are on the brink of damnation, even if you have one foot in hell, even if you have sold your soul to the devil as sorcerers do who practice black magic, and even if you are a heretic as obstinate as a devil, sooner or later you will be converted and will amend your life and will save your soul, if — and mark well what I say — if you say the Holy Rosary devoutly every day until death for the purpose of knowing the truth and obtaining contrition and pardon for your sins."

"If then we are establishing sound devotion to our Blessed Lady, it is only in order to establish devotion to our Lord more perfectly, by providing a smooth but certain way of reaching Jesus Christ."

"As she was the way by which Jesus first came to us, she will again be the way by which he will come to us the second time though not in the same manner."

"Since she is the sure means, the direct and immaculate way to Jesus and the perfect guide to him, it is through her that souls who are to shine forth in sanctity must find him. He who finds Mary finds life, that is, Jesus Christ who is the way, the truth and the life...Mary then must be better known than ever for the deeper understanding and the greater glory of the Blessed Trinity."

Chapter 4: Mary the Great Missionary and Her Children the Saints

"In these latter times Mary must shine forth more than ever in mercy, power and grace; in mercy, to bring back and welcome lovingly the poor sinners and wanderers who are to be converted and return to the Catholic Church; in power, to combat the enemies of God who will rise up menacingly to seduce and crush by promises and threats all those who oppose them; finally, she must shine forth in grace to inspire and support the valiant soldiers and loyal servants of Jesus Christ who are fighting for his cause."

"Mary must become as terrible as an army in battle array to the devil and his followers, especially in these latter times. For Satan, knowing that he has little time—even less now than ever—to destroy souls, intensifies his efforts and his onslaughts every day. He will not hesitate to stir up savage persecutions and set treacherous snares for Mary's faithful servants and children whom he finds more difficult to overcome than others."

"Never will anyone who says his Rosary every day become a formal heretic or be led astray by the devil."

"Never will anyone who says his Rosary every day be led astray. This is a statement that I would gladly sign with my blood."

"When the Holy Rosary is said well, it gives Jesus and Mary more glory and is more meritorious than any other prayer."

"[True devotion to Our Lady] is trustful, that is to say, it fills us with confidence in the Blessed Virgin, the confidence that a child has for its loving Mother. It prompts us to go to her in every need of body and soul with great simplicity, trust and

affection. We implore our Mother's help always, everywhere, and for everything. We pray to her to be enlightened in our doubts, to be put back on the right path when we go astray, to be protected when we are tempted, to be strengthened when we are weakening, to be lifted up when we fall into sin, to be encouraged when we are losing heart, to be rid of our scruples, to be consoled in the trials, crosses and disappointments of life. Finally, in all our afflictions of body and soul, we naturally turn to Mary for help, with never a fear of importuning her or displeasing our Lord."

"As all perfection consists in our being conformed, united and consecrated to Jesus it naturally follows that the most perfect of all devotions is that which conforms, unites, and consecrates us most completely to Jesus. Now of all God's creatures Mary is the most conformed to Jesus. It therefore follows that, of all devotions, devotion to her makes for the most effective consecration and conformity to him. The more one is consecrated to Mary, the more one is consecrated to Jesus.

"That is why perfect consecration to Jesus is but a perfect and complete consecration of oneself to the Blessed Virgin, which is the devotion I teach; or in other words, it is the perfect renewal of the vows and promises of holy baptism."

"By this devotion we give to Jesus all we can possibly give him, and in the most perfect manner, that is, through Mary's hands.

"The Blessed Virgin, mother of gentleness and mercy, never allows herself to be surpassed in love and generosity. When she *sees someone giving himself entirely to her in order to honor and serve her, and depriving himself of what he prizes most in order to adorn her, she gives herself completely in a wondrous manner to him. She engulfs him in the ocean of her graces, adorns him with her merits, supports him with her power, enlightens him with her light, and fills him with her love. She shares her virtues with him — her humility, faith, purity, etc. She makes up for his failings and becomes his representative with Jesus. Just as one who is consecrated belongs entirely to Mary, so Mary belongs entirely to him."*

"St. Thomas assures us that, following the order established by his divine Wisdom, God ordinarily imparts his graces to men through Mary. Therefore, if we wish to go to him, seeking union with him, we must use the same means which he used in coming down from heaven to assume our human nature and to impart his graces to us. That means was a complete dependence on Mary his Mother, which is true devotion to her."

"Have you strayed from the path leading to heaven? Then call on Mary, for her name means "Star of the Sea, the North Star which guides the ships of our souls during the voyage of this life," and she will guide you to the harbor of eternal salvation."

"God the Father has communicated to Mary His fruitfulness, as far as a mere creature was capable of it, in order that He might give her the power to produce His Son, and all the members of His mystical body."

"When Mary has struck her roots in a soul, she produces there marvels of grace, which she alone can produce, because she alone is the fruitful Virgin who never has had, and never will have, her equal in purity and in fruitfulness."

"The works of Jesus and Mary can also be called wonderful flowers; but their perfume and beauty can only be appreciated by those who study them carefully—and who open them and drink in their scent by diligent and sincere meditation."

"In order to rid ourselves of self, we must die ourselves daily. That is to say, we must renounce the operations of the powers of our soul and the senses of our body. We must see as if we saw not, understand as if we understood not, and make use of the things of this world as if we made no use of them at all (1 Cor. 7:29-31). This is what St. Paul calls dying daily (1 Cor. 15:31). "Unless the grain of wheat falling into the ground die, itself remains alone," and bringeth forth no good fruit (Jn. 12:24-25)."

"Mary has produced, together with the Holy Ghost, the greatest thing which has been or ever will be—a God-Man; and she will consequently produce the greatest saints that there will be in the end of time."

"If, then, we establish solid devotion to our Blessed Lady, it is only to establish more perfectly devotion to Jesus Christ, and to provide an easy and secure means for finding Jesus Christ. If devotion to Our Lady removed us from Jesus Christ, we should have to reject it as an illusion of the devil; but so far from this being the case, devotion to Our Lady is, on the contrary, necessary for us—as I have already shown, and will show still *further hereafter—as a means of finding Jesus Christ perfectly, of loving Him tenderly, of serving Him faithfully."*

"She is not the sun, which by the brightness of its rays blinds us because of our weakness; but she is fair and gentle as the moon (Cant. 6:9), which receives the light of the sun, and tempers it to make it more suitable to our capacity."

"Saint Dominic has divided up the lives of Our Lord and Our Lady into fifteen mysteries which stand for their virtues and their most important actions. These are the fifteen tableaux; or pictures whose every detail must rule and inspire our lives."

"Satan, being proud, suffers infinitely more from being beaten and punished by a little and humble handmaid of God, and her humility humbles him more than the Divine power; and, secondly, because God has given Mary such a great power against the devils, that, as they have often been obliged to confess, in spite of themselves, by the mouths of the possessed, they fear one of her sighs for a soul more than the prayers of all the Saints, and one of her menaces against them more than all other torments."

"It is an easy way. It is the way which Jesus Christ Himself trod in coming to us, and in which there is no obstacle in reaching Him. It is true that we can attain divine union by other roads; but it is by many more crosses and strange deaths, and with many more difficulties, which we shall find it hard to overcome. We must pass through obscure nights, through combats, through strange agonies, over craggy mountains, through cruel

thorns and over frightful deserts. But by the path of Mary we pass more gently and more tranquilly."

"God has never made or formed but one enmity; but it is an irreconcilable one, which shall endure and develop even to the end. It is between Mary, His worthy Mother, and the devil,—between the children and the servants of the Blessed Virgin and the children and instruments of Lucifer. The most terrible of all the enemies which God has set up against the devil is His holy Mother, Mary. He has inspired her, even since the days of the earthly Paradise, though she existed then only in His idea, with so much hatred against that cursed enemy of God, with so much industry in unveiling the malice of that old serpent, with so much power to conquer, to overthrow, and to crush that proud impious rebel, that he fears her not only more than all Angels and men, but in some sense more than God Himself. It is not that the anger, the hatred, and the power of God are not infinitely greater than those of the Blessed Virgin, for the perfections of Mary are limited, but it is, first, because Satan, being proud, suffers infinitely more from being beaten and punished by a little and humble handmaid of God, and her humility humbles him more than the Divine power; and, secondly, because God has given Mary such a great power against the devils, that, as they have often been obliged to confess, in spite of themselves, by the mouths of the possessed, they fear one of her sighs for a soul more than the prayers of all the Saints, and one of her menaces against them more than all other torments."

St. Louise de Montfort, Missionary of Mary, Pray for us!

St Isaac Jogues

St. Isaac Jogues is called the "Apostle of the Mohawks," and he was known to the Mohawks themselves as Ondessonk, "the indomitable one." He was born on January 10, 1607, at Orleans, France, into a good bourgeois family; at the age of seventeen he entered the Jesuit novitiate school at Rouen. Later he studied at the royal college of La Fleche, and from one of the teachers there (who had two brothers and a nephew serving as missionaries in Canada), the young man heard stories that may well have turned his thoughts towards the New World. He also had meetings with the pioneers, Brebeuf and Masse, on their return from Canada in 1629, when Quebec was captured by the English. Three years later the province was again in French hands. Isaac Jogues continued his education at the College of Clermont, University of Paris, and in due time was ordained and accepted for missionary service. He was already recognized as an able scholar, with talents for writing and teaching. In the summer of 1636, at the age of twenty-nine, he embarked for Canada with several of his fellows. Drawings of Jogues made at about this time reveal features of unusual refinement; this air of delicacy was, however, deceptive, for beneath it lay heroic powers of physical endurance.

On arrival Jogues wrote as follows to his mother: *"I do not know what it is to enter Heaven, but this I know—that it would be difficult to experience in this world a joy more excessive and more overflowing than I felt in setting foot in the New World, and celebrating my first*

Mass on the day of the Visitation." His later letters show the same exaltation of spirit.

Father Jogues' companions were at once sent on westward to join Father Brebeuf, who in 1626 had established an outpost on the peninsula of Lake Huron, to minister to the Huron Indians, one of the less warlike tribes. Jogues went with them as far as the settlement of Trois Rivieres, and there, some weeks later, he saw a flotilla of canoes descending the St. Lawrence. In the first, wielding a paddle, was Father Anthony Daniel, one of Brebeuf's coworkers, exhausted and emaciated, his cassock in tatters. He was bound for Quebec for a period of recuperation, and Jogues was to replace him. The young missionary lost no time in organizing the expedition. The post was nine hundred miles away, up the river, through forests, across portages. On long trips such as these the missionaries and their guides had to carry provisions.

Arriving at last at the Lake Huron post, Father Jogues collapsed in Brebeuf's arms. Almost at once he fell ill of a fever, which in turn struck down others. At this time the fathers were living in crude huts, and their food was poor and scanty. When the missionaries had recovered, a similar epidemic broke out among the Indians, who, blaming it on the Black Coats, as they called the Jesuits, threatened to kill them all. Brebeuf conciliated them and by the following year relations had so improved that he was able to write in one of his reports: *"We are gladly heard, and there is scarcely a village that has not invited us to go to it.... And at last it is understood from our whole conduct that we have not come to buy skins or to carry on any traffic, but solely to teach them, and to procure for them their souls' health."* Indian good will, however, was fickle, and before long the medicine men had fomented so much hostility that in a tribal council the Indians decided that the Jesuit priests must die. Once more the Indians were pacified. But eventually they were taken prisoners by the Iroquois, along with some Huron converts. Jogues wrote: *"We were made to go up from the shore between two lines of Indians who were armed with clubs, sticks, and knives. I was the last and blows were showered on me. I fell on the ground and thought my end had come, but they lifted me up all streaming with blood and carried me more dead than alive to the platform."* Worse tortures followed. The Iroquois were especially cruel to the Huron converts. At this time and during subsequent torturings Father Jogues suffered the loss of two fingers. The young doctor arrested with him was martyred. Father Jogues wrote of his death: *"Thus on the 28th of September this angel of innocence and martyr of Jesus Christ was immolated in his thirty-fifth year, for Him who had given His life for his ransom. He had consecrated his heart and soul to God and his life and labor to the welfare of the poor Indians."*

Jogues' slavery lasted for more than a year. His record of it, written for his Superior, has been studied by scholars who are amazed at his endurance. *"He would sometimes escape,"* Parkman wrote, *". . . and wander in the forest, praying his beads and repeating passages of Scripture. In a remote and lonely spot he cut the bark in the form of a cross from the trunk of a great tree; and here he made his prayers. This living martyr, half clad in shaggy furs, kneeling in the snow among the icicled rocks and beneath the gloomy pines, bowing in adoration before the emblem of his faith in which was his only consolation and his only hope, is alike a theme for the pen and a subject for the pencil."* Later

Jogues was to report to his spiritual guide, *"The only sin I can remember during my captivity is that I sometimes looked on the approach of death with complacency."* The Indians were not without respect for their strange captive, naming him "the indomitable one." He had at least one good friend among the Mohawks, an old woman whom he called "aunt." She tried to heal his wounds and to warn and protect him when danger threatened. His days were passed in menial work, learning the language, and comforting Huron prisoners who were sometimes brought in. He was taken on fishing and hunting expeditions, where he suffered much from hunger and exposure. As opportunity offered, he baptized children he found dying. During the year he baptized some seventy persons. Eventually Isaac Jogues escaped his Indian captors.

And so, on November 5, 1643, Jogues sailed for France, and on Christmas Day was put ashore in Brittany. Kindly people helped him reach the town of Rennes. At the rector's house, he sent word by a servant that he was the bearer of news from New France. Unknown to Jogues, his own fate was a matter of widespread concern in France, for the latest volume of 'Jesuit Relations' had contained the details of his capture. When the rector came to the door, after an exchange of courtesies, he asked the shabbily-dressed man if he had known Father Jogues. *"Very well indeed,"* was the answer. *"Have they murdered him?" "No, Father, he is alive and free—and I am he!"*

Father Jogues' only desire was to get back to Canada, and in June, 1644, he was again in Quebec. From there he was sent to Montreal, to spend his time helping to build up that new outpost, until the cessation of warfare would permit him to return to the Hurons. Two years later an embassy of Iroquois came to Trois Rivieres to discuss terms of truce and the ransom of prisoners. Many fine speeches were made and gifts were exchanged. The Jesuit priest participated in these conclaves. After the deliberations were concluded, the French thought it prudent to send a conciliatory deputation to meet with other Iroquois chieftains at Ossernenon. This embassy was led by Father Jogues and Sieur Jean Bourdon, an engineer, who represented the government of New France. *"Oh, how I should regret to lose so glorious an occasion,"* wrote the priest to his superior before starting, *"when it may depend only on me that some souls be saved! I hope that His goodness, which has not abandoned me in the hour of trial, will aid me still."*

The party traveled south, stopping first at Fort Orange, where the priest saw again his Dutch friends and reimbursed them for his ransom of the year before. The Dutch were astonished to learn that he was going back to the scene of his painful captivity. Ondessonk indeed deserved his name! The Mohawks, too, when he appeared among them, were impressed by his courage and disarmed by his gentleness, for he showed no trace of ill-will. The old "aunt" greeted with friendly words the man who had been the tribe's despised captive and who now returned as an envoy of peace. *"With us you will always have a mat to lie on and a fire to warm yourself,"* she told him. Gifts were exchanged between Frenchmen and Indians, and belts of wampum offered for the release of the Hurons held captive. Thus, the purpose of the visit was achieved, the pact confirmed, and Jogues went back to Quebec. He was to return to spend the winter among the Mohawks, now that friendly relations were established.

In the meanwhile, after Jogues and Bourdon had left Ossernenon, an epidemic broke out, caterpillars ate the crops, and famine threatened. As usual, the Mohawks blamed all their troubles on Black Coat, even though, on his latest trip, he had not worn priestly garb. But had he not left with them a mysterious box? True, he had showed them its contents, which consisted of personal necessaries, but he had locked it up and asked them to keep it. No doubt a devil was concealed in the box, to bring upon them all manner of evils. They threw the box into the river. Totally unaware of the mounting tension and antagonism, Jogues, with John Lalande, a lay missionary, once more started south for Ossernenon. On the trail they were met by a party of Mohawks on the warpath. The three or four Hurons serving Jogues as guides turned back to escape capture, while the two Frenchmen were led on as prisoners. At Ossernenon Jogues' arguments seemed to affect his hearers. *"I am a man like yourselves,"* he replied to their charges. *"I do not fear death or torture. I do not know why you wish to kill me. I come here to confirm the peace and show you the way to Heaven, and you treat me like a dog."* In the councils the majority were ready to give the brave Ondessonk his freedom, but the minority faction, members of the Bear clan, took matters into their own hands. They invited Jogues to pay them a visit, and as he unsuspectingly entered the cabin of the Bear chief, he was brutally tomahawked. The next day Lalande met the same fate, and both bodies were thrown into a nearby ravine. Their heads were cut off and placed on poles facing the trail by which they had come, as if in warning to other Black Robes. When the news of the martyrdom was carried to Fort Orange, the Dutch pastor hastened to Ossernenon to denounce the Mohawks for their crime. Later on some of the Indians went to the fort with Father Jogues' breviary, missal, and cassock, hoping to make a profitable trade, and the pastor again censured them.

The Iroquois now once more began to attack and plunder the Huron villages, sparing neither Christians nor non-Christians. Garnier, Daniel, Gabriel, Lalemant, and Brebeuf were killed. But in the Mohawk Valley the example of Jogues' heroism was not forgotten, for the gentle priest had possessed in high degree the virtue the Indians most admired, bravery. And when, some years later, there was peace, the three Jesuit priests sent from Canada to establish the Mission of the Martyrs were well received. Before long Mohawk converts were traveling to the seminary in Quebec to be trained as Christian leaders.

What gave St. Isaac Joques such passion to preach the Gospel to the Indians and such courage in the face of death? He said:

> "My confidence is placed in God who does not need our help for accomplishing his designs. Our single endeavor should be to give ourselves to the work and to be faithful to him, and not to spoil his work by our shortcomings. ..."
>
> "The sign of the cross is adorable and could not do anything but good to those who should use it. I have no intention of giving it up."
>
> "Let us love silence till the world is made to die in our hearts. Let us always remember death, and in this thought draw near to God in our heart – and the pleasures of this world will have our scorn."
>
> "We begged God to accept our lives and our blood and unite them to His life and His blood for the salvation of these tribes."

In one of his last letters to a friend before his death he explained further:

> "... *The Iroquois have come to make some presents to our governor, ransom some prisoners he held, and treat of peace with him in the name of the whole country. It has been concluded, to the great joy of France. It will last as long as pleases the Almighty.*
>
> *To maintain, and see what can be done for the instruction of these tribes, it is here deemed expedient to send them some father. I have reason to think I shall be sent, since I have some knowledge of the language and country. You see what need I have of the powerful aid of prayers while amidst these savages. I will have to remain among them, almost without liberty to pray, without Mass, without Sacraments, and be responsible for every accident among the Iroquois, French, Algonquins, and others. But what shall I say? My hope is in God, who needs not us to accomplish his designs. We must endeavor to be faithful to Him and not spoil His work by our shortcomings....*
>
> *My heart tells me that if I have the happiness of being employed in this mission, 'Ibo et non redibo' (I shall go and shall not return); but I shall be happy if our Lord will complete the sacrifice where He has begun it, and make the little blood I have shed in that land the earnest of what I would give from every vein of my body and my heart.*
>
> *In a word, this people is "a bloody spouse" to me (Exodus iv, 25). May our good Master, who has purchased them in His*

blood, open to them the door of His Gospel, as well as to the four allied nations near them.

Adieu, dear Father. Pray Him to unite me inseparably to Him.

Isaac Jogues, S.J.

St. Isaac Jogues, Missionary to the Indians, Pray for us!

St. Vincent de Paul

St. Vincent de Paul (1581 - 1660) was a missionary whose ministry encompassed a vast variety of souls. He is always associated with his work with the poor. However, at one point in time, he was asked by the Queen of France to serve her as her spiritual director and was the adviser to the wealthiest and most powerful woman in France for 10 years! He also served galley slaves, helped greatly in the reform of seminaries and renewed the priesthood in holiness.

St. Vincent de Paul was born to a poor peasant family in the French village of Pouy on April 24, 1581. His first formal education was provided by the Franciscans until the age of 15. He was such a good student that he was hired to tutor the children of a nearby wealthy family. He used the money he earned tutoring to continue his education studying theology at the University of Toulose.

He was ordained in 1600 at the tender age of nineteen. When he was appointed to serve at a parish, it was pointed out that the Council of Trent had established a minimum age for ordination of twenty-four years of age. Vincent resigned the position and continued his studies completing his bachelor's degree at Toulouse in 1604. Later, he would earn a Licentiate in Canon Law from the University of Paris. Vincent intended to live a priestly life of comfort until he heard the deathbed confession of a servant which opened Vincent de Paul's eyes to the crying spiritual needs of the peasantry of France. The Countess (whose servant St. Vincent had helped) had a heart for the poor and asked her husband to fund a group of priests who would serve the rural poor. St. Vincent declined her offer to lead this group out of his own humility -although later on he would accept her offer and form the priestly group of the Vincentians. In the meantime in 1605, while on a ship traveling from Marseilles to Narbone, he was captured, brought to Tunis and sold as a slave. He had three different masters over a two-year period -the final one being a former Franciscan who converted to Islam and was living with three wives. After converting the man's second wife, the man repented of his apostasy and together with St. Vincent managed to escape and both returned to France.

St. Vincent went to Avignon and later to Rome to continue his studies. While there he became a chaplain to the Count of Goigny and was placed in charge of distributing money to the deserving poor. He became pastor of a small parish in Clichy for a short period of time, while also serving as a tutor and spiritual director.

From that point forward he spent his life preaching missions and providing relief to the poor. He even established hospitals for them. The young priest who hoped for a 'comfortable life' now lived passionately and tirelessly for the poor. He later extended his concern and ministry to convicts. He organized the rich women of Paris to collect funds for his missionary projects, founded several hospitals, collected relief funds for the victims of war, and ransomed over 1,200 galley slaves from North Africa. Later, Vincent established confraternities of charity for the spiritual and physical relief of the poor and sick of each parish. The need to evangelize and assist these souls was so great and the demands beyond his own ability to meet that he founded the Ladies of Charity along with St. Louise de Marillac, a lay institute of woman to help, *"whose convent is the sickroom, whose chapel is the parish church, whose cloister is the streets of the city."* He also founded a religious institute of priests - the Congregation of Priests of the Mission, commonly referred to now as the Vincentians. He was zealous in conducting retreats for clergy at a time when there was great laxity, abuse, and ignorance among them. He was a pioneer in clerical training and was instrumental in establishing seminaries. This was at a time when there were not many priests in France and what priests there were, were neither well-formed nor faithful to their way of life. Vincent helped reform the clergy and the manner in which they were instructed and prepared for the priesthood. He did this first through the presentation of retreats and later by helping develop a precursor to our modern-day seminaries. At one point his community was directing 53 upper-level seminaries. His retreats, open to priests and laymen, were so well attended that it is said he infused a "Christian spirit among more than 20,000 persons in his last 23 years." It has been reported that St. Vincent wrote more than 30,000 letters in his lifetime and that nearly 7,000 had been collected in the 18th century. There are at least five collections of his letters in existence today.

He was eighty years old when he died in Paris on September 27, 1660. He had "become the symbol of the successful reform of the French Church". St. Vincent is sometimes referred to as "The Apostle of Charity" and "The Father of the Poor". His mission work continues today through the countless souls that are part of his institutes and who follow his charism. The Vincentians in 2023 have nearly 4,000 members in 86 countries. There are more than 18,000 Daughters today serving the needs of the poor in 94 countries. His incorrupt heart can be found in the Convent of the Sisters of Charity and his bones have been embedded in a wax effigy of the Saint located at the Church of the Lazarist Mission. Both sites are located in Paris, France.

What was the Wisdom that inspired a man so greatly known and loved as a missionary throughout the entire world? We hear it on his own lips. St. Vincent said:

"Humility is nothing but truth, and pride is nothing but lying."

"You will find out that Charity is a heavy burden to carry, heavier than the kettle of soup and the full basket. But you will keep your gentleness and your smile. It is not enough to give soup and bread. This the rich can do. You are the servant of the poor, always smiling and good-humored. They are your masters, terribly sensitive and exacting master you will see. And the uglier and the dirtier they will be, the more unjust and insulting, the more love you must give them. It is only for your love alone that the poor will forgive you the bread you give to them."

"Make it a practice to judge persons and things in the most favorable light at all times and under all circumstances."

"Go to the poor: you will find God."

> "Charity is certainly greater than any rule. Moreover, all rules must lead to charity."
>
> "The kingdom of God is peace in the Holy Spirit; He will reign in you if your heart is at peace. So, be at peace, Mademoiselle, and you will honor in a sovereign way the God of peace and love."
>
> "We are chosen by God as instruments of His immense and fatherly love, which seeks to be established and to spread in souls.... Our vocation is therefore to go not to a parish, nor only to a bishopric, but to the whole world. To do what? To set peoples' hearts on fire, to do what the Son of God did, He who came to bring fire to the world, to set it ablaze with His love."
>
> "Our vocation is to go and enflame the hearts of men, to do what the Son of God did, He Who brought fire into the world to set it alight with His love. What else can we wish for, than for it to burn and consume all things?" – "if our vocation is to go and spread this divine fire in the whole world, if it is so, my brothers, if it is really so, how must I myself burn of this divine fire!"

St. Vincent de Paul, Missionary to the Poor and Orphaned, Pray for us!

St. Therese of Lisieux

Now we move on to a slew of women saints who are powerful missionary intercessors for the Church militant. Ironically, the Patron Saint of Missions is none other than the young cloistered

Carmelite sister -St. Therese of Lisieux! She was born in France in 1873, and was the spoiled youngest daughter of a mother who had wanted to be a saint and a father who had wanted to be monk. The two had gotten married but determined they would be celibate until a priest told them that was not how God wanted a marriage to work! They eventually had nine children. The five children who lived were all daughters who were close all their lives. Four of them -including St. Therese -joined the Carmel in Lisieux. Although St. Therese was pampered and adored by her family, her life was full of suffering. As an infant she almost died until her mother entrusted her to a wet nurse in a village. It was as her mother was kneeling under a statue of St. Joseph begging for the life of her little one to be saved that St. Therese started nursing her wet nurse furiously and recovered her health. At age four and a half her beloved mother died of cancer and she took her older 16-year-old sister Pauline as a 'second mother.' When Pauline entered the Carmelite convent five years later Therese's little heart was crushed again and she became so ill with a fever that people thought she was dying. It was only when people around her were praying a rosary in front of a statue in her bedroom that she saw the Virgin Mother smile at her and she was cured instantly. When her other sisters, Marie and Leonie, left to join religious orders (the Carmelites and Poor Clares, respectively), Therese was left alone with her last sister Celine and her father. She was so spoiled she did not want to help with the housework and was so overly sensitive that the smallest infraction against her sensibilities made her burst into a rage of tears. It was on Christmas when she was 14 that Jesus gave her the grace of healing from her disordered emotions. Therese greatly longed to enter Carmel with her sisters and was, of course, denied because of her young age. But she had a will of steel and during a pilgrimage to Rome although she was forbidden to speak to the Pope, she ran to him during an audience and begged the Holy Father to make an exception and admit her to the Carmel in Lisieux. She had to be carried out by two of the guards! But the Vicar General who had seen her courage was impressed and soon Therese was admitted to the Carmelite convent that her sisters Pauline and Marie had already joined. Therese's dreams of Carmelite life were shattered by great interior suffering as well as persecution from some of the sisters who judged her too young to be serious about a religious vocation. Therese used all obstacles to grow in great virtue and developed a spirituality now known as the 'Little Way' -a way of spiritual childhood before God that allowed Him to carry her to great heights of holiness in a very short time. She once explained this secret to her sister writing:

"Let me tell you, Marie, that my desires for martyrdom are nothing. It is not they which give me the unlimited confidence which I feel in my heart... What pleases God in my little soul is that He sees me loving my littleness and my poverty: it is the blind hope that I have in His mercy. That is my only treasure. Why can't it be yours?... To love Jesus, the more one is weak, without desires and without virtues, the more one is suitable for the operations of God's consuming and transforming love. It is confidence and nothing but confidence that must lead us to love."

Therese was made novice mistress and led the souls entrusted to her with great maturity and wisdom. She dreamed of being a missionary and helping to open a Carmel in the East, but her poor health prevented her from being sent on this mission. St. Therese wrote:

> *"Our vocation, yours and mine, is not to go harvesting in the fields of ripe corn. Jesus does not say to us: "Lower your eyes, look at the fields and go and reap them," our mission is still loftier. Here are Jesus' words: "Lift up your eyes and see....*
> *" See how, in My Heaven, there are places empty; it is for you to fill them ... each one of you is My Moses praying on the mountain (Ex 17:8) ask Me for laborers and I shall send them, I await only a prayer, a sigh from your heart!"* – St Thérèse of the Child Jesus (1873-1897) Carmelite, (Letter 135).
>
> *'I have the vocation of the Apostle. I would like to travel over the whole earth to preach Your Name and to plant Your glorious Cross on infidel soil. But O my Beloved, one mission alone would not be sufficient for me, I would want to preach the Gospel on all the five continents simultaneously and even to the most remote isles. I would be a missionary, not for a few years only but from the beginning of creation until the consummation of the ages.'*

St. Therese of Lisieux was a spiritual sister, mother and guide to a few missionary priests through a relationship of prayer and spiritual direction through letters. And it was the flame of love in her heart that reached all places and times (even down to our own day and age) that won for her the title of 'Patroness of the Missions'. She wrote:

> 'I understood that the Church had a Heart and that this Heart was BURNING WITH LOVE. I understood it was Love alone that made the Church's members act, that if Love ever became extinct, apostles would not preach the Gospel and martyrs would not shed their blood. I understood that LOVE COMPRISED ALL VOCATIONS, THAT LOVE WAS EVERYTHING, THAT IT EMBRACED ALL TIMES AND PLACES ... IN A WORD, THAT IT WAS ETERNAL! At last I have found it ... MY VOCATION IS LOVE! ... in the heart of the Church, my Mother, I shall be LOVE.'
>
> "Jesus has chosen to show me the only way which leads to the Divine Furnace of love; it is the way of childlike self-surrender, the way of a child who sleeps, afraid of nothing, in its father's arms."

At age 24 she died a very painful death from Tuberculosis which she united to the Crucified Lord for the salvation of souls. She promised on her deathbed that she would send a 'shower of roses from heaven' as graces to all who prayed through her intercession after her death -and truly it is rare if one does not receive a physical rose in addition to heavenly help when one prays for her intercession.

St. Therese teaches us that one does not have to be great, rich, powerful, popular or successful to be a great missionary for the Lord. It is sufficient to take the little that one has and is and to offer it to God with all of the passionate love one can muster in their heart. She also shows us that it is not the work we do -but the love and prayer with which we act and speak -that is the conduit for the Holy Spirit to use us as powerful missionary instruments to bring souls to God. St. Therese said, *"Holiness consists simply in doing God's will, and being just what God wants us to be."* And she prayed for us even while still on earth, saying, *"I implore You, cast Your eyes upon a multitude of little souls; choose from this world, I beg of You, a legion of little victims worthy of Your love."* It is by burning with the furnace of Christ's divine Love and being consumed by it as a victim with Him that we will be able to complete the mission that has been entrusted to each one of our vocations.

St. Therese of the Child Jesus and of the Holy Face, Patroness of the Missions, pray for us!

St. Edith Stein

St. Edith Stein was another Carmelite that saw her missionary work as being that of the Apostolate of Prayer, although her writing as a philosopher and witness of martyrdom among her fellow Jews in the Death Camps of WWII were also ways that she served Christ's mission. St. Edith Stein was born in Bresslau, Germany (now Wroclaw, Poland) to a Jewish family. Raised as an Orthodox Jew she became a well-respected philosopher throughout Europe, a feat not common for a woman of her time. She traveled and taught at the most prestigious universities. Upon visiting a Catholic friend whose husband had recently died she was struck by the peace the woman exuded in the face of her beloved's death. Upon questioning her friend -now a young widow -the source of such peace she was given

Chapter 4: Mary the Great Missionary and Her Children the Saints

a glimpse of the power of the Catholic faith's belief in the Resurrection. As St. Edith Stein dove deeper into the faith, she eventually decided to become baptized, causing a rift between her and her loving, Orthodox Jewish Mother. Edith did what she could to soften the blow, but until her Mother's death she never quite understood why her daughter had abandoned her Jewish faith. Edith felt called deeper and deeper into prayer, eventually discerning a vocation to the Carmel in Germany. She abandoned her highly respected profession of teaching and lecturing and became the poor bride of Christ. She who taught so far and wide with words was now preaching the Truth simply by the action of the renunciation of her life for Christ. She said:

> *"The limitless loving devotion to God, and the gift God makes of Himself to you, are the highest elevation of which the heart is capable; it is the highest degree of prayer. The souls that have reached this point are truly the heart of the Church. If anyone comes to me, I want to lead them to Him."*

Recognizing Edith's intellectual prowess, her superiors encouraged her to continue writing. We have very deep and beautiful reflections on the Carmelite spirituality left behind by Edith, who had now taken the name as Teresa Benedicta of the Cross in her Carmelite family. When WWII broke out and the Jews began to be persecuted, St. Edith Stein felt the call of the Lord to suffer with them for their salvation. She wrote:

> "I told our Lord that I knew it was His cross that was now being placed upon the Jewish people; that most of them did not understand this, but that those who did would have to take it up willingly in the name of all. I would do that. At the end of the service, I was certain that I had been heard. But what this carrying of the cross was to consist in, that I did not yet know."
>
> "Things were in God's plan which I had not planned at all. I am coming to the living faith and conviction that - from God's point of view - there is no chance and that the whole of my life, down to every detail, has been mapped out in God's divine providence and makes complete and perfect sense in God's all-seeing eyes."

Her superiors sent her into hiding in the Netherlands (along with her blood sister Rosa who had taken refuge in the convent), but the Nazis eventually found her, arrested her and sent her to the death camps where she was murdered for her Jewish heritage the day following her arrival. St. Edith Stein deeply understood the evils of this world and yet chose to look above them to Jesus Crucified as her strength and hope. She found meaning in her life solely in Him and trusted that He would bear powerful fruit from the path of humility, sacrifice and prayer that she chose as a Carmelite nun. In 1939 she wrote in a reflection for the community:

> "The followers of the Anti-Christ make every effort to tear the cross out of the hands of Christians... Therefore, the Savior today looks at us, solemnly probing us: 'Will you remain faithful to the crucified?' If you decide for Christ, it could cost you

your life… If you intend to be the Bride of Christ, the Crucified, you too must completely renounce your will and no longer have any desire except to fulfill God's will.

The Savior hangs before you with a pierced Heart. He has spilled His Heart's blood to win your heart. If you want to follow Him in holy purity, your heart must be free of every earthly desire. Jesus, the Crucified, is to be the only object of your longings, your wishes, your thoughts… **The world is in flames. Are you impelled to put them out? Look at the Cross. From the open Heart gushes the Blood of the Savior. This extinguishes the flames of hell. Make your heart free… and then the flood of Divine Love will be poured into your heart until it overflows and becomes fruitful to all the ends of the earth. Do you hear the groans of the wounded on the battlefields in the west and the east? You are not a physician and not a nurse and cannot bind up the wounds. You are enclosed in a cell and cannot get to them. Do you hear the anguish of the dying? You would like to be a priest and comfort them. Does the lament of the widows and orphans distress you? You would like to be an angel of mercy and help them. Look at the Crucified. If you are nuptially bound to him by the faithful observance of your holy vows, your being is precious blood. Bound to him, you are omnipresent as he is. You cannot help here or there like the physician, the nurse, the priest. You can be at all fronts, wherever there is grief, in the power of the cross. Your compassionate love takes you** *everywhere, this love from the divine heart. Its precious blood is poured everywhere -soothing, healing, saving.*

The eyes of the Crucified look down on you -asking, probing. Will you make your covenant with the Crucified anew in all seriousness? What will you answer him? 'Lord where shall we go? You have the words of eternal life." September 14, 1939

St. Edith Stein, Carmelite Missionary to Philosophers, Jews and devout souls, pray for us!

St. Mother Teresa of Calcutta

"By blood, I am Albanian. By citizenship, an Indian. By faith, I am a Catholic nun. As to my calling, I belong to the world. As to my heart, I belong entirely to the Heart of Jesus." A missionary of our modern times who changed both the secular as well as religious world was St. Mother Teresa of Calcutta. She, like her namesake St. Therese of Lisieux, followed a spirituality of littleness -allowing the fire of God's love to be the impetus of all her words and actions. She said, *"We cannot all do great things, but we can do small things with great love."* And, *"Love begins at home, and it is not how much we do... but how much love we put in that action."* Not only her words, but the witness of her life shows the power of doing *"ordinary things with extraordinary love,"* for the Lord.

Mother Teresa was born Agnes Gonxha Bojaxhiu on August 26, 1910 in Albania. She left her home in September 1928 at the age of 18 to join the Institute of the Blessed Virgin Mary, known as the Sisters of Loreto, in Ireland. She received the name Sister Mary Teresa after St. Therese of Lisieux. In December of 1929, she departed for her first trip to India, arriving in Calcutta. After making her First Profession of Vows in May 1931, Sister Teresa was assigned to teach in Calcutta at St. Mary's School for girls. Sister Teresa made her Final Profession of Vows, On May 24, 1937, becoming, as she said, the "spouse of Jesus" for "all eternity." From that time on she was called Mother Teresa. In 1944 she became the school's principal and all together spent 20 years serving at the girls' school. Mother Teresa found deep joy in her work and was known for great organizational skills, hard work and deep consecration to Jesus through a faithful living out of her religious vows.

It was on September 10, 1946 during a train ride from Calcutta to Darjeeling for her annual retreat, that Mother Teresa received her *"inspiration, her call within a call."* During this experience Jesus' thirst for love and for souls took hold of her heart and the desire to satiate His thirst became the driving force of her life. By means of interior locutions and visions, Jesus revealed to her the desire of His heart for *"victims of love"* who would *"radiate His love on souls."* *"Come be My light,"'* He begged her. *"I cannot go alone."* Jesus revealed His pain at the neglect of the poor, His sorrow at their ignorance of Him and His longing for their love. He asked Mother Teresa to establish a religious community, Missionaries of Charity, dedicated to the service of the poorest of the poor.

Nearly two years of testing and discernment passed before Mother Teresa received permission to begin. On August 17, 1948, she dressed for the first time in a white, blue-bordered sari and passed through the gates of her beloved Loreto convent to enter the world of the poor. After a short course with the Medical Mission

Sisters in Patna, Mother Teresa returned to Calcutta and found temporary lodging with the Little Sisters of the Poor. On December 21, she went for the first time to the slums. She visited families, washed the sores of some children, cared for an old man lying sick on the road and nursed a woman dying of hunger and tuberculosis. She started each day with communion and then went out, rosary in her hand, to find and serve Him amongst "*the unwanted, the unloved, the uncared for.*" After some months, she was joined, one by one, by her former students.

On October 7, 1950 the new congregation of the Missionaries of Charity was officially established in the Archdiocese of Calcutta. By the early 1960s, Mother Teresa began to send her Sisters to other parts of India. The Decree of Praise granted to the Congregation by Pope Paul VI in February 1965 encouraged her to open a house in Venezuela. It was soon followed by foundations in Rome and Tanzania and, eventually, on every continent. Starting in 1980 and continuing through the 1990s, Mother Teresa opened houses in almost all of the communist countries, including the former Soviet Union, Albania and Cuba.

In order to respond better to both the physical and spiritual needs of the poor, Mother Teresa founded the Missionaries of Charity Brothers in 1963, in 1976 the contemplative branch of the Sisters, in 1979 the Contemplative Brothers, and in 1984 the Missionaries of Charity Fathers. Yet her inspiration was not limited to those with religious vocations. She formed the Co-Workers of Mother Teresa and the Sick and Suffering Co-Workers, people of many faiths and nationalities with whom she shared her spirit of prayer, simplicity, sacrifice and her apostolate of humble works of love. This spirit later inspired the Lay Missionaries of Charity. In answer to the requests of many priests, in 1981 Mother Teresa also began the Corpus Christi Movement for Priests as a "little way of holiness" for those who desire to share in her charism and spirit.

By 1997 Mother Teresa's community had 4000 sisters, 610 foundations in 123 countries. During the last years of her life, despite increasingly severe health problems, Mother Teresa continued to govern her Society and respond to the needs of the poor and the Church. In March 1997 she blessed her newly-elected successor as Superior General of the Missionaries of Charity and then made one more trip abroad. After meeting Pope John Paul II for the last time, she returned to Calcutta and spent her final weeks receiving visitors and instructing her Sisters. On September 5, 1997 Mother Teresa died. Because of her widespread witness of virtue and holiness throughout the world, she was Beatified by 2003 and later Canonized in 2015.

St. Mother Teresa's spirituality was very simple and very deep. It is best described by herself:

> "I try to give to the poor people for love what the rich could get for money. No, I wouldn't touch a leper for a thousand pounds; yet I willingly cure him for the love of God."
>
> "Love is a one-way street. It always moves away from self in the direction of the other. Love is the ultimate gift of ourselves to others. When we stop giving, we stop loving, when we stop loving we stop growing, and unless we grow we will never attain personal fulfillment; we will never open out to receive the life of God. It is through love we encounter God."
>
> "If you can't feed a hundred people, then feed just one."

"Let us touch the dying, the poor, the lonely and the unwanted according to the graces we have received and let us not be ashamed or slow to do the humble work."

"Some time ago a man to our house and he said, 'Mother, there is a family, a Hindu family, that has eight children. They have not eaten for a long time. Do something for them.' So, I took some rice and I went. When I arrived at their house, I could see the hunger in the children's eyes. Their eyes were shining with hunger. I gave the rice to the mother, and she took the rice. She divided it into two, and then she went out. When she came back, I asked her, 'Where did you go?' She said, 'They are hungry also.' Next door neighbor, they were also hungry. What struck me most, not that she gave the rice but she knew they were hungry. And because she knew, she shared. And this is what we have to come to know.... Love, to be true, has to hurt and this woman who was hungry – she knew that her neighbor was also hungry, and that family happened to be a Muslim family. So it was touching, so real."

"We think sometimes that poverty is only being hungry, naked and homeless. The poverty of being unwanted, unloved and uncared for is the greatest poverty. We must start in our own homes to remedy this kind of poverty."

"At the end of life, we will not be judged by how many diplomas we have received, how much money we have made, how many great things we have done. We will be judged by "I was hungry, and you gave me something to eat, I was naked and you clothed me. I was homeless, and you took me in."

"I see God in every human being. When I wash the leper's wounds, I feel I am nursing the Lord himself. Is it not a beautiful experience?"

"I am everything. Every country I love and I am a child of God to love the humans," she said in a 1995 interview when asked about her nationality.

"I see somebody dying, I pick him up. I find somebody hungry, I give him food. He can love and be loved. I don't look at his color, I don't look at his religion. I don't look at anything. Every person whether he is Hindu, Muslim or Buddhist, he is my brother, my sister."

"Let us always meet each other with a smile, for the smile is the beginning of love."

"I'm a little pencil in the hand of a writing God, who is sending a love letter to the world."

"Kind words can be short and easy to speak, but their echoes are truly endless."

"Do not think that love in order to be genuine has to be extraordinary. What we need is to love without getting tired."

"I alone cannot change the world, but I can cast a stone across the waters to create many ripples."

"Love is a fruit in season at all times and within reach of every hand."

"God doesn't require us to succeed, he only requires that you try."

"If you are humble nothing will touch you, neither praise nor disgrace, because you know what you are."

"Do not wait for leaders; do it alone, person to person."

"Be kind and merciful. Let no one ever come to you without coming away better and happier."

"One of the realities we're all called to go through is to move from repulsion to compassion and from compassion to wonderment."

"Never worry about numbers. Help one person at a time and always start with the person nearest you."

"Love to be real, it must cost—it must hurt—it must empty us of self."

"Do not allow yourselves to be disheartened by any failure as long as you have done your best."

"One filled with the joy preaches without preaching."

"I do not pray for success; I ask for faithfulness."

"I know I am touching the living body of Christ in the broken bodies of the hungry and the suffering."

"Each one of them is Jesus in disguise."

"Joy is a net of love in which you can catch souls."

"We ourselves feel that what we are doing is just a drop in the ocean. But the ocean would be less because of that missing drop."

"Yes, you must live life beautifully and not allow the spirit of the world that makes gods out of power, riches, and pleasure make you to forget that you have been created for greater things."

"We must know that we have been created for greater things, not just to be a number in the world, not just to go for

Chapter 4: Mary the Great Missionary and Her Children the Saints

diplomas and degrees, this work and that work. We have been created in order to love and to be loved."

"Spread love everywhere you go. Let no one ever come to you without leaving happier."

"I never look at the masses as my responsibility. I look at the individual. I can love only one person at a time. I can feed only one person at a time. Just one, one, one." Mother Teresa

"Be the living expression of God's kindness; kindness in your face, kindness in your eyes, kindness in your smile."

"The more you have, the more you are occupied, the less you give. But the less you have the more free you are. Poverty for us is a freedom. It is not mortification, a penance. It is joyful freedom. There is no television here, no this, no that. But we are perfectly happy."

"I can do things you cannot, you can do things I cannot; together we can do great things."

"Even the rich are hungry for love, for being cared for, for being wanted, for having someone to call their own."

"What can you do to promote world peace? Go home and love your family."

"Words which do not give the light of Christ increase the darkness." Mother Teresa

"If you are kind, people may accuse you of selfish, ulterior motives: Be kind anyway. If you are successful, you will win some false friends and true enemies: Succeed anyway. If you are honest and frank people will try to cheat you: Be honest anyway. What you spend years building, someone could

destroy overnight: Build anyway. If you find serenity and happiness, they may be jealous of you: Be happy anyway. The good you do today, will often be forgotten by tomorrow: Do good anyway. Give the world the best you have, and it may never be enough: Give your best anyway."

"If I ever become a Saint–I will surely be one of 'darkness.' I will continually be absent from Heaven–to light the light of those in darkness on earth."

St. Mother Teresa, Missionary to the Poor, pray for us!

St. Katherine Drexel

St. Katherine Drexel was an incredible American missionary sister to the Indians and African American people. She was born in Philadelphia on November 26, 1858, the second child of a prominent and wealthy banker, Francis Anthony Drexel and his wife, Hannah Langstroth. When Katherine was just five weeks old, her mother died. In 1860 her father remarried to a faithful Catholic woman Emma Bouvier and together they had another daughter. All three Drexel girls received a wonderful education from private tutors and traveled throughout the United States and Europe. The family was very well off -both financially and spiritually. Virtue took center stage in their family as they devoutly practiced their faith and both Francis and Emma lived morally upright and prayerful lives giving daily witness to the practice of both the spiritual and corporal works of mercy.

Katharine always remembered as a child watching her father pray for 30 minutes each evening. She also witnessed her stepmother regularly opening their doors to house and care for the poor. The couple distributed food, clothing and provided rent assistance to those in need.

Though Katharine made her social debut in 1879, she never let her family's money adversely affect the way she lived her life and faith. She was an example of a Christian with a proper understanding that the goods of this earth are given for the common good. After watching her stepmother suffer with terminal cancer for three straight years, Katharine also learned that no amount of money could shelter them from pain or suffering. From this moment, Katharine's life took a turn. She became imbued with a passionate love for God and neighbor, and she took an avid interest in the material and spiritual well-being of black and native Americans. In 1884, while her family was visiting the Western states, Katharine saw first-hand the troubling and poor situation of the Native Americans. She desperately wanted to help them.

When her father passed away a year later, he donated part of his $15.5 million estate to a few charities and then left the remainder to be equally split amongst his three daughters. He set up his will in a way to protect his daughters from men who were only seeking their money. If his daughters should die, the money was then to go on to his would-be grandchildren. If there were no grandchildren, the Drexel estate would be distributed to several different religious orders and charities, including the Society of Jesus, the Religious of the Sacred Heart, a Lutheran hospital and the Christian Brothers. As one of their first acts following their father's death, Katharine and her sisters contributed money to assist the St. Francis Mission of South Dakota's Rosebud Reservation.

Katherine soon concluded that more was needed to help the Native Americans and the lacking ingredient was people. In 1887, while touring Europe, the Drexel sisters were given a private audience with Pope Leo XIII. They were seeking missionaries to help with the Indian missions they were financing. The Pope looked to Katharine and suggested she, herself, become a missionary. He surprised her by responding, *"Why don't you go? Why don't you become one?"* As a teenager, Katharine had considered convent life, but in a letter to Bishop James O'Connor, stated that: *"she couldn't bear separation from her family, she hated community life and the thought of living with "old-maidish" dispositions, did not like to be alone, and could not part with luxuries"*. At that time, the Bishop discouraged her from entering the convent. After speaking with the Pope and her spiritual director back in Pennsylvania, Father O' Connor, Katharine changed her mind. Watching her step mother suffer for years with cancer had helped her to see that no amount of family happiness or money could save a person from suffering. She learned that only the eternal mattered. And so she decided she would give herself and her inheritance to God through service to both Native Americans and African Americans. She once again wrote the Bishop, stating that she wanted to give herself completely to the Lord, adding, *"The world cannot give me peace."* She later wrote reflecting on this decision, *"The feast of St. Joseph brought me the grace to give the remainder of my life to the Indians and the Colored."*

Katharine began her six-month postulancy at the Sisters of Mercy Convent in Pittsburgh in 1889. On February 12, 1891, Katharine made her first vows as a religious and dedicated herself to working for the American Indians and African-Americans in the

Chapter 4: Mary the Great Missionary and Her Children the Saints

Western United States. Taking the name Mother Katharine, she established a religious congregation called the Sisters of the Blessed Sacrament for Indians and Colored, whose members would work for the betterment of those they were called to serve. From the age of 33 until her death in 1955, she dedicated her life and her fortune to this work. In 1894, Mother Katharine took part in opening the first mission boarding school called St. Catherine's Indian School, in Santa Fe, New Mexico. Other schools quickly followed - for Native Americans west of the Mississippi River, and for the blacks in the southern part of the United States. In 1897, Katharine asked the friars of St. John the Baptist Province of the Order of Friars Minor to help staff a mission for the Navajos in Arizona and New Mexico, and she would help finance their work with the Pueblo Native Americans. In 1910, Katharine also financed the printing of 500 copies of A Navaho-English Catechism of Christian Doctrine for the Use of Navaho Children. In 1915, Katherine founded Xavier University in New Orleans, the first Catholic University in the United States for African-Americans.

By the time of her death, she had more than 500 Sisters teaching in 63 schools throughout the country and she established 50 missions for Native Americans in 16 different states. Katharine suffered a heart attack at 77-years-old and was forced to retire. She spent the remainder of her life in quiet and intense prayer. Mother Katharine died on March 3, 1955 at the age of 96. She is buried at her order's motherhouse. Neither of Katharine's sisters had any children, so after her death, the Sisters of the Blessed Sacrament lost the Drexel fortune that supported their ministries. However, the order continues to pursue Katharine's mission with the African-Americans and Native Americans in 21 states and in Haiti.

Katharine was remembered for her love of the Eucharist. She once said:

> "Ours is the Spirit of the Eucharist, the total Gift of Self.... The Eucharist is a never-ending sacrifice. It is the Sacrament of love, the supreme love, the act of love.
>
> My sweetest Joy is to be in the presence of Jesus in the holy Sacrament. I beg that when obliged to withdraw in body, I may leave my heart before the holy Sacrament. How I would miss Our Lord if He were to be away from me by His presence in the Blessed Sacrament!"

St. Katherine Drexel was courageous and took the initiative to address social inequality within minorities. She believed all should have access to a quality education and her selfless service, including the donation of her inheritance, helped many reach that goal. St. Katharine was beatified on November 20, 1988 and canonized on October 1, 2000 by Pope John Paul II. St. Katharine Drexel teaches missionaries that it is by surrendering oneself and all that one has to Providence's designs that one finds peace and fulfillment in this life. Only in such surrender does one retain peace, even in the midst of the Cross. At the end of her life Katherine Drexel prayed and wrote much in her notebooks leaving a spiritual treasury of teaching and inspirations to the souls who would carry on her work after her. Some bits of her wisdom are:

"The patient and humble endurance of the cross, whatever nature it may be, is the highest work we have to do."

"If we wish to serve God and love our neighbor well, we must manifest our joy in the service we render to Him and them. Let us open wide our hearts. It is joy which invites us. Press forward and fear nothing."

"It is a lesson we all need - to let alone the things that do not concern us. He has other ways for others to follow Him; all do not go by the same path. It is for each of us to learn the path by which He requires us to follow Him, and to follow Him in that path."

"Peacefully do at each moment what at that moment ought to be done. If we do what each moment requires, we will eventually complete God's plan, whatever it is. We can trust God to take care of the master plan when we take care of the details."

"Often in my desire to work for others I find my hands tied, something hinders my charitable designs, some hostile influence renders me powerless. My prayers seem to avail nothing, my kind acts are rejected, I seem to do wrong things when I am trying to do my best. In such cases I must not grieve. I am only treading in my Master's steps."

"Union with God alone gives us life and abundance of life. We are not sufficient in ourselves."

"O Mary, make me endeavor, by all the means in my power, to extend the kingdom of your Divine Son and offer incessantly my prayers for the conversion of those who are yet in darkness or estranged from His fold."

St. Katherine Drexel, Missionary to the American Indians and African-Americans, pray for us!

St. Rose Philippine Duchesne

Our next saint was also a great missionary to the American Indians, although she lived 100 years before St. Katherine Drexel. St. Rose Philippine Duchesne was born in Grenoble, France in 1769 to a wealthy and prominent family. From early on she had an iron will, which eventually was the battlefield of her holiness as well as the tool God used to make her a great missionary in the New World. At 19 despite family opposition Rose entered the convent. As the French Revolution broke, the convent was closed, and she began taking care of the poor and sick, opened a school for homeless children, and risked her life helping priests in the underground. When the situation cooled, Rose personally rented the former convent, now a shambles, and tried to revive its religious life. The spirit was gone, however, and soon there were only four nuns left. They joined the infant Society of the Sacred Heart, whose young superior, Mother Madeleine Sophie Barat, would be her lifelong friend. She shortly became a superior of the novitiate and school. But because she had heard about missionary work in Louisiana since the time she was a small girl, she greatly desired to go to America to work among the Indians. Finally in 1818 when she was 49 years old, she left with four other sisters and spent 11 weeks at sea on her way to New Orleans, followed by 7 more weeks on the Mississippi river to St. Louis. She was greatly disappointed to find out that the Bishop had no place for them to live and work among the Indians. In St. Louis she founded a boarding school for girls. One biographer explained:

> *"In her first decade in America, Mother Duchesne suffered practically every hardship the frontier had to offer, except the threat of Indian massacre—poor lodging, shortages of food, drinking water, fuel and money, forest fires and blazing chimneys, the vagaries of the Missouri climate, cramped living quarters and the privation of all privacy, and the crude manners of children reared in rough surroundings and with only the slightest training in courtesy"* (Louise Callan, R.S.C.J., Philippine Duchesne).

Finally at age 72, retired and in poor health, Rose got her lifelong wish. A mission was founded at Sugar Creek, Kansas, among the Potawatomi and she was taken along. Rose struggled greatly to learn the Potawatomi language, and because she failed all there was left to do was sit in the chapel and pray for those who were teaching. Because of this the Indians soon named her "Woman-Who-Prays-Always." This exemplified Rose's teaching that one should *"Preach by example of your lives rather than by words. Example is the very best sermon."* Rose Duchesne died in 1852, at the age of 83, and was canonized in 1988.

In all of the hardships that Rose faced in her life, her strength and peace came in surrendering to God's will and trusting His plan. In doing this, even the natural disappointments of mission life found great meaning in uniting her to the God who she loved. St. Rose said:

"Do not look back to the past, nor forward to the future. Claim only the present, for it holds God's will."

"I am where God wills me to be, and so I have found rest and security. His wisdom governs me, His power defends me, His grace sanctifies me, His mercy encompasses me, His joy sustains me and all will go well with me."

"We cultivate a very small field for Christ, but we love it, knowing that God does not require great achievements but a heart that holds back nothing for self."

"Let us never lose courage or despair of God's mercy. We have only to humble ourselves before God in order to obtain grace to become all that we ought to be."

"He will never let the trial surpass the strength He gives you, and at the very moment you think yourself overwhelmed by sorrow, He will lift you up and give you peace."

"It fills me with joy to realize that I can lay down my life daily for God, that I can sacrifice it willingly for Him. I may not be a martyr for the faith, but I can be a martyr of charity."

"Lord, I lean on You alone for strength. Give me your arm to support me, your shoulders to carry me, your breast on which to lay my head, your Cross to uphold me, your Eucharist to nourish me. On you Lord, I shall sleep and rest in peace."

"Let us bear our cross and leave it to God to determine the length and the weight."

"Never forget that the road to Heaven is the Way of the Cross. Jesus has called us to follow Him, bearing the Cross as He did."

St. Rose Philippine Duchesne, Missionary to the New World, pray for us!

St. Mother Francis Xavier Cabrini

St. Francis Xavier Cabrini is the last missionary saint we will discuss. Although born in Italy, she too became a missionary to the New World. St. Frances Xavier Cabrini was born in Lombardi, Italy in 1850. She was born two months premature and the youngest of thirteen children. Unfortunately, only three of her siblings survived past adolescence and Frances would live most of her life in a fragile and delicate state of health. Enthralled with stories of missionaries, she dreamed as a child of joining a religious order, but hindered by poor health the congregation who were her teachers and mentors denied her entry. Instead, a priest asked her to teach at the House of Providence Orphanage in Cadagono, Italy. And so, she became a teacher, teaching at a girl's school for six years.

Frances took religious vows in 1877, adding Xavier to her name to honor St. Francis Xavier. In 1880, Frances founded her own order with seven other young women—the Institute of the Missionary Sisters of the Sacred Heart of Jesus. She and her Sisters wanted to be missionaries in China and despite all obstacles; she visited Rome to obtain an audience with Pope Leo XIII. The Pope told Frances to go *"not to the East, but to the West"* to New York rather than to China as she had expected. She was to help the thousands of Italian immigrants already in the United States.

And so, Mother Cabrini crossed the Atlantic ocean in spite of her great fear of water. On March 31, 1889, Frances arrived in New York

City along with six other sisters ready to begin her new journey. However, right from the beginning she encountered many disappointments and hardships. In 1889, New York seemed to be filled with chaos and poverty. The house originally attended for her new orphanage was no longer available, but Frances did not give up, even though the archbishop insisted she return to Italy. After she refused, the Archbishop found them housing with the convent of the Sisters of Charity. Frances then received permission to found an orphanage. Cabrini organized catechism and education classes for the Italian immigrants and provided for the needs of the many orphans. She established schools and orphanages despite tremendous odds. Filled with a deep trust in God and endowed with a wonderful administrative ability, Frances founded 67 institutions, including orphanages, schools, and hospitals, within 35 years dedicated to caring for the poor, uneducated, sick, abandoned, and especially for the Italian immigrants. Her institutions were spread out in places all over the United States, including New York, Colorado, and Illinois. In 1909, Frances became a naturalized citizen of the United States. Frances was known for being as resourceful as she was prayerful. She was always able to find people to donate their money, time, and support for her institutions.

Soon, requests for her to open schools came to Frances Cabrini from all over the world. She traveled to Europe, Central and South America, and throughout the United States. She made 24 trans-Atlantic trips. In addition to the United States, her sisters worked in England, France, Spain and South America. Mother Cabrini died from malaria at the age of 67, on December 22, 1917, at Columbus

Hospital in Chicago, IL. Her legacy of love and service remain throughout the cities of the United States.

Like many other missionary saints, Mother Cabrini was able to do so much for Christ simply because she kept following His lead and saying 'yes' to what He laid before her. Once she said, *"The Heart of Jesus does things in such a hurry that I can barely keep up with Him."* And yet regardless of the work she felt heaped by God upon her plate, she continued to trust in the fire and strength of His Love to accomplish all that He was asking of her. She said, *"I will go anywhere and do anything in order to communicate the love of Jesus to those who do not know Him or have forgotten Him."* Mother Cabrini knew that prayer was the fuel that made her work fruitful. She said:

> *"We must pray without tiring, for the salvation of mankind does not depend upon material success . . . but on Jesus alone."*
>
> *"If you are in danger, if your hearts are confused, turn to Mary; she is our comfort, our help; turn towards her and you will be saved."*
>
> *"Prayer is powerful! It fills the earth with mercy, it makes the Divine clemency pass from generation to generation; right along the course of the centuries wonderful works have been achieved through prayer."*
>
> *"They who pray with faith have fervor and fervor is the fire of prayer. This mysterious fire has the power of consuming all our faults and imperfections, and of giving to our actions, vitality, beauty and merit."*

St. Francis Cabrini saw firsthand the evil of sin and the pain of the Cross in her work in New York, Chicago and among the immigrants wherever she went. And yet her faith, her fearless embracing of the Cross with Christ, her humility and her trust in God's plan strengthened her to plow forward accomplishing the Divine Will. She said:

> *"I travel, work, suffer my weak health, meet with a thousand difficulties, but all these are nothing, for this world is so small. To me, space is an imperceptible object, as I am accustomed to dwell in eternity."*
>
> *"The world is poisoned with erroneous theories, and needs to be taught sane doctrines, but it is difficult to straighten what has become crooked."*
>
> *"Did a Magdalene, a Paul, a Constantine, an Augustine become mountains of ice after their conversion? Quite the contrary. We should never have had these prodigies of conversion and marvelous holiness if they had not changed the flames of human passion into volcanoes of immense love of God."*
>
> *"I trust in you, my Jesus. I place my poor soul in your hands – mold me according to your divine will,"* she wrote in 1877.
>
> *"Live abandoned to God and let Him treat you according to His pleasure,"* she wrote, *"What does it matter if it be Golgotha, Tabor, or Gethsemane? It is enough to know that we are with Him."*
>
> *"If you carry the Cross willingly, the Cross will carry you."*

"A single act of humility is worth more than the proud exhibition of any virtue" she advised one Sister. To another she wrote, "The proud always do damage because the grace of heaven cannot fall on them."

"Fortify me with the grace of Your Holy Spirit and give Your peace to my soul that I may be free from all needless anxiety, solicitude and worry. Help me to desire always that which is pleasing and acceptable to You so that Your will may be my will. Amen"

"Stretch every fiber of my being, dear Lord, that I may more easily fly towards you. May your Spirit, which once breathed over the chaos of the earth, give life to all the powers of my soul."

In 1931, Mother Cabrini's body was exhumed, found partially incorrupt, and is now enshrined under glass in the altar at St. Frances Cabrini Shrine in Manhattan.

St. Francis Xavier Cabrini, Missionary to the Immigrants, pray for us!

Chapter 5

Characteristics of a Missionary

The Holy Spirit is the source of all missionary work. The greater the Holy Spirit fills a soul, the more efficacious that soul will be in saving souls. Every human life is in the hands of God -but when a soul surrenders to God without holding anything back, then the Grace of His Love (being the Holy Spirit) can consume him in full and flow out of that soul as a fountain to the world around him. And wherever the Holy Spirit goes, along follows the effects of His presence in His gifts, fruits, charisms and virtues. Although every creative action of the Holy Spirit is important for missionaries to surrender to, there are specific characteristics that are particularly helpful for a missionary to pray for the Holy Spirit to pour out upon their interior life, as well as upon their work. St. Bonaventure says, *"In all your deeds and words you should look upon this Jesus as your model. Do so whether you are walking or keeping silence, or speaking, whether you are alone or with others."* But what does this 'looking like Christ our model' consist of if not the particular imitation of His concrete virtue in our lives? In this chapter we will consider what sorts of characteristic virtues should emanate from a missionary's life. This list is by no way exhaustive -instead it is meant to be an inspiration to those seeking to enflame the missionary spirit of their own hearts to primarily focus on, thus allowing these graces to change them completely into another Christ in the world.

Humility

The most important characteristic for a missionary to embrace is humility. The saints highlight this virtue as the basis of spiritual growth and holiness, and this remains true for every missionary:

"The three most important virtues are humility, humility, and humility."- Bernard of Clairvaux

"To be taken with love for a soul, God does not look on its greatness, but the greatness of its humility." -St. John of the Cross

"In the difficulties which are placed before me, why should I not act like a donkey? When one speaks ill of him - the donkey says nothing. When he is mistreated - he says nothing. When he is forgotten - he says nothing. When no food is given him - he says nothing. When he is made to advance - he says nothing. When he is despised - he says nothing. When he is overburdened - he says nothing. The true servant of God must do likewise, and say with David: "Before Thee I have become like a beast of burden."" -- St. Alphonsus Rodriguez

"The most powerful weapon to conquer the devil is humility... Humility and charity are the two master-chords: one, the lowest; the other, the highest; all the others are dependent on them. Therefore, it is necessary, above all, to maintain ourselves in these two virtues; for observe well that the preservation of the

Chapter 5: Characteristics of a Missionary

whole edifice depends on the foundation and the roof." -St. Vincent de Paul

One of the best definitions of humility we have from the saints comes from a conversation St. Catherine of Sienna had with God in prayer. Catherine writes about Jesus saying to her, *"Do you know who you are and who I am? If you know these two things, you will be blessed and the Enemy will never deceive you. I am He who is; and you are she who is not."* This is the essence of humility -knowing who God is and knowing in His light who He created us to be (which is not a god). God is the center of all the of universe. He is all powerful, all love - and we are not. We are merely His creatures and we can only do anything because of His gift of grace. Everything depends on Him and the work of His will, His active Love in this world. This is something a missionary must know not only with his mind, but embrace with his heart and live with his life.

God is the one who calls a missionary to a work. He goes before him to prepare the way -the circumstances of a missionary's work and to till the souls he will encounter. God provides the seeds of grace, of teachings, of words, of work and He helps a missionary plant them in the souls that God Himself brings to him. And then, it is God to who nurtures the seeds of grace in each soul that a missionary encounters and it is ultimately God who bears fruit.

A missionary is not simply a raw instrument in the hands of God in a detached way. His cooperation with grace is much more than simply being an inanimate shovel in the hands of a gardener. Because a missionary himself has a relationship of love with God -he himself being a creation of God as well as creating with Him -a missionary's relationship is being less of a tool and more like a student, a helper, a child of God. It is the living relationship that a missionary has with God that will be the first 'work' he does in any given mission. His relationship will speak and do more than any words and actions he performs. St. John of the Cross said, *"One act of pure love is more valuable to the Church than all other works combined."* What enables a missionary to be that close to God -not only as an instrument, but as His very child, is grace. And a soul can only be full of grace to the degree that they are humble -empty of themselves -knowing full well how great is our God and how little and empty we are by ourselves and how dependent we are on Him for everything. Humility is not a hatred for oneself, but a recognition of truth -the truth of who we are and the truth of who God is. A humble soul is so absorbed in his love for God that he forgets to think of himself. He is totally other-focused -with the object of his focus being his Creator and Redeemer. Our Lady -the Queen of Humility -prays in the Magnificat *'He has filled the empty with great things and lifted up the lowly.'* (Luke 1:52) Because of this, in order for a missionary to be a vessel of God's love in a mission, he has to be totally humble and empty of himself -so that God's divine Love can fill, radiate and work through him.

Littleness

A virtue very related to humility is littleness. Humility basically is the truth about oneself -and the truth about all people is that we are little children in the big hands of God. Humility recognizes that. Jesus said that *'Unless you become like a little child you cannot enter the Kingdom of Heaven. Whoever humbles himself like this child is the*

Chapter 5: Characteristics of a Missionary 163

greatest in the kingdom of heaven." (Mt 18:3-4) When we are little before God, He can purify us, teach us, fill us and guide us. When we are little before other people, we are approachable in their eyes. Little children are not afraid of other children. Even the most prideful person has the heart of a child within them -and when we are little before them, they are called back to the core of who they are before God. You might not see them crack before you, but in some quiet moment of their day the humility of a missionary living littleness filled with Love will move and change the most hardened of people.

Littleness is not only important for a missionary in regards to a missionary's humility which empties him before God to be filled, but it is also important for a missionary to understand that it is in the little things he does with great love that mountains will be moved for the Lord. *"Amen, I say to you, if you have faith the size of a mustard seed, you will say to this mountain, 'Move from here to there,' and it will move. Nothing will be impossible for you."* (Matthew 17:20) The greatest saints were those who knew they were little and instead of fighting it, embraced it and in the simplicity that comes with littleness turned it over to God Who is able to do mighty things with such surrender. Our Lady is the greatest example of this as She prayed in the Magnificat: *"He has shown might with his arm, dispersed the arrogant of mind and heart. He has thrown down the rulers from their thrones but lifted up the lowly."* (Luke 1:51-52) Also well known for her littleness is St. Therese of Lisieux, who said:

> *"I can prove my love only by scattering flowers, that is to say, by never letting slip a single little sacrifice, a single glance, a single word; by making profit of the very smallest*

actions, by doing them for love. Jesus points out to me the only way which leads to Love's furnace – that way is self-surrender – it is the confidence of the little child who sleeps without fear in its father's arms.

How shall I show my love is proved by deeds? Well – the little child will strew flowers...she will embalm the Divine Throne with their fragrance, will sing with silvery voice the canticle of love.

The Divine Heart's Goodness and Merciful Love are little known! It is true that to enjoy these treasures we must humble ourselves, must confess our nothingness – and here is where many a soul draws back.

You know well enough that Our Lord does not look so much at the greatness of our actions, nor even at their difficulty, but at the love with which we do them.

Miss no single opportunity of making some small sacrifice, here by a smiling look, there by a kindly word; always doing the smallest right and doing it all for love.

I too, would like to find an elevator to lift me up to Jesus for I am too little to climb the rough staircase of perfection. The elevator which must raise me to the Heavens is Your Arms, O Jesus...I must necessarily remain small."*

Mother Teresa explained her missionary work by saying, 'Not all of us can do great things. But we can do small things with great love.'

And St. Dominic Savio similarly professed, *"I am not capable of doing big things, but I want to do everything, even the smallest things, for the greater glory of God."*

St. André Bessette put it best when he said, *"It is with the smallest brushes that the artist paints the most exquisitely beautiful pictures."*

Not only the words of these saints -but even more profoundly their actions -show to us that the greatest missionary work is accomplished simply through each little moment, word and action being filled by the great fire of God's Love.

Openness and Docility to the Holy Spirit

Because the Holy Spirit is the catalyst of all missionary activity, it is very necessary for every missionary to be open and docile to the Holy Spirit –to be 'willing' to do God's will and to be obedient to God. The Blessed Mother is the best example of this in Luke 1:38 when in response to St. Gabriel's message She responded with Her answer to God being, *"Behold, I am the handmaid of the Lord. May it be done to me according to your word."* Our Lady didn't qualify Her surrender to God with excuses or a list of stipulations. Her 'yes' was a total surrender to God allowing Him to love Her, fill Her and use Her as He saw fit. And it is only to the souls who surrender the most to His Love that God can give the most gifts of His grace. St. Bernadette Soubirous said, *"Jesus gives all to those who surrender all."*

St. Ignatius of Loyola -the great missionary founder of the Jesuits -also believed that the key to all holiness and being used by God as a source of grace for others was that of surrendering oneself to God. He speaks of such holy abandonment saying, *"There are very few men* who realize what God would make of them if they abandoned themselves entirely to his hands, and let themselves be formed by His Grace." And, "What has He done for me? He has loved me and given me His whole self. What shall I do for Him? I shall love Him and give myself to Him without reserve."

To those wondering how to go about growing in openness and docility to the Holy Spirit I would suggest simply praying for these graces daily. Pope John Paul II daily prayed a prayer to the Holy Spirit. And St. Charles de Foucauld wrote a beautiful prayer of surrender that I offer to you here:

Father,
I abandon myself into your hands; do with me what you will.
Whatever you may do, I thank you:
I am ready for all, I accept all.
Let only your will be done in me, and in all your creatures.
I wish no more than this, O Lord.
Into your hands I commend my soul;
I offer it to you
with all the love of my heart,
for I love you, Lord,
and so need to give myself,
to surrender myself into your hands,
without reserve,
and with boundless confidence,
for you are my Father.

Simplicity

I think it is because of her deep understanding of a missionary's heart that St. Therese of Lisieux was named the patroness of the missions. Here we turn to her again for an explanation as to why a missionary must encompass the virtue of simplicity. She said: *"Because your soul is extremely simple, but when you will be perfect, you will be even more simple; the closer one approaches to God, the simpler one becomes."* If a missionary is called to draw souls close to God, then he himself must already be close to God. And we are only able to be drawn close to our Lord when we enter in the path of simplicity. When we are simple, God has room to enter in to arrange everything in our lives. And as we begin to experience the power of the fire of His divine Love, we become even simpler from just being in His presence. Those who embark on the missionary life with a complicated plan will not get very far. All God wants from a missionary heart is littleness and simplicity offered to Him *in great love* and He then uses that love to transform all those gathering around the missionary's life. As Padre Pio says, *"Love and practice simplicity and humility and don't worry about the opinion of the world, because if the world had nothing to say against us, we would not be real servants of God."*

St. Thomas Aquinas offers this advice to souls who want to draw others to God. He said, *"To convert somebody, go and take them by the hand and guide them."* Its that simple -taking another by the hand *in love* is all God needs for us to do in order to create room for Him to act. St. Anthony of Padua seconds that word of advice saying, *"Actions speak louder than words; let your words teach and your actions speak."*

St. Francis de Sales often recommended simplicity as the necessary state in which to keep one's soul. He said, *"In everything, love simplicity." "Go in all simplicity..." "I recommend to you holy simplicity."*

When a missionary is simple, he is approachable by those who he serves. His love shines forth so powerfully in such simplicity that others are immediately attracted to him and able to easily follow his footsteps, thus giving them confidence as they begin their new journey with Jesus. Also, simplicity helps a missionary's soul be single-hearted for God. It allows all complicated matters that tend to confuse one's judgment to fall away so that 'God Alone' may reign from his mind and heart. Jesus Himself said, *"Where your treasure is that is where your heart will be."* (Matthew 6:21). When one tries to remain simple, little and poor, Jesus Christ becomes His greatest treasure -without distractions -and such a soul is quickly transformed into 'another Christ' in the world.

Poor

"Blessed are the poor in spirit..." Christ says in Matthew 5:3. To be poor in spirit means to keep oneself little, humble and simple in the hands of God. Being poor in spirit (and living an exterior life of sacrifice -fleeing all self-indulgence or excess riches) gives God a space to enter and work. The more one denies himself, the more God can give to a soul and direct him. Fr. Jean-Baptiste Chautard once put it this way:

"Bossuet has a sentence which is beyond the comprehension of an apostle who does not realize what must be the soul of his apostolate. It

runs: "When God desires a work to be wholly from His hand, he reduces all to impotence and nothingness, and then He acts." Nothing wounds God so much as pride."

Chaste

"*Blessed are the pure of heart...*" (Matthew 5:8) Only those who are pure will ever be believed or followed by souls seeking Christ and His truth. Purity of heart allows God to consume a soul. We look to the Immaculate Heart of Mary in this -being totally sinless She had nothing at all to obscure the radiance of God -the Holy Trinity - dwelling within Her and flowing forth from Her onto all of humanity. Our Lady was the translucent glass that allowed God to give Himself to us through Her in full. St. Faustina describes the power of Her Immaculate Heart thus:

"To give worthy praise to the Lord's mercy, we unite ourselves with Your Immaculate Mother, for then our hymn will be more pleasing to You, because She is chosen from among men and angels. Through Her, as through a pure crystal, Your mercy was passed on to us. Through Her, man became pleasing to God; Through Her, streams of grace flowed down upon us."

If Our Lady is the Archetype of Purity and our example of what God can do through a small soul totally on fire with the purity of Divine Love, then we should strive in all things to imitate the absolute beauty of Her purity. Purity in this sense is not the absence of man -it is the complete presence of God (without the smallest obstruction of sin) consuming and flowing through a soul. This is the degree of purity all missionaries should strive to attain. It is a purity of thought, of speech, of action -even of intention. It is a natural commitment to keeping great custody of the eyes and ears so that evil may not taint the mind and heart of a soul through them. And as I said, it is even more the gift of one's heart in total fullness to the Godhead to be consumed and annihilated by His Holy Love.

"Holy Purity, the queen of virtues, the angelic virtue, is a jewel so precious that those who possess it become like the angels of God in heaven, even though clothed in mortal flesh," said Saint John Bosco. Saint John Vianney proclaimed, "The pure soul is a beautiful rose, and the Three Divine Persons descend from Heaven to inhale its fragrance." And Saint Peter Julian Eymard explained, "The state of grace is nothing other than purity, and it gives heaven to those who clothe themselves in it. Holiness, therefore, is simply the state of grace purified, illuminated, beautified by the most perfect purity, exempt not only from mortal sin but also from the smallest faults; purity will make saints of you! Everything lies in this!"

Selfless and Generous

Jesus said, "*The Son of Man did not come to be served but to serve and to give his life as a ransom for many.*" (Matthew 20:28) This is the duty of a missionary. He also said in John 10:11, "*I am the good shepherd. A good shepherd lays down his life for the sheep.*" Jesus came to serve. Jesus came to sacrifice. Jesus was not absorbed in Himself, but instead was constantly focused on fulfilling the will of God for the sake of those He loved (being the entire world.) Jesus did not count the cost. St. Therese of Lisieux said, "*When one loves, one does not calculate.*" Jesus was Love Incarnate and so He naturally was inclined

Chapter 5: Characteristics of a Missionary

to always remain focused on the Father in Heaven and the needs of those around Him. He was so generous, in fact, He was willing to give His entire life in the agony of the Passion to save us all from hell. When we consider this (and that as missionaries He is to be our model), then no sacrifice should be too great to offer to God in order to fulfill His will among those He sent us to serve.

Joyful

St. Mother Teresa of Calcutta said, *"Joy is prayer -Joy is strength -Joy is love -Joy is a net of love by which you can catch souls... A joyful heart is the inevitable result of a heart burning with love. Never let anything so fill you with sorrow as to make you forget the joy of the Christ risen."*

Joy is not an act of the will in itself, because it is something that flows from charity. In the *Summa* St. Thomas Aquinas says that *"joy is caused by love, either through the presence of the thing loved, or because of the proper good of the thing loved exists and endures in it."* In simple words, spiritual joy results from loving God. He later states, *"Hence joy is not a virtue distinct from charity, but an act, or effect, of charity: for which reason it is numbered among the Fruits (Galatians 5:22)."* And yet, even considering all of that, I would argue that one can in most circumstances 'choose to be joyful.' This is not by choosing joy with the will, but instead by choosing in whatever situation one encounters to live love. When one chooses charity, joy will naturally flow from this as a fruit. And so, in order to spread joy to the world, a missionary is simply called to 'love now', 'love now', 'love now' -with every heartbeat. To live joy always one simply needs to seek to love in the present moment. This will naturally cause joy to overflow from one's loving heart to reach those around them.

One example of this, I remember, was when I was in Poland many years ago. I was really suffering at the time over a few things and when I left Mass one day I was simply offering my heavy heart to the Lord to use as He saw fit. While leaving the Church an older lady came up to me and said, *"Madam, I don't know who you are but you always radiate such peace and joy wherever you go!"* I had to chuckle in my heart because I was not feeling anything near peaceful nor joyful. But I was accepting my interior cross in great love offering it to Jesus and this caused the fruit of the Holy Spirit's peace and joy to flow to this stranger around me.

Even if one cannot control one's emotion of feeling joy, one can always strive to give joy to others through one's words and gestures. Avoiding complaining is one way to offer joy. Also choosing to hum or sing in a difficult situation often inserts joy. And, as Mother Teresa always said -joy can be given through the loving gesture of a smile. In fact, this great missionary saint spoke so much about the theology of the smile that I would consider her an expert on the subject. She said:

> *"Every time you smile at someone, it is an action of love, a gift to that person, a beautiful thing."*
>
> *"Let us always meet each other with smile, for the smile is the beginning of love."*
>
> *"Be the living expression of God's kindness; kindness in your face, kindness in your eyes, kindness in your smile."*

> *"Smile at each other. Smile at your wife, smile at your husband, smile at your children, smile at each other- it doesn't matter who it is- and that will help to grow up in greater love for each other."*
>
> *"Peace beings with a smile."*
>
> And lastly, *"I will never understand all the good that a simple smile can accomplish."*

Mother Teresa was not the only saint who spoke about the importance of spreading joy in the midst of any mission the Lord might assign to us. Many others have written and spoken about the importance of a joyful spirit. St. Padre Pio taught that *"Joy, with peace, is the sister of charity. Serve the Lord with laughter."* Not all souls will naturally have a sanguine personality, but all souls are called to a life of ardent charity and this will naturally spread joy to the world. One must focus simply and solely on growing in love daily -and the joy will simply overflow from that.

St. John of the Cross said, *"The soul of the one who serves God always swims in joy, always keeps holiday, and is always in the mood for singing."* How can that be in the midst of persecution, suffering and pain? It is by uniting whatever difficulty we encounter to the Jesus suffering on the Cross, trusting in the truth that He will resurrect it and *'make all things new.'* (Rev. 21:5) This does not happen simply at the end of time in heaven, but can begin here and now while we are on earth. The closer we draw near to God, the more heaven can begin to drip over into our hearts even while still making our earthly journey. This is because the purpose of our life is to contain God - and thus to be beacons of His Love, Peace and Joy. St. Pope John Paul

II says that *"God made us for joy."* He explained that, *"We who are Christians have a further cause for joy: like Jesus, we know that we are loved by God our Father. This love transforms our lives and fills us with joy. It makes us see that Jesus did not come to lay burdens upon us. He came to teach us what it means to be fully happy and fully human. Therefore, we discover joy when we discover truth -the truth about God our Father, the truth about Jesus our Savior, the truth about the Holy Spirit who lives in our hearts."* In this way, so many martyrs have found great joy radiating from their hearts and on their faces as they proclaimed the Truth of the Gospel, even while facing death.

Joy is not a gift that God only grants a few chosen souls -it is the eternal destiny of all of humanity and a reality that by living today can easily attract souls to God. Living joy in the midst of confusion and darkness is like being a lighthouse pointing the way for souls to find the way to heaven. It is what people crave and it can be everyone's if they begin to live according to God's statutes and allow His Redemption to take full root in one's heart. Joy comes from Love - love of God by obeying His will and love of neighbor by sacrificing ourselves for him. And we are always free to Love. In today's world it takes courage to live joyfully because it takes courage to love fiercely. But God gives us the fortitude we need to live joy always through the gift of the Holy Spirit. St. Katharine Drexel exhorts us, *"If we wish to serve God and love our neighbor well, we must manifest our joy in service we render to Him and them. Let us open wide our hearts. It is joy which invites us. Press forward and fear nothing."*

Forgiveness

"Blessed are the meek...blessed are the merciful, for they will be shown mercy..." (Matthew 5:5,7) Forgiveness and Mercy are also extremely important characteristics for a missionary to live. First of all, the evil one loves to divide. The name of the devil itself comes from Latin and Greek '*diabolos*' which means '*the accuser*,' '*the slanderer*', and '*to divide*.' To accuse or slander means basically to lie and to do it in such a way as to destroy another person. Satan hates the love of Christ that came '*that they all may be one.*' (John 17:21) He fights against the Truth of Christ because he is the 'father of lies'. He strives to enter all relationships to cause division because as Christ said, *"Every kingdom divided against itself will be laid waste, and no town or house divided against itself will stand."* (Matthew 12:25) In order for a missionary to touch many hearts he will have to deeply live the forgiveness Christ taught and be a beacon of His Merciful Love. Jesus came from heaven to earth to save us from hell. And yet His mission -although directly from God and untainted by any mistakes because He was God -was rejected. He -Love Itself -was betrayed, denied, rejected and killed. Yet Jesus took all of this sin thrown at Him and on the Cross He forgave. He prayed during those agonizing hours, *"Father, forgive them, they know not what they do."* (Luke 23:34) He not only prayed these words, but He took our very sins onto Himself and by offering His wounded body and heart to the Father as a Victim of Love for our sins He won the graces needed for our conversion, healing and very salvation. If this was true of Jesus Christ's mission, it will also be asked of all missionaries who follow in His footsteps. Jesus' meek, humble, forgiving, merciful love shared with souls

through the lips and lives of missionaries will be the greatest sermon they ever preach -the greatest witness that could ever attract and win souls for Christ. Our Lord told St. Faustina, *"Apostle of My mercy, proclaim to the whole world My unfathomable mercy"* (Diary, 1142). In His words to this obscure, Polish nun (who became through her writing and the witness of her heroic life of virtue one of the greatest missionaries of modern times), Jesus was emphasizing for all missionaries the absolute primacy of the message of His Mercy being taught and lived in each and every mission. What is this message of Mercy He is calling all missionaries to preach and live? Here are some excerpts directly from St. Faustina's *Diary* explaining:

> St. Faustina wrote: *"He who knows how to forgive prepares for himself many graces from God. As often as I look upon the cross, so often will I forgive with all my heart"* (390)
>
> Jesus said: **"My daughter, in this meditation, consider the love of neighbor. Is your love for your neighbor guided by My love? Do you pray for your enemies? Do you wish well to those who have, in one way or another, caused you sorrow or offended you? Know that whatever good you do to any soul, I accept it as if you had done it to Me"** (Diary, 1768)
>
> "During Holy Mass, I saw Jesus stretched out on the Cross, and He said to me, **'My pupil, have great love for those who cause you suffering. Do good to those who hate you.'**" She answered, "O my Master, You see very well that I feel no love for them, and that troubles me." Jesus said, **"It is not always within your power to control your feelings. You will**

recognize that you have love if, after having experienced annoyance and contradiction, you do not lose your peace, but pray for those who have made you suffer and wish them well" (Diary, 1628).

Jesus told Sr. Faustina, *"The greater the sinner, the greater the right he has to My mercy"* (Diary, 723). He also said, *"If someone causes you trouble, think what good you can do for the person who caused you to suffer."* (Diary, 1760)

"Mankind will not have peace until it turns with trust to My Mercy." —Diary 300

"My Heart overflows with great mercy for souls, and especially for poor sinners. If only they could understand that I am the best of Fathers to them and that it is for them that the Blood and Water flowed from My Heart as from a fount overflowing with mercy." —Diary 367

"I desire trust from My creatures. Encourage souls to place great trust in My fathomless mercy. Let the weak, sinful soul have no fear to approach Me, for even if it had more sins than there are grains of sand in the world, all would be drowned in the unmeasurable depths of My mercy." —Diary 1059

An incredible example of a missionary living Christ's message of Divine Mercy is Fr. Augustus Tolton -the first African-American ever ordained a priest. He was born into slavery and escaped with his mother. He had a burning desire to serve Christ as a priest, but no seminary in the US at the time would accept a black seminarian. He was tutored by compassionate priests in Latin and Theology and eventually was able to travel to Rome to be educated for the missions. The original thought was because the US was still so hostile to the idea of African American priests that Rome would then send him to Africa to serve. But a few days after his ordination he was called into the meeting and informed that he was being sent back to his home country to a parish in Illinois to serve black Catholics. He replied to this appointment saying, *"But you don't understand. There are no black priests in America."* The Cardinals he was meeting with simply replied, *"Now there is one black priest in America. You."* Fr. Tolton upon his return to the US continued to suffer the prejudice that he had experienced before he had left to study in Rome. This was both from the laity he served as well as from others ordained by the Church. But his forgiveness and mercy was a great light that led many to a path of healing that primarily came through forgiveness and Christian love of one's enemies. He was a great encourager of black Americans seeking holiness within the Catholic Church. In a speech delivered to the first Black Catholic Conference in Washington, D.C. in 1889 Fr. Tolton said:

> *"The Catholic Church deplores a double slavery – that of the mind and that of the body. She endeavors to free us of both. I was a poor slave boy but the priests of the Church did not disdain me. It was through the influence of one of them that I became what I am tonight. I must now give praise to that son of the Emerald Isle, Father Peter McGirr, pastor of St. Peter's Church in Quincy, who promised me that I would be educated*

and who kept his word. It was the priests of the Church who taught me to pray and to forgive my persecutors... it was through the direction of a Sister of Notre Dame, Sister Herlinde, that I learned to interpret the Ten Commandments; and then I also beheld for the first time the glimmering light of truth and the majesty of the Church. In this Church we do not have to fight for our rights because we are black. She had colored saints – Augustine, Benedict the Moor, Monica. The Church is broad and liberal. She is the Church for our people."

Another great missionary example of living meekness, forgiveness and mercy is St. Pope John Paul II. On May 13, 1981 while being driven through St. Peter's Square he was shot by a 23-year-old Turkish man, Mehmet Ali Ağca. On the Sunday morning after the shooting, the Pope addressed the faithful in a recorded message from his hospital bed, asking people to pray for the man who pulled the trigger, whom he referred to as "my brother" and offered his "sincere forgiveness." Sustaining two gunshot wounds, Saint John Paul II claimed that, *"one hand pulled the trigger, another guided the bullet,"* and it was Our Lady herself who saved him from certain death. He later visited the man in prison and sat in a prison cell for 20 minutes with him alone, in quiet conversation. About the meeting Pope John Paul II said, *"What we said to each other is a secret between him and me. I spoke to him as I would speak to a brother whom I have forgiven and who enjoys my confidence."* After leaving the prisoner he spoke about the encounter as something providentially allowed by our heavenly Father for great good. He said:

> "I have been able to meet the person whose name is known by all who in the year 1981, on May 13, made an attempt on my life. But providence guided matters in its way - exceptional, I would say, marvelous - so that today, after more than two years, I could meet my assailant and repeat my pardon, which I had offered immediately and also offered publicly as soon as it became possible in the hospital.
>
> "I think that this meeting, too, in the framework of the Holy Year of Redemption, was providential and was not planned or prepared but took place. The Lord has given me the grace to let us meet as men, as brothers, because all the events of our lives must confirm that God is our father, and we are all his children in Jesus Christ and thus are all brothers."

St. Pope John Paull II was one of the greatest missionary Popes in the history of the Church. He traveled to 129 countries --several repeatedly -- on 104 trips and logging more than 700,000 miles in a papacy that lasted more than 27 years. He always tried to learn a few words or phrases in the native language of the places he visited. He truly "ate what they ate, danced like they danced, prayed like they prayed' and drew each soul regardless of ethnicity to his own heart in fatherly love. The forgiveness he offered his would-be assassin leaves all missionaries with a clear Christ-like example of how a missionary shepherd should love each of his 'sheep' with the Heart of Christ.

St. John of the Cross wrote about the power of such love for one's enemies in a letter to a discalced Carmelite nun in Segovia, *"Have a great love for those who contradict and fail to love you, for in this way* love is begotten in a heart that has no love. God so acts with us, for he loves us that we might love by means of the very love he bears toward us." (Letter #33 Ubeda, October-November 1591) And in another place he writes similarly, *"When there is no love, pour in love and you shall draw out love."* In this way, loving one's enemies, having much to forgive those who one serves, practicing long-suffering and encountering trials are all means of actually growing love, and therefore the fruitfulness, of one's mission work with God.

For those who find such radical forgiveness and meekness in the face of great injustice difficult, St. Phillip Neri suggests that we prepare through prayer before we meet such trials in life. He says, *"During mental prayer, it is well, at times, to imagine that many insults and injuries are being heaped upon us, that misfortunes have befallen us, and then strive to train our heart to bear and forgive these things patiently, in imitation of our savior. This is the way to acquire a strong spirit."*

Lastly, I must mention that in order for a missionary to live with a truly merciful heart, he must first experience God's mercy by humbly drawing near to Him often in the Sacrament of Confession. Weekly or bi-weekly Confession of one's sins to God will keep a missionary as a pure vessel for God's grace. St. Pope John Paul II desired to go to Confession daily while Pope, recognizing that no human is able to live without making mistakes. He also clearly understood the importance of being a pure vessel for the Holy Spirit to be able to use to pour out His Love on the world. May all missionaries keep their own experience of God's mercy and forgiveness -especially in the Sacrament of Confession -as a central point of their own spiritual life. And when a missionary sees that he has offended God or neighbor, may he run to repair the damage of his own defects and sins -asking forgiveness of all whom he offends. In this way, he will grow as a child on the Vine of Jesus' Heart.

Peaceful

"Acquire the Spirit of Peace and a thousand souls around you will be saved," said St. Seraphim of Serov. This quote makes saving souls seem easy -and yet acquiring the Spirit of Peace is a difficult journey learning to trust God so much that His all-encompassing Love is able to surround you and truly consume you with peace. I remember a priest once encouraging me to be a peace-maker in all I said and did by telling me to speak with a quiet voice, to walk lightly, to never slam a door, to put a dish or boiling kettle of water down gently. He said that by practicing doing everything peacefully, I would grow in my union with God who is the source of all peace daily through my ordinary life.

St. Francis of Assisi who was a missionary and inspirer of souls taught us how to not only live peace within ourselves but how to become instruments of God's peace in the world around us. He wrote the prayer that I shared in the previous chapter, but I will print it here again. It is an important reflection of how each and every missionary should strive to be a bearer of peace to the world:

"Lord, make me an instrument of thy peace.
Where there is hatred, let me sow love,
Where there is injury, pardon;
Where there is doubt, faith;

Where there is despair, hope;
Where there is darkness, light;
And where there is sadness, joy.
O Divine Master, grant that I may not so much seek
to be consoled as to console,
to be understood as to understand,
to be loved, as to love.
For it is in giving that we receive,
It is in pardoning that we are pardoned,
and it is in dying that we are born to eternal life."

If Jesus taught, *"Blessed are the peacemakers…"* (Matthew 5:9), it means that He especially held dear to His heart this virtue. Many saints highlighted this virtue as one of the quintessential goals of the interior life. St. Francis de Sales wrote, *"Never be in a hurry; do everything quietly and in a calm spirit. Do not lose your inner peace for anything whatsoever, even if your whole world seems upset."* St. Margaret Mary Alacoque said, *"But above all preserve peace of heart. This is more valuable than any treasure."* St. John of the Cross encouraged souls, *"Abide in peace, banish cares, take no account of all that happens, and you will serve God according to His good pleasure and rest in Him."*

St. Faustina even encouraged those who were worried about good things (like accomplishing God's will) to instead find peace and rest in trusting God. She exhorted, *"Be at Peace. What God has started He will finish."* As St. Teresa of Avila prayed:

> *"Let nothing disturb you.*
> *Nothing frighten you.*
> *God never changes.*
> *Patience obtains all things.*
> *Nothing is wanting to he who possesses God.*
> *God alone suffices."*

Polite and Kind

In 1 Corinthians 13:5 St. Paul writes, 'Love is never rude.' This is an important Christian attribute that is easily overlooked in our world today. And yet it holds an important place in the life of grace and virtue. Our world has become quite rude and this is no little thing. If St. Paul wrote that 'Love is never rude' than the lack of manners in our modern world is actually a sad sign of a lack of authentic Christian love. All missionaries must be sure to cultivate this aspect of love in their everyday encounters. Imagine that -simply saying 'please', 'thank you,' 'excuse me', 'I'm sorry', answering people in a timely manner with patience and love, being hospitable and gracious are ways of actually sharing the Gospel and winning souls for Christ. Jesus Christ was polite and courteous -even if He broke some social norms of His day. He was not mean or rude to souls. And if a missionary is called to be conformed to Him, then all missionaries should brush up on their manners and be attentive to the way they interact with others around them.

Many saints highlighted the importance of being polite -and most namely kind -as a coveted virtue worth striving to live daily. St. Therese of Lisieux wrote in her diary entitled "The Story of a Soul,"

"Kindness is my only guiding star. In its light, I sail a straight route, I have my motto written on my sail: 'To live in love.'"

Mother Teresa said, "Let us more and more insist on raising funds of love, of kindness, of understanding, of peace. Money will come if we seek first the Kingdom of God - the rest will be given."

Saint Basil the Great's often preached on kindness. The saint once said "A tree is known by its fruit; a man by his deeds. A good deed is never lost; he who sows courtesy reaps friendship, and he who plants kindness gathers love."

St. Padre Pio wrote in a letter, "You need to hold fast to two virtues: kindness toward your neighbor and humility toward God."

St. Jean Baptiste de la Salle sums this virtue up saying:

'It is surprising that most Christians look upon decorum and politeness as merely human and worldly qualities and do not think of raising their minds to any higher views by considering them as virtues that have reference to God, to their neighbor, and to themselves. This illustrates very well how little true Christianity is found in the world and how few among those who live in the world are guided by the Spirit of Jesus Christ. Still, it is this Spirit alone which ought to inspire all our actions, making them holy and agreeable to God.'

Prayerful, Eucharistic and Marian

I do not want to skip over these three characteristics of a missionary -as they are of the most importance for every missionary to reflect. And yet, they are so important that I will explain them in their own chapter -following this one. This is because they are of central importance to any and every missionary work.

Martyr's Heart

"Lord Jesus, by the Blood of Thy Crucifixion, inflame with ever-increasing zeal the dispensers of Thy Blood. Grant that thirsting like Thee for souls, they may continue the work of Thy Bloody Passion, increasing its efficacy by applying its merits. Succor, most of all, the poor missionaries, who after watering with their sweat and their tears the soil in which they have sown the divine seed, may still be called upon to dye with their blood the land upon which they planted the cross.

Our Lady of the Precious Blood, watch over the living chalices of the Blood of Jesus. Amen."

This prayer, taken from the offerings of the Precious Blood for priests, beautifully exemplifies the heart of a missionary -which should be the heart of a martyr. Not every missionary will be called to give their life for Christ physically, and yet all missionaries are called to have a 'martyr's heart." For Jesus said, *"Amen, amen, I say to you, unless a grain of wheat falls to the ground and dies, it remains just a grain of wheat; but if it dies, it produces much fruit. Whoever loves his life loses it, and whoever hates his life in this world will preserve it for eternal life."* (John 12:24-25)

Chapter 5: Characteristics of a Missionary

Regardless if a missionary will live a red or white martyrdom, their heart must be given so fully to God that they love Him more than they love their very own life. They must be single-hearted in their devotion and pure of heart in their intention to spread the Gospel. A physical martyr is formed to be heroic in the sacrifice of their life for Christ by first living the Gospel radically day in and day out in all sorts of different circumstances. A heart becomes a martyr before a body does -and this martyrdom of heart is what Our Lady lived with Jesus on the Cross. In the Presentation in the Temple, the priest Simeon said to Our Lady, ""*Behold, this child is destined for the fall and rise of many in Israel, and to be a sign that will be contradicted (and you yourself a sword will pierce) so that the thoughts of many hearts may be revealed.*" (Luke 2:34-35) Our Lady was destined to suffer as much as She loved. And since Her love of Jesus -both Her Son and Her God -was infinite, so too was Her compassion and suffering with Him. All missionaries will be called to imitate Her in this -to the degree that they allow their love for Christ to grow, is the degree they will suffer with Him. Some will be called to give their blood and life for Him. But all will be called to die daily with Him to their own will and ego, so that the Father's will and Holy Spirit's Love can rule all from within them.

As a missionary tries to prepare one's heart to be such a fiery temple of love for God and with God -willing to sacrifice himself even unto death, I offer these words of St. Jane de Chantel on the white martyrdom of love as inspiration and place of reflection:

> "*One day Saint Jane spoke the following eloquent words, which listeners took down exactly as spoken:*

"My dear daughters, many of our holy fathers in the faith, men who were pillars of the Church, did not die martyrs. Why do you think this was?" Each one present offered an answer; then their mother continued. *"Well, I myself think it was because there is another martyrdom: the martyrdom of love. Here God keeps His servants and handmaids in this present life so that they may labor for Him, and He makes of them both martyrs and confessors. I know,"* she added, *"that the Daughters of the Visitation are meant to be martyrs of this kind and that, by the favor of God, some of them, more fortunate than others in that their desire has been granted, will actually suffer such a martyrdom."*

One sister asked what form this martyrdom took. The saint answered: *"Yield yourself fully to God, and you will find out! Divine love takes its sword to the hidden recesses of our inmost soul and divides us from ourselves. I know one person whom love cut off from all that was dearest to her, just as completely and effectively as if a tyrant's blade had severed spirit from body."*

We realized that she was speaking of herself. When another sister asked how long the martyrdom would continue, the saint replied: *"From the moment when we commit ourselves unreservedly to God, until our last breath. I am speaking, of course, of great-souled individuals who keep nothing back for themselves, but instead are faithful in love. Our Lord does not intend this martyrdom for those who are weak in love and perseverance. Such people He lets continue on their mediocre way, so that they will not be lost to Him; He never does violence to our free will."*

Finally, the saint was asked whether this martyrdom of love could be put on the same level as martyrdom of the body. She answered: "We should not worry about equality. I do think, however, that their martyrdom of love cannot be relegated to a second place, for love is as strong as death. For the martyrs of love suffer infinitely more in remaining in this life so as to serve God, than if they died a thousand times over in testimony to their faith and love and fidelity."

Sometimes this idea of living with a martyr's heart instills fear in faint-hearted souls. And yet, Jesus Himself while warning that all of His followers would suffer in one way or another as He did, also spoke great words of encouragement to inspire us all to move forward with trust. In Matthew 10 after warning His disciples of various sufferings they would endure in His Name, comforts them in saying:

"Therefore **do not be afraid of them.** *Nothing is concealed that will not be revealed, nor secret that will not be known. What I say to you in the darkness, speak in the light; what you hear whispered, proclaim on the housetops. And do not be afraid of those who kill the body but cannot kill the soul; rather, be afraid of the one who can destroy both soul and body in Gehenna.* **Are not two sparrows sold for a small coin? Yet not one of them falls to the ground without your Father's knowledge. Even all the hairs of your head are counted. So**

do not be afraid; you are worth more than many sparrows. Everyone who acknowledges me before others I will acknowledge before my heavenly Father. But whoever denies me before others, I will deny before my heavenly Father." (Matthew 10:26-33)

In Conclusion

And a word at the end of this chapter to those readers who might feel intimidated by the inspiring virtues needed by a missionary and lived so vibrantly by saints before us. To those tempted to discouragement because of one's own shortcomings, St. Angela Merici answers, *"Do not lose heart, even if you should discover that you lack qualities necessary for the work to which you are called. He who called you will not desert you, but the moment you are in need he will stretch out his saving hand."*

These virtues do not always come easily, and yet when we focus the eyes of our hearts on Christ and lean upon Him, He will supply all we need. It is in the midst of feeling inadequate and in uniting the suffering this causes to the Passion of Christ that one will find the remedy of needed grace. St. Anthony of Padua says that, *"Christians must lean on the Cross of Christ just as travelers lean on a staff when they begin a long journey. They must have the Passion of Christ deeply embedded in their minds and hearts, because only from it can they derive peace, grace, and truth."* And so, the more we feel these virtues crucified and we unite the struggle to Him, the faster we will be swept up in the fires of Divine Charity which in turn will do all to provide us with these graces.

Photos

Mary Kloska serving the 200,000 people who lived in the trash dump called 'Smokey Mountain' in Manila, Philippines.

A second photo of 'Smokey Mountain' trash dump in Manila, Philippines.

Mary Kloska with girls from a Russian youth group in Achinsk, Siberia.

Mary Kloska with youth in a rural village near Komga, South Africa.

Mary 'going for a walk' with her orphan babies
from Upendo Children's Home in Moshi, Tanzania.

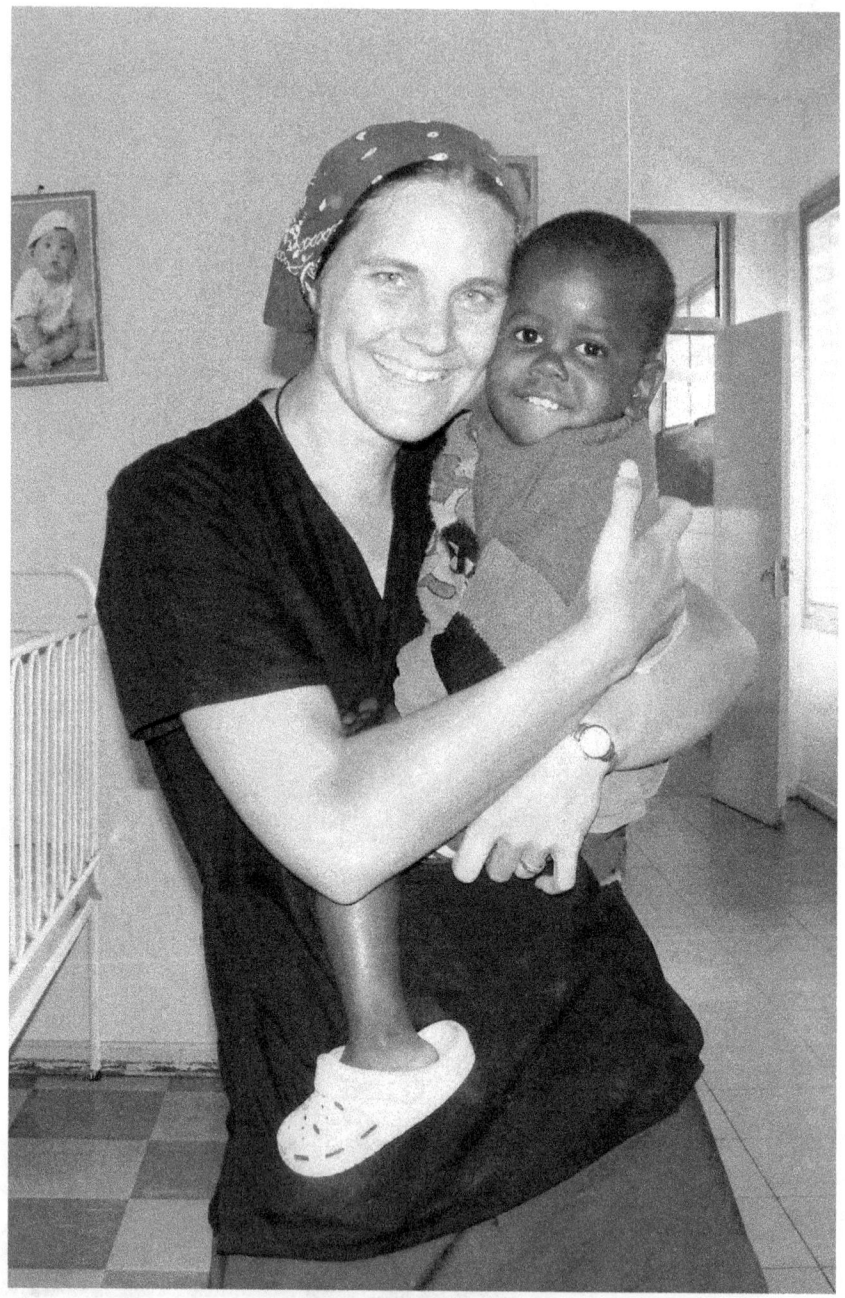

Mary with little Polycarp from Upendo Children's Home in Moshi, Tanzania.

Mary with 'Dima' -an 18-year-old mentally handicapped patient at a medical institution in Gagarinka, Russia (photo taken in 1994).

Mary with Muslim twins entrusted to the orphanage run by the Precious Blood Sisters in Moshi, Tanzania after their mother died in childbirth.

Mary Kloska with some of the 20+ infants entrusted to her care at the Precious Blood orphanage in Moshi, Tanzania.

Mary speaking to a women's prayer group in Achinsk, Siberia (Russia) about 'The Holiness of Womanhood'.

(Both top and bottom) Mary Kloska visiting the Yenisey River that flows through Krasnoyarsk, Russia.

Mary Kloska visiting with the Precious Blood Sisters and a Sister of Charles Barromeo in Achinsk, Russia.

Mary Kloska giving a retreat on 'The Holiness of Womanhood' in Krzydlina Mala, Poland (with her interpreter Hania Przybylo).

Mary Kloska with her close Siberian friend Natasha
and her two nephews whom she adopted.

Mary Kloska in Krasnoyarsk, Russia with Babuska Anna. ('Baba Anna' was one of the old church ladies who personally knew Fr. Walter Ciszek - author of *With God in Russia* and *He Leadeth Me* when he was exiled to work camps in Siberia.)

Mary Kloska in Achinsk, Russia
with the Polish Sisters of the Most Precious Blood

Mary Kloska on retreat in the Tatri mountains of Zakopane, Poland.

Mary Kloska with Sasha in Bagatol, Siberia. (Mary took care of Sasha on many children's retreats when he was young, and also met up with him many years later when she re-visited his parish).

Mary Kloska with her little brother Joey in the Tatri mountains of Zakopane, Poland.

Chapter 6

Prayer, Mass, Eucharistic Adoration and the Rosary as the Center of Every Mission (and Missionary Life)

Prayer

Prayer is the soul of the Apostolate. St. John of the Cross believed that *"One small act carried out with pure love is more valuable to the church than all other works combined."* And how can one's love be made pure if not through long hours in prayer? St. John Vianney taught, *"Prayer is the inner bath of love into which the soul plunges itself."*

To love purely means to follow the path of virtue and the will of God so fiercely that you become one heart with Him. And yet St. Ephraem of Syria explains, *"Virtues are formed by prayer. Prayer preserves temperance. Prayer suppresses anger. Prayer prevents emotions of pride and envy. Prayer draws into the soul the Holy Spirit, and raises man to Heaven."* St. John Chrysostom adds, *"It is simply impossible to lead, without the aid of prayer, a virtuous life."* We grow in love by prayer. St. Alphonsus Maria de Liguori said, *"Without prayer we have neither light nor strength to advance in the way which leads to God."* Fr. Jean-Baptiste Chautard once wrote:

> *"Let the men eaten up with activity,"* he says, *"and who imagine they are able to shake the world with their preaching and other*

outward works, stop and reflect a moment. It will not be difficult for them to understand that they would be much more useful to the Church and more pleasing to the Lord, not to mention the good example they would give to those around them, if they devoted more time to prayer and to the exercises of the interior life."

This strongly echoes St. John Marie Vianney who said, *"Man has a noble task: That of prayer and love. To pray and love, that is the happiness of man on earth."*

If the job of a missionary is to save souls, then prayer has to take primacy in all that a missionary says and does. It is through prayer that one plans the work needed to be done, gains the grace to do it, waters it afterwards so that it takes root in hearts and blooms forth a large harvest. Prayer makes any work of a mission spread as a vine from person to person rippling out to the entire world. *"Have confidence in prayer. It is the unfailing power which God has given us. By means of it you will obtain the salvation of the dear souls whom God has given you and all your loved ones. "Ask and you shall receive", Our Lord said, be yourself good with the Lord,"* says Bl. Peter Julian Eymard. Yes, this prayer should be at set aside times devoted solely to God, but it also should continue throughout the time the missionary works. St. Paul the great missionary said we should, *'Pray without ceasing'* (1 Thess 5:17). If we love while we are working then we are praying while we are working -because love is something we can only do in union with God. It is His constant gift to us that we must receive in our hearts and respond to in grace. But there are some ways to consciously keep our hearts united to Him, too. To do this St.

Phillip Neri offers practical advice, "*It is an old custom of the saints of God to have some little prayers ready and to be frequently darting them up to heaven during the day, lifting their minds to God out of the mire of this world. He who adopts this plan will obtain great fruits with little pain.*"

This sort of prayer offers the missionary wisdom to discern the best way to fulfill one's work. The Holy Spirit Who fills our hearts in prayer will help us reach souls in their deepest core. St. Vincent de Paul explained, "*We should to keep our hearts open to the sufferings and wretchedness of other people, and pray continually that God may grant us that spirit of compassion which is truly the spirit of God.*"

Prayer also offers endurance to the weary missionary who finds himself exhausted, overwhelmed or without strength. St. John Chrysostom says, "*Prayer is the place of refuge for every worry, a foundation for cheerfulness, a source of constant happiness, a protection against sadness.*" And St. Charles Borromeo similarly teaches, "*We meditate before, during and after everything we do. The prophet says: "I will pray, and then I will understand." This is the way we can easily overcome the countless difficulties we have to face day after day, which, after all, are part of our work. In meditation we find the strength to bring Christ to birth in ourselves and in others.*"

Prayer also ensures fruitfulness in our work. The Holy Spirit inspires all mission work, imbues all mission work and follows all mission work to help bear good fruits in the souls of those who are touched by it. As St. Teresa of Avila wrote, prayer ensures 'many great graces and favors' will come from a missionary's blood, sweat and tears. She said, "*Prayer is the only channel through which God's great graces and favors may flow into the soul; and if this be once closed, I know no other way He can communicate them." And if St. Alphonsus Maria de Liguori is correct in saying, "He who prays most receives most," then a missionary simply must pray much in order to bear great fruit. For it is God who bears all fruit. St. Thomas Aquinas reminds us, "We set forth our petitions before God, not in order to make known to Him our needs and desires, but rather so that we ourselves may realize that in these things it is necessary to turn to God for help."

St. Anthony Mary Claret also puts great emphasis on prayer, sacrifice and love as being central to a missionary's life. He said, "Christian perfection consists in three things: praying heroically, working heroically, and suffering heroically." We cannot suffer or work heroically unless we love, and we cannot love heroically without prayer, which is a joining of our heart, mind and soul to God Who is Love Itself.

The Eucharist and Our Lady

St. Don Bosco was a missionary in Italy to street boys for whom he set up homes and provided education. He is known for his many prophetic dreams, but his most famous dream regards future troubles for the Church and is known as the Prophecy of the Two Columns. In his words, here is the dream:

> "Try to picture yourselves with me on the seashore, or, better still, on an outlying cliff with no other land in sight. The vast expanse of water is covered with a formidable array of ships in battle formation, prows fitted with sharp spear-like beaks capable of breaking through any defense. All are heavily armed

with cannons, incendiary bombs, and firearms of all sorts - even books - and are heading toward one stately ship, mightier than them all. As they try to close in, they try to ram it, set it afire, and cripple it as much as possible.

"This stately vessel is shielded by a flotilla escort. Winds and waves are with the enemy. **In this midst of this endless sea,**

two solid columns, a short distance apart, soar high into the sky: one is surmounted by a statue of the Immaculate Virgin at whose feet a large inscription reads: Help of Christians; the other, far loftier and sturdier, supports a [Communion] Host of proportionate size and bears beneath it the inscription Salvation of believers.

"The flagship commander - the Roman Pontiff [the Pope]- seeing the enemy's fury and his auxiliary ships very grave predicament, summons his captains to a conference. However, as *they discuss their strategy, a furious storm breaks out and they must return to their ships. When the storm abates, the Pope again summons his captains as the flagship keeps on its course. But the storm rages again. Standing at the helm, the Pope strains every muscle to steer his ship between the two columns from whose summits hang many anchors and strong hooks linked to chains.*

"*The entire enemy fleet closes in to intercept and sink the flagship at all costs. They bombard it with everything they have: books and pamphlets, incendiary bombs, firearms, cannons. The battle rages ever more furious. Beaked prows ram the flagship again and again, but to no avail, as, unscathed and undaunted, it keeps on its course. At times a formidable ram splinters a gaping hole into its hull, but, immediately, a breeze from the two columns instantly seals the gash.*

"*Meanwhile, enemy cannons blow up, firearms and beaks fall to pieces, ships crack up and sink to the bottom. In blind fury the enemy takes to hand-to-hand combat, cursing and blaspheming. Suddenly the Pope falls, seriously wounded. He is instantly helped up but, struck down a second time, dies. A shout of victory rises from the enemy and wild rejoicing sweeps their ships. But no sooner is the Pope dead than another takes his place. The captains of the auxiliary ships elected him so quickly that the news of the Pope's death coincides with that of his successor's election. The enemy's self-assurance wanes.*

"*Breaking through all resistance, the new Pope steers his ship safely between the two columns and moors it to the two*

Chapter 6: Prayer, Mass, Eucharistic Adoration and the Rosary

columns; first to the one surmounted by the Host, and then to the other, topped by the statue of the Virgin. At this point something unexpected happens. The enemy ships panic and disperse, colliding with and scuttling each other. Some auxiliary ships which had gallantly fought alongside their flagship are the first to tie up at the two columns.

"Many others, which had fearfully kept far away from the fight, stand still, cautiously waiting until the wrecked enemy ships vanish under the waves. Then, they too head for the two columns, tie up at the swinging hooks, and ride safe and tranquil beside their flagship. A great calm now covers the sea."

And in conclusion to this dream:

"Very grave trials await the Church. What we have suffered so far is almost nothing compared to what is going to happen. The enemies of the Church are symbolized by the ships which strive their utmost to sink the flagship. **Only two things can save us in such a grave hour: devotion to Mary and frequent Communion.** *Let us do our very best to use these two means and have others use them everywhere."*

We have already spoken of the great devotion many missionary saints had to the Eucharist and to Our Lady. Daily Mass and hours of prayer in adoration, as well as daily reciting the Most Holy Rosary of Our Lady will surely be the most important anchors of every missionary's life.

The Holy Eucharist: Mass and Adoration

St. John Vianney said:

> "All the good works in the world are not equal to the Holy Sacrifice of the Mass because they are the works of men; but the Mass is the work of God. Martyrdom is nothing in comparison for it is but the sacrifice of man to God; but the Mass is the sacrifice of God for man."

Instead of living day to day, a missionary should cling so tightly to the Holy Eucharist that it becomes the center of time for him. Thus, a true missionary lives from Mass to Mass. The Eucharist becomes his very lifeblood and breath. St. John Vianney explains:

> "When we go before the Blessed Sacrament, let us open our heart; our good God will open His. We shall go to Him; He will come to us; the one to ask, the other to receive. It will be like a breath from one to the other."
>
> "Upon receiving Holy Communion, the Adorable Blood of Jesus Christ really flows in our veins and His Flesh is really blended with ours."
>
> "What does Jesus Christ do in the Eucharist? It is God who, as our Savior, offers himself each day for us to his Father's justice. If you are in difficulties and sorrows, he will comfort and relieve you. If you are sick, he will either cure you or give you strength to suffer so as to merit Heaven. If the devil, the world, and the flesh are making war upon you, he will give you the

weapons with which to fight, to resist, and to win victory. If you are poor, he will enrich you with all sorts of riches for time and eternity. Let us open the door of his sacred and adorable Heart, and be wrapped about for an instant by the flames of his love, and we shall see what a God who loves us can do. O my God, who shall be able to comprehend?"

And it is not only at Holy Mass that we benefit from Christ's Sacramental Presence, but instead many times a day we should draw near to His Eucharistic Heart -especially in the Practice of Eucharistic Adoration -to be filled with the grace needed for the work He entrusts to us. The saints could do nothing without their hearts continually turned to the Sacred Heart of Jesus pouring out torrents of grace from His Eucharistic Presence:

> "We must always have courage, and if some spiritual languor comes upon us, let us run to the feet of Jesus in the Blessed Sacrament, and let us place ourselves in the midst of the heavenly perfumes, and we will undoubtedly regain our strength." - St Padre Pio
>
> "Let weak and frail man come here suppliantly to adore the Sacrament of Christ, not to discuss high things, or wish to penetrate difficulties, but to bow down to secret things in humble veneration, and to abandon God's mysteries to God, for Truth deceives no man—Almighty God can do all things. Amen." - St. Paul of the Cross
>
> "Gaze upon him, consider him, contemplate him, as you desire to imitate him." -St Clare of Assisi

"I no longer take pleasure in perishable food or in the delights of this world. I want only God's bread, which is the Flesh of Jesus Christ, formed of the seed of David, and for drink I crave His Blood which is love that cannot perish." - St. Ignatius of Antioch

"My sweetest Joy is to be in the presence of Jesus in the holy Sacrament. I beg that when obliged to withdraw in body, I may leave my heart before the holy Sacrament. How I would miss Our Lord if He were to be away from me by His presence in the Blessed Sacrament!" - St. Katharine Drexel

"O Jesus! on this day, you have fulfilled all my desires. From now on, near the Eucharist, I shall be able to sacrifice myself in silence, to wait for Heaven in peace. Keeping myself open to the rays of the Divine Host, in this furnace of love, I shall be consumed, and like a seraphim, Lord, I shall love You." - St. Therese of Lisieux

"Heaven for me is hidden in a little Host Where Jesus, my Spouse, is veiled for love. I go to that Divine Furnace to draw out life, and there my Sweet Savior listens to me night and day." - St. Therese of Lisieux

"We must visit Jesus in the Blessed Sacrament a hundred thousand times a day." -St Francis de Sales

"Good friends find pleasure in one another's company. Let us know pleasure in the company of our best Friend, a Friend who can do everything for us, a friend who loves us beyond measure. Here in the Blessed Sacrament we can talk to him straight from the heart." -St Alphonsus de Liguori

"Our Lord in the Blessed Sacrament has His hands full of graces, and He is ready to bestow them on anyone who asks for them." -St Peter of Alcantara

"From the Eucharist comes strength to live the Christian life and zeal to share that life with others." - Pope John Paul II

"I understand that, each time we contemplate with desire and devotion the Host in which is hidden Christ's Eucharistic Body, we increase our merits in heaven and secure special joys to be ours later in the beatific vision of God." - St. Gertrude

"The Eucharist bathes the tormented soul in light and love. Then the soul appreciates these words, 'Come all you who are sick, I will restore your health.'" - St. Bernadette Soubirous

"As a man must be born before he can begin to lead his physical life, so he must be born to lead a Divine Life. That birth occurs in the Sacrament of Baptism. To survive, he must be nourished by Divine Life; that is done in the Sacrament of the Holy Eucharist." - Archbishop Fulton J. Sheen

"What happiness do we not feel in the presence of God, when we find ourselves alone at his feet, before the holy tabernacle! ... 'Come, my soul, redouble your ardor! You are here alone to adore your God! His look rests on you alone!' Ah! if we only had the angels' eyes! Seeing our Lord Jesus Christ here, on that altar, and looking at us, how we should love him! We should want to stay always at his feet; it would be a foretaste of heaven; everything else would become insipid to us." - St. John Vianney

> "The Eucharist had so powerful an attraction for the Blessed Virgin that she could not live away from it. She lived in it and by it. She passed her days and her nights at the feet of her divine Son.... Her love for her hidden God shone in her countenance and communicated its ardor to all about her." - St. Peter Julian Eymard

> **"I have a burning thirst to be honored by men in the Blessed Sacrament, and I find hardly anyone who strives, according to My desire, to allay this thirst by making Me some return of love."** - Words of Jesus to St. Margaret Mary

Devotion to Our Lady and the Holy Rosary

By always keeping a holy rosary in one's hands and the 'Hail Mary' on one's lips, a missionary will march forward with the Light of Our Lady, Star of the Sea and be protected by Her loving Mantle. Clinging to Her as a child She will lead a missionary forward in the night -destroying the enemy who tries to destroy a missionary on all sides. And She also will perfect all of our prayers. St. John Vianney explains, "When our hands have touched spices, they give fragrance to all they handle. Let us make our prayers pass through the hands of the Blessed Virgin. She will make them fragrant."

Every devotion to Our Lady will be powerful help in one's mission work. Particularly powerful is the practice of Consecrating oneself and one's mission to Her Heart -entrusting everything into Her hands. St. Louis de Montfort who gave his entire life to preaching this practice of Marian Consecration explains why:

"[True devotion to Our Lady] is trustful, that is to say, it fills us with confidence in the Blessed Virgin, the confidence that a child has for its loving Mother. It prompts us to go to her in every need of body and soul with great simplicity, trust and affection. We implore our Mother's help always, everywhere, and for everything. We pray to her to be enlightened in our doubts, to be put back on the right path when we go astray, to be protected when we are tempted, to be strengthened when we are weakening, to be lifted up when we fall into sin, to be encouraged when we are losing heart, to be rid of our scruples, to be consoled in the trials, crosses and disappointments of life. Finally, in all our afflictions of body and soul, we naturally turn to Mary for help, with never a fear of importuning her or displeasing our Lord."

"As all perfection consists in our being conformed, united and consecrated to Jesus it naturally follows that the most perfect of all devotions is that which conforms, unites, and consecrates us most completely to Jesus. Now of all God's creatures Mary is the most conformed to Jesus. It therefore follows that, of all devotions, devotion to her makes for the most effective consecration and conformity to him. The more one is consecrated to Mary, the more one is consecrated to Jesus."

"That is why perfect consecration to Jesus is but a perfect and complete consecration of oneself to the Blessed Virgin, which is the devotion I teach; or in other words, it is

> the perfect renewal of the vows and promises of holy baptism."
>
> "The Blessed Virgin, mother of gentleness and mercy, never allows herself to be surpassed in love and generosity. When she sees someone giving himself entirely to her in order to honor and serve her, and depriving himself of what he prizes most in order to adorn her, she gives herself completely in a wondrous manner to him. She engulfs him in the ocean of her graces, adorns him with her merits, supports him with her power, enlightens him with her light, and fills him with her love. She shares her virtues with him — her humility, faith, purity, etc. She makes up for his failings and becomes his representative with Jesus. Just as one who is consecrated belongs entirely to Mary, so Mary belongs entirely to him."

And the most powerful way to live one's Consecration to Our Lady is by the daily recitation of the Holy Rosary. The miracles that abound from this powerful prayer are recounted in St. Louis de Montfort's book *'The Secret of the Rosary'*. This Apostle of the Rosary has said:

> "It would hardly be possible for me to put into words how much Our Lady thinks of the Holy Rosary and of how she vastly prefers it to all other devotions. Neither can I sufficiently express how highly she rewards those who work to preach the

devotion, to establish it and spread it, nor on the other hand how firmly she punishes those who work against it."

"The rosary is the most powerful weapon to touch the Heart of Jesus, Our redeemer, who loves His Mother."

"When the Holy Rosary is said well, it gives Jesus and Mary more glory and is more meritorious than any other prayer."

And yet many saints besides St. Louis de Montfort have spoken about the fact that the Holy Rosary is the most powerful prayer we can pray after the Sacrifice of the Mass itself:

"The greatest method of praying is to pray the Rosary." -St. Francis de Sales

"Those who say the Rosary daily and wear the Brown Scapular and who do a little more, will go straight to Heaven." -St. Alphonsus Ligouri

"The Rosary is THE WEAPON." -St. Padre Pio

"Give me an army saying the Rosary and I will conquer the world." – Blessed Pope Pius IX

"The Rosary is the most excellent form of prayer and the most efficacious means of attaining eternal life. It is the remedy for all our evils, the root of all our blessings. There is no more excellent way of praying." -Pope Leo XIII

> "Among all the devotions approved by the Church none has been favored by so many miracles as the devotion of the most Holy Rosary."-Pope Pius IX

Our Lady Herself has even said:

> "One day through the Rosary and the Scapular I will save the world." -Blessed Virgin Mary to St. Dominic

> "Say the Rosary every day to obtain peace for the world." -Our Lady of Fatima, 1917

I cannot emphasize enough the vital, central importance that daily Mass, adoration and the Holy Rosary must be for a missionary to remain faithful and to bear fruit.

Chapter 7

The Missionary as Priest (Victim), Prophet (speaking God's word), and King (choosing God's will and the authority of love)

The Catechism of the Catholic Church states in Paragraph 783: ***"Jesus Christ is the one whom the Father anointed with the Holy Spirit and established as priest, prophet, and king. The whole People of God participates in these three offices of Christ and bears the responsibilities for mission and service that flow from them."***

Every Catholic missionary is called to a radical transformation into being the face of Jesus Christ in the world to those around him. And in this calling one will particularly find himself identifying with Christ as a priest (victim), prophet (speaking God's word) and king (self-mastery of choosing God's will and exercising an authority of love) to those who he serves.

A Missionary as Priest-Victim

Jesus Christ is the Eternal High Priest -the one who offers sacrifice on behalf of the entire world -as well as the Victim being Sacrificed and the Altar on which the Sacrifice is consumed. On the Cross Jesus Christ offered the ultimate sacrifice of Himself -through all of the woundedness and suffering He accepted -in a fragrant fire of God's Love for the sake of the entire world. As a missionary draws close to this Perfect Sacred Heart of Complete Love, he will begin to love as Jesus Christ loves. And that means his heart will be stretched way beyond the natural borders of human affection (attraction, likes and dislikes) and pulled into the furnace of Divine Love that encompasses all of the souls in the whole world. Often people tell me that I cannot know a mother's love because I do not have my own physical children. This might be true on some superficial, human level -but it is not the least bit true if one considers the union of my heart with Our Lady and how I love the souls entrusted to me with Her Own Motherly Love. A missionary might not feel an attraction to the culture of East Africa or an obscure Asian island -and they might also not understand the ways of the people there -but when that soul is a missionary called and sent by God to bring the Gospel to these people, God will fill his soul with a Divine Love (being the Holy Spirit) who also fills them with a Wisdom, Knowledge and Understanding of their hearts along with a burning zeal for their salvation. This is a special grace given to those called to serve these people. The same can be said on an individual level. A parish priest in the US might not know a particular parishioner well -nor spend lots of time learning about his or her life, but when God calls that priest to be an instrument of His Voice through spiritual direction for them, suddenly a Divine Wisdom that comes through Divine Love will be granted to that priest, along with a determination to work ardently without counting the cost to lead that soul towards heaven.

If God grants His special Divine Love for souls to those Who He calls to serve them, then that means that the missionary called is transformed by that Love himself. His eyes begin to see with a Divine perspective, his ears hear with a Divine understanding, his lips speak with Divine words, his mind judges according to God's Love and perfect will -all of this guided by the Holy Spirit (God's Love) Who is the source of these gifts. And as a missionary soul is united to the Heart of Jesus Christ in these flames of Love, he will also be given the desire to sacrifice courageously all of himself along with Christ for the salvation of souls. In this way, he partakes in Christ's role as the Eternal High Priest, not only being an instrument of His grace to reach the souls he serves, but also adding to Jesus' Sacrifice his own sacrifices for others.

St. Paul writes that Christ *'makes peace by the blood of his cross'* (Colossians 1:20). He explains that Jesus endures all of His bloody Passion to convert, heal and purify us so that we can reach heaven (the only place of perfect Peace). He writes, *"And you who once were alienated and hostile in mind because of evil deeds he has now reconciled in his fleshly body through his death, to present you holy, without blemish, and irreproachable before him."* (Colossians 1: 21-22) In the same way, missionaries are called to participate in His priesthood as little victims offering sacrifices of love along with Him for the souls they love and serve. St. Paul wrote, *"Now I rejoice in my sufferings for your sake, and in my flesh I am filling up what is lacking in the afflictions of Christ on behalf of his body, which is the church."* (Colossians 1:24) St. Paul also encourages those who he served to join in this co-redemption with Christ. He writes to the Romans, *"I urge you therefore, brothers, by the mercies of God, to offer your bodies as a living sacrifice, holy and pleasing to God, your spiritual worship."* (Romans 12:1) In offering the sacrifice of our lives along with Christ both as a priest and the victim, we become incense rising to heaven to cover the stench of the world's sin. *"For we are the aroma of Christ for God* among those who are being saved and among those who are perishing." (2 Corinthians 2:15)

Priests offer sacrifice for the people -and a missionary is called to offer the sacrifice of his own being -emptying himself out alongside Christ -for those he is called to serve. His prayer is a fragrant offering of Love. And hopefully, his words and actions all are intertwined with Jesus' Priestly Mission as our Redeemer. Particularly when a missionary priest offers the Sacraments, he will intimately do so in union with Christ and no other work in a mission is as important as this. But even when religious and laity are called into mission work, they must remember that their participation in the Sacraments and their leading others to them as well is the most important work that they can ever do for souls. And it is their lay priestly prayer and suffering offered to God on behalf of their people which will reach the Heart of Jesus on the Altar of the Cross and win graces way beyond human expectation.

Missionary as Prophet (speaking God's word)

"Go forth and set the world on fire." -Saint Ignatius of Loyola

This is what it means to be a missionary prophet. To go forth after entering in the furnace of God's Love and to allow His flames to set all you encounter on fire. This can be done in a myriad of ways. In the Old Testament, prophets not only heard the words of the Lord and repeated them to the Israelites as His mouthpiece, often they also were called to live out prophesy with their lives. Oftentimes we read about Old Testament prophets being commanded to do certain things so that the action of their lives would give a message to God's people. Sometimes these actions were accompanied by explanations with words and at other times God wanted the actions to speak for themselves to all of those who had 'eyes to see and ears to hear' His message. And so even if most of the time God will ask a missionary to relay His message to a people through his words, it is always necessary that a prophet first and foremost speaks to a people through his own example and life. Saint Teresa of Ávila said, *"We must all try to be preachers through our deeds."* Pope Paul VI also said this: *"Modern man listens more willingly to witnesses than to teachers, and if he does listen to teachers, it is because they are witnesses."* And so, when Christ in Mark 16:15 commanded his disciples, *"Go into all the world and proclaim the gospel to the whole creation,"* He was demanding not only that they proclaim His words to the world, but also that they teach by the example of their lives which were supposed to be conformed to His through Love.

The message that Christ entrusts to the disciples is the message of the Beatitudes. A new way of living and thinking not according to human understanding, but instead an echo of Divine Wisdom. He taught:

Blessed are the poor in spirit, for theirs is the kingdom of heaven.
Blessed are they who mourn, for they will be comforted.
Blessed are the meek, for they will inherit the land.
Blessed are they who hunger and thirst for righteousness, for they will be satisfied.
Blessed are the merciful, for they will be shown mercy.

> *Blessed are the clean of heart, for they will see God.*
>
> *Blessed are the peacemakers, for they will be called children of God.*
>
> *Blessed are they who are persecuted for the sake of righteousness, for theirs is the kingdom of heaven. Blessed are you when they insult you and persecute you and utter every kind of evil against you [falsely] because of me. Rejoice and be glad, for your reward will be great in heaven. Thus they persecuted the prophets who were before you." (Matthew 5:3-12)*

And yet, Jesus' message was not new. When He revealed Himself in the temple in Nazareth, He chose a reading from the prophet Isaiah and followed that reading with the statement, *"Today this scripture passage is fulfilled in your hearing."* (Luke 4:21) This message that Christ was fulfilling is the same message that all missionaries are called to live. Isaiah 61:1-3 says:

> *"The Spirit of the Lord God is upon me, because the Lord has anointed me to bring good news to the poor; he has sent me to bind up the brokenhearted, to proclaim liberty to the captives, and the opening of the prison to those who are bound; to proclaim the year of the Lord's favor, and the day of vengeance of our God; to comfort all who mourn; to grant to those who mourn in Zion— to give them a beautiful headdress instead of ashes, the oil of gladness instead of mourning, the garment of praise instead of a faint spirit; that they may be called oaks of*

righteousness, the planting of the Lord, that he may be glorified."

Missionaries, like Christ, are to give preference to the poor, the broken-hearted, the humble and outcasts. And not only are missionaries supposed to firstly direct their message to them, their very presence among them should bring light to their darkness, healing to their suffering, freedom to their chains, comfort and hope to the despairing. A missionary may feel incapable of doing such great things -and yet, if one looks away from himself and instead focuses on the Heart of God and His Grace, God will do the work Himself simply through the missionary's surrender -his freewill offering of 'fiat', of 'yes.' Many saints and prophets of old felt incapable -and yet God often *"chose the foolish of the world to shame the wise, and God chose the weak of the world to shame the strong, and God chose the lowly and despised of the world, those who count for nothing, to reduce to nothing those who are something, so that no human being might boast before God."* (1 Cor 1:27-29) We even see this in the Old Testament:

> *"Amos answered Amaziah, "I am not a prophet, nor do I belong to a company of prophets. I am a herdsman and a dresser of sycamores, but the LORD took me from following the flock, and the LORD said to me, 'Go, prophesy to my people Israel.'"* (Amos 7:14-15)

> *"The word of the LORD came to me: Before I formed you in the womb I knew you, before you were born I dedicated you, a prophet to the nations I appointed you. "Ah, Lord GOD!" I said,*

"I do not know how to speak. I am too young!" But the LORD answered me, "Do not say, "I am too young." To whomever I send you, you shall go; whatever I command you, you shall speak. Do not be afraid of them, for I am with you to deliver you"—oracle of the LORD. Then the LORD extended his hand and touched my mouth, saying to me, "See, I place my words in your mouth! Today I appoint you over nations and over kingdoms, to uproot and to tear down, to destroy and to demolish, to build and to plant." The word of the LORD came to me: What do you see, Jeremiah? "I see a branch of the almond tree," I replied. Then the LORD said to me: You have seen well, for I am watching over my word to carry it out." (Jeremiah 1:4-12)

"But Moses said to the Lord, "Oh, my Lord, I am not eloquent, either in the past or since you have spoken to your servant, but I am slow of speech and of tongue." Then the Lord said to him, "Who has made man's mouth? Who makes him mute, or deaf, or seeing, or blind? Is it not I, the Lord? Now therefore go, and I will be with your mouth and teach you what you shall speak."" (Exodus 4:10-12)

The first disciples and apostles of Jesus were very convicted of their duty to preach the Gospel. Timothy wrote, *"Preach the word; be ready in season and out of season; reprove, rebuke, and exhort, with complete patience and teaching."* (2 Timothy 4:2) And St. Paul proclaimed:

> *"If I preach the gospel, this is no reason for me to boast, for an obligation has been imposed on me, and woe to me if I do not preach it! If I do so willingly, I have a recompense, but if unwillingly, then I have been entrusted with a stewardship. What then is my recompense? That, when I preach, I offer the gospel free of charge so as not to make full use of my right in the gospel."* (1 Corinthians 9:16-18)

> *"How then will they call on him in whom they have not believed? And how are they to believe in him of whom they have never heard? And how are they to hear without someone preaching?"* (Romans 10:14)

It is a duty of every missionary to preach the Truth. For if people do not hear or know the Truth, then they can never be brought back from their errors or be freed from the chains of sin. St. Boniface -a great missionary to the Germanic people -understood this well. He taught:

> *"In her voyage across the ocean of this world, the Church is like a great ship being pounded by the waves of life's different stresses. Our duty is not to abandon ship but to keep her on her course."*
>
> *"Let us be careful shepherds watching over Christ's flock. Let us preach the whole of God's plan, to the powerful and to the humble, to rich and to poor, to men of every rank and age, as far as God gives us the strength, in season and out of season."*

And this mandate to preach the Truth does not come with a price -many who hear the message of Jesus will reject it and even persecute those who sacrifice so much to give it to them. St. Boniface mentioned above was eventually martyred for the faith. Another martyr for the faith was Blessed Titus Brandsma -a Carmelite priest who spoke about the evil being done by the Nazis in World War II and who eventually was arrested and put to death. And yet, he firmly taught (and lived) his belief that *"They who want to win the world for Christ must have the courage to come into conflict with it."*

The message of Christ is not always easy to preach because it necessitates upon the listener a response -often a radical change of life and a willingness to suffer along with their Savior. And yet this message of the Cross should never be avoided -as it is central to our faith and the meaning behind all that we believe. St. Paul makes this clear in his writing:

> *"For Christ did not send me to baptize but to preach the gospel, and not with words of eloquent wisdom, lest the cross of Christ be emptied of its power."* (1 Corinthians 1:17)

> *"And I, when I came to you, brothers, did not come proclaiming to you the testimony of God with lofty speech or wisdom. For I decided to know nothing among you except Jesus Christ and him crucified. And I was with you in weakness and in fear and much trembling, and my speech and my message were not in plausible words of wisdom, but in demonstration of the Spirit and of power, so that your faith might not rest in the wisdom of men but in the power of God."* (1 Corinthians 2:1-8)

> *"But we preach Christ crucified, a stumbling block to Jews and folly to Gentiles..."* (1 Corinthians 1:23)

Oftentimes it is the radical witness of the message of the Cross that eventually converts hardened sinners. Sometimes the murderers of the martyrs eventually convert because of their witness. This was true of St. Isaac Jogues among the Indians in Canada. There is a more recent story of 21 men martyred by the Islamic State in Libya in 2015. Twenty of these men were Coptic Orthodox from Libya and one of whom was from Ghana. The terrorists gave the men a chance: renounce Christianity and embrace Islam. Or die. They chose to die. Captured on the video were the last words of some of the men, "Ya Rabb Yeshua!" ("O Lord Jesus!"). The Ghanian, Matthew Ayariga, was not Coptic. Some accounts say that he was already a Christian, others that he was not but regardless he said, *"Their God is my God"*, knowing that he would be killed. He was inspired by the example of those Coptic Christians willing to die for their faith that he also was baptized in blood right alongside them.

Missionary as King (choosing God's will and the authority of love)

All missionaries -priestly, religious and lay - participate in Christ's kingly office as well. First of all, this is by self-governance and mastery and using God's gift of freewill to always choose what is good and holy. *The Catechism of the Catholic Church* explains:

> *908 By his obedience unto death, Christ communicated to his disciples the gift of royal freedom, so that they might "by the*

self-abnegation of a holy life, overcome the reign of sin in themselves". (Lumen Gentium)

That man is rightly called a king who makes his own body an obedient subject and, by governing himself with suitable rigor, refuses to let his passions breed rebellion in his soul, for he exercises a kind of royal power over himself. And because he knows how to rule his own person as king, so too does he sit as its judge. He will not let himself be imprisoned by sin, or thrown headlong into wickedness. (St. Ambrose)

That missionaries should practice self-control and use their freewill to always choose a path of highest virtue is a given -for they are the Face of Christ to those who they serve. But the priestly role of Christ extends further than a missionary's own governance of self. The vocation of being called into mission (and most often lived out through an official assignment by the authority of the Church) constitutes being a person of great spiritual authority to those that one serves. In this way, a missionary is called to wield his authority as the Good Shepherd did – *'seeking and saving the lost'* (Luke 19:10) – *'carrying the wounded on His shoulders'* (Luke 15:5) – *'laying down His life for the sheep.'* (John 10:11). The authority that a missionary is given over the souls entrusted to his care is an authority of love. Even when he may be in a position to 'rule' in a way -making practical decisions that will affect the people he serves intimately -he must rule through love -as the Good Shepherd. In fact, he will particularly need the Holy Spirit's gift of Wisdom to do so -for Wisdom is a 'listening heart' that receives knowledge from God through his love for

God and those he serves. Wisdom is a knowledge of love. The saints teach this importance of the primacy of love in all decisions we make in life. We must always be led by God's love and choose God's love. And such love will cost us sacrifice. Mother Teresa said, *"Love to be real, it must cost—it must hurt—it must empty us of self."* And, *"Intense love does not measure, it just gives."* Saint Pope John Paul II taught, *"Real love is demanding. I would fail in my mission if I did not tell you so. Love demands a personal commitment to the will of God."* St. Teresa of Avila reminds us, *"It is not so essential to think much as to love much."* And Saint Catherine of Siena observed, *"Everything comes from love, all is ordained for the salvation of man, God does nothing without this goal in mind."*

It would be good here to briefly visit the places in Scripture where Jesus Christ's love as the Good Shepherd is described. For he is to be the model for all missionaries carrying out their role of kingly authority:

> *"Like a shepherd he feeds his flock; in his arms he gathers the lambs, carrying them in his bosom, leading the ewes with care."* (Isaiah 40: 11)

> *"What man of you, having a hundred sheep, if he has lost one of them, does not leave the ninety-nine in the open country, and go after the one that is lost, until he finds it? And when he has found it, he lays it on his shoulders, rejoicing. And when he comes home, he calls together his friends and his neighbors,*

saying to them, 'Rejoice with me, for I have found my sheep that was lost.'" (Luke 15:4-7)

"For thus says the Lord God: Behold, I, I myself will search for my sheep and will seek them out. As a shepherd seeks out his flock when he is among his sheep that have been scattered, so will I seek out my sheep, and I will rescue them from all places where they have been scattered on a day of clouds and thick darkness. And I will bring them out from the peoples and gather them from the countries, and will bring them into their own land. And I will feed them on the mountains of Israel, by the ravines, and in all the inhabited places of the country. I will feed them with good pasture, and on the mountain heights of Israel shall be their grazing land. There they shall lie down in good grazing land, and on rich pasture they shall feed on the mountains of Israel. I myself will be the shepherd of my sheep, and I myself will make them lie down, declares the Lord God. I will seek the lost, and I will bring back the strayed, and I will bind up the injured, and I will strengthen the weak, and the fat and the strong I will destroy. I will feed them in justice." (Ezekiel 34:11-16)

In Conclusion

As we reflect on a missionary's need to reflect Jesus Christ as priest (victim), prophet and king (shepherd) to those he serves, we see that following Our Savior's footsteps means following His Way of the Cross. And yet, Jesus' bloody footsteps of self-sacrificial love up the road of Calvary are actually light posts for us -enlightening the good and holy path we are called to walk through this dark world of sin, brokenness, and error. As we see His bloody footsteps glow, we are given courage to follow Him -the Light of the World -trusting that even more than we will be called to carry those we are called to serve on our backs, Jesus Who is Our Good Shepherd will carry us when Golgotha's terrain is too dangerous or difficult for our feeble feet. He said to us: *"Come to me, all you who labor and are burdened, and I will give you rest. Take my yoke upon you and learn from me, for I am meek and humble of heart; and you will find rest for yourselves. For my yoke is easy, and my burden light."* (Matthew 11:28-30) And we simply must trust His promise.

Chapter 8

Church Documents on Mission Life

As we reflected in the last chapter on how the missionary is called to imitate Christ the Good Shepherd, it makes sense that we now turn to the teachings of the Magisterium on missionary life -for Christ was speaking to His disciples teaching them to imitate His Sherherdly Love -and this is passed on to us through the Apostolic Succession of the Church. The Popes throughout the centuries have been entrusted with a particular call by Jesus Christ to teach the faithful how best to imitate Christ the Missionary. And it is from Church documents -Encyclicals, Papal Homilies, Documents of the various Church Counsels and other Exhortations from Church Hierarchy -that keep us grounded in how the Catholic Church is asking each of us to follow the missionary footsteps of Jesus Christ and His Church.

I would like to open this chapter with a few small excerpts from Pope John XXIII in his Encyclical about Missionary Work entitled *'Princeps Pastorum'* ("The Prince of the Shepherds") promulgated on 28 November 1959. In these few excerpts he reminds the Church of the primacy that love takes in the missionary life -a love we first experience and then learn to share through our own personal prayer. And he emphasizes how we are called to live such charity not just in a spiritual way, but also concretely offering material help to those we serve to the degree possible:

1-3. On the day when "the Prince of the Shepherds" entrusted to Us His lambs and sheep, God's flock, which dwells all over the earth, We responded to the sweet invitation of His love with a sense of Our unworthiness but with trust in His all-powerful assistance. And the magnitude, the beauty, and the importance of the Catholic Missions have been constantly on Our mind. For this reason, We have never ceased to devote to them Our greatest solicitude and attention.

37- 37. Union in prayer and in active participation in the mysteries of the sacred liturgy enormously enriches and completes the Christian life of individuals and of the whole community, and it greatly helps educate the soul to charity, which is the distinguishing mark of the true Christian; a charity, We say, which overcomes all differences between languages and nationalities, and amicably embraces all men, whether brothers or enemies. In this connection, We like to repeat the words of Our predecessor Pope Clement: "When they (the pagans) hear from us that God says, 'You have no merit if you love those who love you, but you have merit if you love your enemies and those who hate you'[65] --when they hear this, they admire the grace of your charity; but when they see that we not only do not love those who hate us, but do not even reciprocate the love of those who love us, they will mock us and God's name will be blasphemed." The greatest missionary of all, St. Paul the Apostle, at the time when he was on the point of bringing the message of God's word to the people, as far as the farthest reaches of the Western world, wrote to the Romans and exhorted them to practice "love without pretense." Earlier, with sublime expression, he had praised that virtue--without which a Christian is nothing.

38. Charity also becomes visible through material help; as Our predecessor Pius XII stated: "The body also requires a multitude of members, which are joined together for the purpose of helping one another. If in our mortal organism one member ails, all the other members suffer with it; and those members which are sound, come to the help of the sick one; by the same token, in the Church, the individual members do not live only for themselves, but also to help the others, and all of them help one another for their mutual comfort, as well as for a better development of the Mystical Body."

39. The material necessities which affect the faithful also affect the life and structure of the Church. It is therefore necessary that native Christians become accustomed to supporting, spontaneously and within the limits of their means, their churches, institutions, and clergy, who are entirely devoting themselves to them. It does not matter whether they can give much, but it is of the greatest importance that what is contributed is proof of a conscience that is practicing Christian discipline.

40. The Christian faithful, members of a living organism, cannot remain aloof and think that they have done their duty when they have satisfied their own spiritual needs; every individual must give his assistance to those who are working for the increase and propagation of God's kingdom. Our predecessor Pius XII reminded all of their common duty in these words: "A principal note of the Church is catholicity; consequently, a man is no true member of the Church unless he is likewise a true member of the entire body of Christian believers and is filled with an ardent desire to see her take root and flourish in every land."

Who God calls missionaries to be…

In Pope Pius XI's 1926 Encyclical *'Rerum Ecclesiae'* on promoting Catholic Missions, he writes extensively about the roots of Catholic Missions and the call and qualities of a missionary to such a work. He speaks about the missionary call to all vocations -priests, sisters and laity alike -and I will simply include here a powerful excerpt of his writing on this topic:

ON CATHOLIC MISSIONS

7. This missionary activity derives its reason from the will of God, "who wishes all men to be saved and to come to the knowledge of the truth. For there is one God, and one mediator between God and men, Himself a man, Jesus Christ, who gave Himself as a ransom for all" (1 Tim. 2:45), "neither is there salvation in any other" (Acts 4:12). Therefore, all must be converted to Him, made known by the Church's preaching, and all must be incorporated into Him by baptism and into the Church which is His body. For Christ Himself "by stressing in express language the necessity of faith and baptism (cf.

Mark 16:16; John 3:5), *at the same time confirmed the necessity of the Church, into which men enter by baptism, as by a door. Therefore those men cannot be saved, who though aware that God, through Jesus Christ founded the Church as something necessary, still do not wish to enter into it, or to persevere in it." Therefore though God in ways known to Himself can lead those inculpably ignorant of the Gospel to find that faith without which it is impossible to please Him (Heb. 11:6), yet a necessity lies upon the Church (1 Cor. 9:16), and at the same time a sacred duty, to preach the Gospel. And hence missionary activity today as always retains its power and necessity.*

MISSIONARIES

23. Although every disciple of Christ, as far in him lies, has the duty of spreading the Faith, Christ the Lord always calls whomever He will from among the number of His disciples, to be with Him and to be sent by Him to preach to the nations (cf. Mark 3:13). Therefore, by the Holy Spirit, who distributes the charismata as He wills for the common good (1 Cor. 12:11), He inspires the missionary vocation in the hearts of individuals, and at the same time He raises up in the Church certain institutes which take as their own special task the duty of preaching the Gospel, a duty belonging to the whole Church.

They are assigned with a special vocation who, being endowed with a suitable natural temperament, and being fit as regards talent and other qualities, have been trained to undertake mission work; or be they autochthonous or be they foreigners: priests, Religious, or laymen. Sent by legitimate authority, they go out in faith and obedience to those who are far from Christ. They are set apart for the work for which they have been taken up (cf. Acts 13:2), as ministers of the Gospel, "that the offering up of the Gentiles may become acceptable, being sanctified by the Holy Spirit" (Rom. 15:16).

24. Yet man must respond to God Who calls, and that in such a way, that without taking counsel with flesh and blood (Gal. 1:16), he devotes himself wholly to the work of the Gospel. This response, however can only be given when the Holy Spirit gives His inspiration and His power. For he who is sent enters upon the life and mission of Him Who "emptied Himself, taking the nature of a slave" (Phil. 2:7). Therefore, he must be ready to stay at his vocation for an entire lifetime, and to renounce himself and all those whom he thus far considered as his own, and instead to "make himself all things to all men" (1 Cor. 9:22).

Announcing the Gospel to all nations, he confidently makes known the mystery of Christ, whose ambassador he is, so that in him he dares to speak as he ought (cf. Eph. 6:19; Acts 4:31), not being ashamed of the scandal of the Cross. Following in his Master's footsteps, meek and humble of heart, he proves that His yoke is easy and His burden light (Matt. 11:29ff.) By a truly evangelical life, in much patience, in long - suffering, in kindness, in unaffected love (cf. 2 Cor. 6:4ff.), he bears witness to his Lord, if need be to the shedding of his *blood. He will ask of God the power and strength, that he may know that there is an overflowing of joy amid much testing of tribulation and deep poverty (2 Cor. 8:2). Let him be convinced that obedience is the hallmark of the servant of Christ, who redeemed the human race by His obedience.*

The heralds of the Gospel lest they neglect the grace which is in them, should be renewed day by day in the spirit of their mind (cf. 1 Tim. 4:14; Eph. 4:23; 2 Cor. 4:16). Their Ordinaries and superiors should gather the missionaries together from time to time, that they be strengthened in the hope of their calling and may be renewed in the apostolic ministry, even in houses expressly set up for this purpose.

25. For such an exalted task, the future missionary is to be prepared by a special spiritual and moral training. For he must have the spirit of initiative in beginning, as well as that of constancy in carrying through what he has begun; he must be persevering in difficulties, patient and strong of heart in bearing with solitude, fatigue, and fruitless labor. He will encounter men with an open mind and a wide heart; he will gladly take up the duties which are entrusted to him; he will with a noble spirit adapt himself to the people's foreign way of doing things and to changing circumstances; while in the spirit of harmony and mutual charity, he will cooperate with his brethren and all who dedicate themselves to the same task, so that together with the faithful, they will be one heart and one soul (cf. Acts 2:42; 4:32) in imitation of the apostolic community.

> *These habits of mind should be earnestly exercised already in his time of training; they should be cultivated, and should be uplifted and nourished by the spiritual life. Imbued with a living faith and a hope that never fails, the missionary should be a man of prayer. Let him have an ardent spirit of power and of love and of prudence (cf. 2 Tim. 1:7). Let him learn to be self-sufficing in whatever circumstances (Phil. 4:11); always bearing about in himself the dying of Jesus, so that the life of Jesus may work in those to whom he is sent (2 Cor. 4:10ff.), out of zeal of souls, let him gladly spend all and be spent himself for souls (cf. 2 Cor. 12:15ff.), so that "by the daily practice of his duty he may grow in the love of God and neighbor." Thus obedient to the will of the Father together with Christ, he will continue His mission under the hierarchical authority of the Church.*
>
> *30. In order that the proper goals and results may be obtained, all missionary workers should have but "one heart and one soul" (Acts 4:32) in the actual carrying out of mission work itself.*

The last papal document that I want to share in this chapter is Pope Paul VI's 1975 Apostolic Exhortation '*Evangelii Nuntiandi*' ('Proclaiming the Gospel...') In this writing the Holy Father first touches upon the mission of Christ Himself Who was sent by the Father into the world to proclaim a message of Salvation and the coming of the Kingdom of Heaven. Pope Paul VI writes:

1. There is no doubt that the effort to proclaim the Gospel to the people of today, who are buoyed up by hope but at the same time often oppressed by fear and distress, is a service rendered to the Christian community and also to the whole of humanity.

6. The witness that the Lord gives of Himself and that Saint Luke gathered together in his Gospel - "I must proclaim the Good News of the kingdom of God" - without doubt has enormous consequences, for it sums up the whole mission of Jesus: "That is what I was sent to do." These words take on their full significance if one links them with the previous verses, in which Christ has just applied to Himself the words of the prophet Isaiah: "The Spirit of the Lord has been given to me, for he has anointed me. He has sent me to bring the good news to the poor."

Going from town to town, preaching to the poorest - and frequently the most receptive - the joyful news of the fulfillment of the promises and of the Covenant offered by God is the mission for which Jesus declares that He is sent by the Father. And all the aspects of His mystery - the Incarnation itself, His miracles, His teaching, the gathering together of the disciples, the sending out of the Twelve, the cross and the resurrection, the permanence of His presence in the midst of His own - were components of His evangelizing activity.

7. During the Synod, the bishops very frequently referred to this truth: Jesus Himself, the Good News of God, was the very first and the greatest evangelizer; He was so through and through: to perfection and to the point of the sacrifice of His earthly life.

8. As an evangelizer, Christ first of all proclaims a kingdom, the kingdom of God; and this is so important that, by comparison, everything else becomes "the rest," which is "given in addition." Only the kingdom therefore is absolute and it makes everything else relative. The Lord will delight in describing in many ways the happiness of belonging to this kingdom (a paradoxical happiness which is made up of things that the world rejects), the demands of the kingdom and its Magna Charta, the heralds of the kingdom, its mysteries, its children, the vigilance and fidelity demanded of whoever awaits its definitive coming.

9. As the kernel and center of His Good News, Christ proclaims salvation, this great gift of God which is liberation from everything that oppresses man but which is above all liberation from sin and the Evil One, in the joy of knowing God and being known by Him, of seeing Him, and of being given over to Him. All of this is begun during the life of Christ and definitively accomplished by His death and resurrection. But it must be patiently carried on during the course of history, in order to be realized fully on the day of the final coming of Christ, whose date is known to no one except the Father.

10. This kingdom and this salvation, which are the key words of Jesus Christ's evangelization, are available to every human being as grace and mercy, and yet at the same time each individual must gain them by force - they belong to the

violent, says the Lord, through toil and suffering, through a life lived according to the Gospel, through abnegation and the cross, through the spirit of the beatitudes. But above all each individual gains them through a total interior renewal which the Gospel calls metanoia; it is a radical conversion, a profound change of mind and heart.

11. Christ accomplished this proclamation of the kingdom of God through the untiring preaching of a word which, it will be said, has no equal elsewhere: "Here is a teaching that is new, and with authority behind it." "And he won the approval of all, and they were astonished by the gracious words that came from his lips. There has never been anybody who has spoken like him." His words reveal the secret of God, His plan and His promise, and thereby change the heart of man and his destiny.

12. But Christ also carries out this proclamation by innumerable signs, which amaze the crowds and at the same time draw them to Him in order to see Him, listen to Him and allow themselves to be transformed by Him: the sick are cured, water is changed into wine, bread is multiplied, the dead come back to life. And among all these signs there is the one to which He attaches great importance: the humble and the poor are evangelized, become His disciples and gather together "in His name" in the great community of those who believe in Him. For this Jesus who declared, "I must preach the Good News of the Kingdom of God" is the same Jesus of whom John the Evangelist said that He had come and was to die "to gather together in unity the scattered children of God." Thus He accomplishes His revelation, completing it and confirming it by the entire revelation that He makes of Himself, by words and deeds, by signs and miracles, and more especially by His death, by His resurrection and by the sending of the Spirit of Truth.

13. Those who sincerely accept the Good News, through the power of this acceptance and of shared faith therefore gather together in Jesus' name in order to seek together the kingdom, build it up and live it. They make up a community which is in its turn evangelizing. The command to the Twelve to go out and proclaim the Good News is also valid for all Christians, though in a different way. It is precisely for this reason that Peter calls Christians "a people set apart to sing the praises of God," those marvelous things that each one was able to hear in his own language. Moreover, the Good News of the kingdom which is coming and which has begun is meant for all people of all times. Those who have received the Good News and who have been gathered by it into the community of salvation can and must communicate and spread it.

14. The Church knows this. She has a vivid awareness of the fact that the Savior's words, "I must proclaim the Good News of the kingdom of God," apply in all truth to herself. She willingly adds with St. Paul: "Not that I boast of preaching the gospel, since it is a duty that has been laid on me; I should be punished if I did not preach it." It is with joy and consolation that at the end of the great Assembly of 1974 we heard these illuminating words: "We wish to confirm once more that the task of evangelizing all people constitutes the essential mission of the Church." It is a task and mission which the vast and profound changes of present-day society make all the more urgent. Evangelizing is in fact the grace and vocation proper to the Church, her deepest identity. She exists in order to evangelize, that is to say, in order to preach and teach, to be the channel of the gift of grace, to reconcile sinners with God, and to perpetuate Christ's sacrifice in the Mass, which is the memorial of His death and glorious resurrection.

15. Anyone who rereads in the New Testament the origins of the Church, follows her history step by step and watches her live and act, sees that she is linked to evangelization in her most intimate being:

- The Church is born of the evangelizing activity of Jesus and the Twelve. She is the normal, desired, most immediate and most visible fruit of this activity: "Go, therefore, make disciples of all the nations." Now, "they accepted what he said and were baptized. That very day about three thousand were added to their number.... Day by day the Lord added to their community those destined to be saved." - Having been born consequently out of being sent, the Church in her turn is sent by Jesus. The Church remains in the world when the Lord of glory returns to the Father. She remains as a sign - simultaneously obscure and luminous - of a new presence of Jesus, of His departure and of His permanent presence. She prolongs and continues Him. And it is above all His mission and His condition of being an evangelizer that she is called upon to continue.

For the Christian community is never closed in upon itself. The intimate life of this community - the life of listening to the Word and the apostles' teaching, charity lived in a fraternal way, the sharing of bread this intimate life only acquires its full meaning when it becomes a witness, when it evokes admiration and conversion, and when it becomes the preaching and proclamation of the Good News. Thus it is the whole Church that receives the mission to evangelize, and the work of each individual member is important for the whole.

- The Church is an evangelizer, but she begins by being evangelized herself. She is the community of believers, the community of hope lived and communicated, the community of brotherly love, and she needs to listen unceasingly to what she must believe, to her reasons for hoping, to the new commandment of love. She is the People of God immersed in the world, and often tempted by idols, and she always needs to hear the proclamation of the "mighty works of God" which converted her to the Lord; she always needs to be called together afresh by Him and reunited. In brief, this means that she has a constant need of being evangelized, if she wishes to retain freshness, vigor and strength in order to proclaim the Gospel. The Second Vatican Council recalled and the 1974 Synod vigorously took up again this theme of the Church which is evangelized by constant conversion and renewal, in order to evangelize the world with credibility.

- The Church is the depositary of the Good News to be proclaimed. The promises of the New Alliance in Jesus Christ, the

Chapter 8: Church Documents on Mission Life

teaching of the Lord and the apostles, the Word of life, the sources of grace and of God's loving kindness, the path of salvation - all these things have been entrusted to her. It is the content of the Gospel, and therefore of evangelization, that she preserves as a precious living heritage, not in order to keep it hidden but to communicate it.

- Having been sent and evangelized, the Church herself sends out evangelizers. She puts on their lips the saving Word, she explains to them the message of which she herself is the depositary, she gives them the mandate which she herself has received and she sends them out to preach. To preach not their own selves or their personal ideas, but a Gospel of which neither she nor they are the absolute masters and owners, to dispose of it as they wish, but a Gospel of which they are the ministers, in order to pass it on with complete fidelity.

16. There is thus a profound link between Christ, the Church and evangelization. During the period of the Church that we are living in, it is she who has the task of evangelizing. This mandate is not accomplished without her, and still less against her.

Pope Paul VI then goes on to explain how the Church continues Jesus Christ's work of evangelization -and he explains what that should look like in the modern world. He speaks about both the importance of the witness of one's life, as well as the actual preaching of the Truth of the Gospel, in the work of missionary evangelization:

26. It is not superfluous to recall the following points: to evangelize is first of all to bear witness, in a simple and direct way, to God revealed by Jesus Christ, in the Holy Spirit, to bear witness that in His Son God has loved the world - that in His Incarnate Word He has given being to all things and has called men to eternal life. Perhaps this attestation of God will be for many people the unknown God whom they adore without giving Him a name, or whom they seek by a secret call of the heart when they experience the emptiness of all idols. But it is fully evangelizing in manifesting the fact that for man the Creator is not an anonymous and remote power; He is the Father: "...that we should be called children of God; and so we are." And thus we are one another's brothers and sisters in God.

27. Evangelization will also always contain - as the foundation, center, and at the same time, summit of its dynamism - a clear proclamation that, in Jesus Christ, the Son of God made man, who died and rose from the dead, salvation is offered to all men, as a gift of God's grace and mercy. And not an immanent salvation, meeting material or even spiritual needs, restricted to the framework of temporal existence and completely identified with temporal desires, hopes, affairs and struggles, but a salvation which exceeds all these limits in order to reach fulfillment in a communion with the one and only divine Absolute: a transcendent and eschatological salvation, which indeed has its beginning in this life but which is fulfilled in eternity.

Chapter 8: Church Documents on Mission Life

28. Consequently evangelization cannot but include the prophetic proclamation of a hereafter, man's profound and definitive calling, in both continuity and discontinuity with the present situation: beyond time and history, beyond the transient reality of this world, and beyond the things of this world, of which a hidden dimension will one day be revealed - beyond man himself, whose true destiny is not restricted to his temporal aspect but will be revealed in the future life. Evangelization therefore also includes the preaching of hope in the promises made by God in the new Covenant in Jesus Christ; the preaching of God's love for us and of our love for God; the preaching of brotherly love for all men - the capacity of giving and forgiving, of self-denial, of helping one's brother and sister - which, springing from the love of God, is the kernel of the Gospel; the preaching of the mystery of evil and of the active search for good. The preaching likewise - and this is always urgent - of the search for God Himself through prayer which is principally that of adoration and thanksgiving, but also through communion with the visible sign of the encounter with God which is the Church of Jesus Christ; and this communion in its turn is expressed by the application of those other signs of Christ living and acting in the Church which are the sacraments. To live the sacraments in this way, bringing their celebration to a true fullness, is not, as some would claim, to impede or to accept a distortion of evangelization: it is rather to complete it. For in its totality, evangelization - over and above the preaching of a message - consists in the implantation of the Church, which does not exist without the driving force which is the sacramental life culminating in the Eucharist.

29. But evangelization would not be complete if it did not take account of the unceasing interplay of the Gospel and of man's concrete life, both personal and social. This is why evangelization involves an explicit message, adapted to the different situations constantly being realized, about the rights and duties of every human being, about family life without which personal growth and development is hardly possible, about life in society, about international life, peace, justice and development- a message especially energetic today about liberation.

41. Without repeating everything that we have already mentioned, it is appropriate first of all to emphasize the following point: for the Church, the first means of evangelization is the witness of an authentically Christian life, given over to God in a communion that nothing should destroy and at the same time given to one's neighbor with limitless zeal. As we said recently to a group of lay people, **"Modern man listens more willingly to witnesses than to teachers, and if he does listen to teachers, it is because they are witnesses."** St. Peter expressed this well when he held up the example of a reverent and chaste life that wins over even without a word those who refuse to obey the word. It is therefore primarily by her conduct and by her life that the Church will evangelize the world, in other words, by her living witness of fidelity to the Lord Jesus- the witness of poverty and detachment, of freedom in the

face of the powers of this world, in short, the witness of sanctity.

42. Secondly, it is not superfluous to emphasize the importance and necessity of preaching. "And how are they to believe in him of whom they have never heard? And how are they to hear without a preacher?... So faith comes from what is heard and what is heard comes by the preaching of Christ." This law once laid down by the Apostle Paul maintains its full force today.

Preaching, the verbal proclamation of a message, is indeed always indispensable. We are well aware that modern man is sated by talk; he is obviously often tired of listening and, what is worse, impervious to words. We are also aware that many psychologists and sociologists express the view that modern man has passed beyond the civilization of the word, which is now ineffective and useless, and that today he lives in the civilization of the image. These facts should certainly impel us to employ, for the purpose of transmitting the Gospel message, the modern means which this civilization has produced. Very positive efforts have in fact already been made in this sphere. We cannot but praise them and encourage their further development. The fatigue produced these days by so much empty talk and the relevance of many other forms of communication must not however diminish the permanent power of the word, or cause a loss of confidence in it. The word remains ever relevant, especially when it is the bearer of the power of God. This is why St. Paul's axiom, "Faith comes from what is heard," also retains its relevance: it is the Word that is heard which leads to belief.

43. This evangelizing preaching takes on many forms, and zeal will inspire the reshaping of them almost indefinitely. In fact there are innumerable events in life and human situations which offer the opportunity for a discreet but incisive statement of what the Lord has to say in this or that particular circumstance. It suffices to have true spiritual sensitivity for reading God's message in events. But at a time when the liturgy renewed by the Council has given greatly increased value to the Liturgy of the Word, it would be a mistake not to see in the homily an important and very adaptable instrument of evangelization. Of course it is necessary to know and put to good use the exigencies and the possibilities of the homily, so that it can acquire all its pastoral effectiveness. But above all it is necessary to be convinced of this and to devote oneself to it with love. This preaching, inserted in a unique way into the Eucharistic celebration, from which it receives special force and vigor, certainly has a particular role in evangelization, to the extent that it expresses the profound faith of the sacred minister and is impregnated with love. The faithful assembled as a Paschal Church, celebrating the feast of the Lord present in their midst, expect much from this preaching, and will greatly benefit from it provided that it is simple, clear, direct, well-adapted, profoundly dependent on Gospel teaching and faithful to the magisterium, animated by a balanced apostolic ardor coming from its own characteristic nature, full of hope, fostering belief, and productive of peace and unity. Many parochial or other communities live and are held together thanks to the Sunday homily, when it possesses these qualities.

Let us add that, thanks to the same liturgical renewal, the Eucharistic celebration is not the only appropriate moment for the homily. The homily has a place and must not be neglected in the celebration of all the sacraments, at paraliturgies, and in assemblies of the faithful. It will always be a privileged occasion for communicating the Word of the Lord.

44. A means of evangelization that must not be neglected is that of catechetical instruction. The intelligence, especially that of children and young people, needs to learn through systematic religious instruction the fundamental teachings, the living content of the truth which God has wished to convey to us and which the Church has sought to express in an ever richer fashion during the course of her long history. No one will deny that this instruction must be given to form patterns of Christian living and not to remain only notional. Truly the effort for evangelization will profit greatly- at the level of catechetical instruction given at church, in the schools, where this is possible, and in every case in Christian homes- if those giving catechetical instruction have suitable texts, updated with wisdom and competence, under the authority of the bishops. The methods must be adapted to the age, culture and aptitude of the persons concerned, they must seek always to fix in the memory, intelligence and heart the essential truths that must impregnate all of life. It is necessary above all to prepare good instructors- parochial catechists, teachers, parents- who are desirous of perfecting themselves in this superior art, which is indispensable and requires religious instruction. Moreover, without neglecting in any way the training of children, one sees that present conditions render ever more urgent catechetical instruction, under the form of the catechumenate, for innumerable young people and adults who, touched by grace, discover little by little the face of Christ and feel the need of giving themselves to Him.

45. Our century is characterized by the mass media or means of social communication, and the first proclamation, catechesis or the further deepening of faith cannot do without these means, as we have already emphasized.

When they are put at the service of the Gospel, they are capable of increasing almost indefinitely the area in which the Word of God is heard; they enable the Good News to reach millions of people. The Church would feel guilty before the Lord if she did not utilize these powerful means that human skill is daily rendering more perfect. It is through them that she proclaims "from the housetops" the message of which she is the depositary. In them she finds a modern and effective version of the pulpit. Thanks to them she succeeds in speaking to the multitudes.

Nevertheless the use of the means of social communication for evangelization presents a challenge: through them the evangelical message should reach vast numbers of people, but with the capacity of piercing the conscience of each individual,

Chapter 8: Church Documents on Mission Life

of implanting itself in his heart as though he were the only person being addressed, with all his most individual and personal qualities, and evoke an entirely personal adherence and commitment.

46. *For this reason, side by side with the collective proclamation of the Gospel, the other form of transmission, the person-to-person one, remains valid and important. The Lord often used it (for example, with Nicodemus, Zacchaeus, the Samaritan woman, Simon the Pharisee), and so did the apostles. In the long run, is there any other way of handing on the Gospel than by transmitting to another person one's personal experience of faith? It must not happen that the pressing need to proclaim the Good News to the multitudes should cause us to forget this form of proclamation whereby an individual's personal conscience is reached and touched by an entirely unique word that he receives from someone else. We can never sufficiently praise those priests who through the sacrament of Penance or through pastoral dialogue show their readiness to guide people in the ways of the Gospel, to support them in their efforts, to raise them up if they have fallen, and always to assist them with discernment and availability.*

47. *Yet, one can never sufficiently stress the fact that evangelization does not consist only of the preaching and teaching of a doctrine. For evangelization must touch life: the natural life to which it gives a new meaning, thanks to the evangelical perspectives that it reveals; and the supernatural life, which is*

not the negation but the purification and elevation of the natural life.

This supernatural life finds its living expression in the seven sacraments and in the admirable radiation of grace and holiness which they possess.

Evangelization thus exercises its full capacity when it achieves the most intimate relationship, or better still, a permanent and unbroken intercommunication, between the Word and the sacraments. In a certain sense it is a mistake to make a contrast between evangelization and sacramentalization, as is sometimes done. It is indeed true that a certain way of administering the sacraments, without the solid support of catechesis regarding these same sacraments and a global catechesis, could end up by depriving them of their effectiveness to a great extent. The role of evangelization is precisely to educate people in the faith in such a way as to lead each individual Christian to live the sacraments as true sacraments of faith- and not to receive them passively or reluctantly.

51. To reveal Jesus Christ and His Gospel to those who do not know them has been, ever since the morning of Pentecost, the fundamental program which the Church has taken on as received from her Founder. The whole of the New Testament, and in a special way the Acts of the Apostles, bears witness to a privileged and in a sense exemplary moment of this missionary effort which will subsequently leave its mark on the whole history of the Church.

She carries out this first proclamation of Jesus Christ by a complex and diversified activity which is sometimes termed "pre-evangelization" but which is already evangelization in a true sense, although at its initial and still incomplete stage. An almost indefinite range of means can be used for this purpose: explicit preaching, of course, but also art, the scientific approach, philosophical research and legitimate recourse to the sentiments of the human heart.

52. This first proclamation is addressed especially to those who have never heard the Good News of Jesus, or to children. But, as a result of the frequent situations of dechristianization in our day, it also proves equally necessary for innumerable people who have been baptized but who live quite outside Christian life, for simple people who have a certain faith but an imperfect knowledge of the foundations of that faith, for intellectuals who feel the need to know Jesus Christ in a light different from the instruction they received as children, and for many others.

Pope Paul VI then goes on to answer the concrete question: But who then has the mission of evangelizing?

59. If people proclaim in the world the Gospel of salvation, they do so by the command of, in the name of and with the grace of Christ the Savior. "They will never have a preacher unless one is sent," wrote he who was without doubt one of the greatest evangelizers. No one can do it without having been sent.

But who then has the mission of evangelizing?

The Second Vatican Council gave a clear reply to this question: it is upon the Church that "there rests, by divine mandate, the duty of going out into the whole world and preaching the gospel to every creature." And in another text: "...the whole Church is missionary, and the work of evangelization is a basic duty of the People of God."

We have already mentioned this intimate connection between the Church and evangelization. While the Church is proclaiming the kingdom of God and building it up, she is establishing herself in the midst of the world as the sign and instrument of this kingdom which is and which is to come. The Council repeats the following expression of St. Augustine on the missionary activity of the Twelve: "They preached the word of truth and brought forth Churches."

60. The observation that the Church has been sent out and given a mandate to evangelize the world should awaken in us two convictions.

The first is this: evangelization is for no one an individual and isolated act; it is one that is deeply ecclesial. When the most obscure preacher, catechist or pastor in the most distant land preaches the Gospel, gathers his little community together or administers a sacrament, even alone, he is carrying out an ecclesial act, and his action is certainly attached to the evangelizing activity of the whole Church by institutional relationships, but also by profound invisible links in the order of grace. This presupposes that he acts not in virtue of a mission which he attributes to himself or by a personal inspiration, but in union with the mission of the Church and in her name.

From this flows the second conviction: if each individual evangelizes in the name of the Church, who herself does so by virtue of a mandate from the Lord, no evangelizer is the absolute master of his evangelizing action, with a discretionary power to carry it out in accordance with individualistic criteria and perspectives; he acts in communion with the Church and her pastors.

We have remarked that the Church is entirely and completely evangelizing. This means that, in the whole world and in each part of the world where she is present, the Church feels responsible for the task of spreading the Gospel.

...76. Let us now consider the very persons of the evangelizers.

It is often said nowadays that the present century thirsts for authenticity. Especially in regard to young people it is said that they have a horror of the artificial or false and that they are searching above all for truth and honesty.

These "signs of the times" should find us vigilant. Either tacitly or aloud- but always forcefully- we are being asked: **Do you really believe what you are proclaiming? Do you live what you believe? Do you really preach what you live? The witness of life has become more than ever an essential condition for real effectiveness in preaching.** *Precisely because of this we are, to a certain extent, responsible for the progress of the Gospel that we proclaim.*

Lastly, Pope Paul VI details the crucial and central role of the Holy Spirit in all evangelization and missionary work:

> 75. *Evangelization will never be possible without the action of the Holy Spirit. The Spirit descends on Jesus of Nazareth at the moment of His baptism when the voice of the Father- "This is my beloved Son with whom I am well pleased"- manifests in an external way the election of Jesus and His mission. Jesus is "led by the Spirit" to experience in the desert the decisive combat and the supreme test before beginning this mission. It is "in the power of the Spirit" that He returns to Galilee and begins His preaching at Nazareth, applying to Himself the passage of Isaiah: "The Spirit of the Lord is upon me." And He proclaims: "Today this Scripture has been fulfilled." To the disciples whom He was about to send forth He says, breathing on them, "Receive the Holy Spirit."*
>
> *In fact, it is only after the coming of the Holy Spirit on the day of Pentecost that the apostles depart to all the ends of the earth in order to begin the great work of the Church's evangelization. Peter explains this event as the fulfillment of the prophecy of Joel: "I will pour out my spirit." Peter is filled with the Holy Spirit so that he can speak to the people about Jesus, the Son of God. Paul too is filled with the Holy Spirit before dedicating himself to his apostolic ministry, as is Stephen when he is chosen for the ministry of service and later on for the witness of blood. The Spirit, who causes Peter, Paul and*

the Twelve to speak, and who inspires the words that they are to utter, also comes down "on those who heard the word."

It is in the "consolation of the Holy Spirit" that the Church increases. The Holy Spirit is the soul of the Church. It is He who explains to the faithful the deep meaning of the teaching of Jesus and of His mystery. It is the Holy Spirit who, today just as at the beginning of the Church, acts in every evangelizer who allows himself to be possessed and led by Him. The Holy Spirit places on his lips the words which he could not find by himself, and at the same time the Holy Spirit predisposes the soul of the hearer to be open and receptive to the Good News and to the kingdom being proclaimed.

Techniques of evangelization are good, but even the most advanced ones could not replace the gentle action of the Spirit. The most perfect preparation of the evangelizer has no effect without the Holy Spirit. Without the Holy Spirit the most convincing dialectic has no power over the heart of man. Without Him the most highly developed schemas resting on a sociological or psychological basis are quickly seen to be quite valueless.

We live in the Church at a privileged moment of the Spirit. Everywhere people are trying to know Him better, as the Scripture reveals Him. They are happy to place themselves under His inspiration. They are gathering about Him; they want to let themselves be led by Him. Now if the Spirit of God has a preeminent place in the whole life of the Church, it is in her evangelizing mission that He is most active. It is not by chance that the great inauguration of evangelization took place on the morning of Pentecost, under the inspiration of the Spirit.

It must be said that the Holy Spirit is the principal agent of evangelization: it is He who impels each individual to proclaim the Gospel, and it is He who in the depths of consciences causes the word of salvation to be accepted and understood. But it can equally be said that He is the goal of evangelization: He alone stirs up the new creation, the new humanity of which evangelization is to be the result, with that unity in variety which evangelization wishes to achieve within the Christian community. Through the Holy Spirit the Gospel penetrates to the heart of the world, for it is He who causes people to discern the signs of the times- signs willed by God- which evangelization reveals and puts to use within history.

The Bishops' Synod of 1974, which insisted strongly on the place of the Holy Spirit in evangelization, also expressed the desire that pastors and theologians- and we would also say the faithful marked by the seal of the Spirit by Baptism- should study more thoroughly the nature and manner of the Holy Spirit's action in evangelization today. This is our desire too, and we exhort all evangelizers, whoever they may be, to pray without ceasing to the Holy Spirit with faith and fervor and to let themselves prudently be guided by Him as the decisive inspirer of their plans, their initiatives and their evangelizing activity.

Saint Pope John Paul II's 1990 Encyclical *'Redemptoris Missio'* ('The Mission of the Redeemer') has such a magnitude of wisdom which would be very helpful in forming our future missionary disciples, that I have decided to dedicate the following entire chapter to this specific work of this great saint.

Chapter 9

John Paul II's *Redemptoris Missio: The Mission of the Redeemer* (on the Permanent Validity of the Church's Missionary Mandate)

Saint Pope John Paul II opens his Encyclical 'The Mission of the Redeemer' ('*Redemptoris Missio*') with these words:

> 1. The mission of Christ the Redeemer, which is entrusted to the Church, is still very far from completion. As the second millennium after Christ's coming draws to an end, an overall view of the human race shows that this mission is still only beginning and that we must commit ourselves wholeheartedly to its service. It is the Spirit who impels us to proclaim the great works of God: "For if I preach the Gospel, that gives me no ground for boasting. For necessity is laid upon me. Woe to me if I do not preach the Gospel!" (1 Cor 9: 16)
>
> In the name of the whole Church, I sense an urgent duty to repeat this cry of St. Paul. From the beginning of my Pontificate I have chosen to travel to the ends of the earth in order to show this missionary concern. My direct contact with peoples who do not know Christ has convinced me even more of the urgency of missionary activity, a subject to which I am devoting the present encyclical.

He continues explaining the dire need in the modern world for missionaries to spread the Gospel and he exhorts both the individual, as well as the Church collectively, to 'open the doors' of their hearts to Christ and this work He wants to live through each and every Christian:

> *(2)... I wish to invite the Church to renew her missionary commitment. The present document has as its goal an interior renewal of faith and Christian life. For missionary activity renews the Church, revitalizes faith and Christian identity, and offers fresh enthusiasm and new incentive. Faith is strengthened when it is given to others! It is in commitment to the Church's universal mission that the new evangelization of Christian peoples will find inspiration and support.*
>
> *But what moves me even more strongly to proclaim the urgency of missionary evangelization is the fact that it is the primary service which the Church can render to every individual and to all humanity in the modern world, a world which has experienced marvelous achievements but which seems to have lost its sense of ultimate realities and of existence itself. "Christ the Redeemer," I wrote in my first encyclical, "fully reveals man to himself.... The person who wishes to understand himself thoroughly...must...draw near to Christ.... [The] Redemption that took place through the cross has definitively restored to man his dignity and given back meaning to his life in the world."*

3. Peoples everywhere, open the doors to Christ! His Gospel in no way detracts from man's freedom, from the respect that is owed to every culture and to whatever is good in each religion. By accepting Christ, you open yourselves to the definitive Word of God, to the One in whom God has made himself fully known and has shown us the path to himself.

The number of those who do not know Christ and do not belong to the Church is constantly on the increase. Indeed, since the end of the Council it has almost doubled. When we consider this immense portion of humanity which is loved by the Father and for whom he sent his Son, the urgency of the Church's mission is obvious.

On the other hand, our own times offer the Church new opportunities in this field: we have witnessed the collapse of oppressive ideologies and political systems; the opening of frontiers and the formation of a more united world due to an increase in communications; the affirmation among peoples of the gospel values which Jesus made incarnate in his own life (peace, justice, brotherhood, concern for the needy); and a kind of soulless economic and technical development which only stimulates the search for the truth about God, about man and about the meaning of life itself.

God is opening before the Church the horizons of a humanity more fully prepared for the sowing of the Gospel. I sense that the moment has come to commit all of the Church's energies to a new evangelization and to the mission ad gentes.

No believer in Christ, no institution of the Church can avoid this supreme duty: to proclaim Christ to all peoples.

In the First Chapter of this Encyclical, the Holy Father discusses how Jesus Christ is the only Savior. He explains how in many cases in the modern world the Church's missionary mandate has been replaced by interreligious dialogue -and this should not be. While respecting all religions and leaving people in freedom to choose truth, the truth remains that Jesus Christ was sent by the Father into the world to redeem all of mankind and as He Himself said, *'No one can come to the Father except through me.'* John 14:6 The Acts of the Apostles echoes, *"And there is salvation in no one else, for there is no other name under heaven given among men by which we must be saved.' (Acts 4:12)* Paul's first letter to Timothy also adds, *"for there is one God, and there is one mediator between God and men, the man Christ Jesus, who gave himself as a ransom for all, the testimony to which was borne at the proper time." (1 Timothy 2:5-7)* The missionary mandate of Christ is not obsolete, but in contrast as the number of unbelievers grows throughout the world the Church as a deeper obligation to offer the world the only answer that will lead to eternal life -faith in Jesus Christ and acceptance of the Salvation He won for us on the Cross, offered to us through the Catholic church.

Offering the Truth of Jesus Christ as He revealed Himself through the Church to souls is actually offering them freedom. Jesus said, *'The Truth will set you Free.'* (John 8:32) And Pope John Paul II explains:

7. The urgency of missionary activity derives from the radical newness of life brought by Christ and lived by his followers. This new life is a gift from God, and people are asked to accept and develop it, if they wish to realize the fullness of their vocation in conformity to Christ. The whole New Testament is a hymn to the new life of those who believe in Christ and live in his Church. Salvation in Christ, as witnessed to and proclaimed by the Church, is God's self-communication: "It is love which not only creates the good, but also grants participation in the very life of God: Father, Son and Holy Spirit. For he who loves desires to give himself."

God offers mankind this newness of life. "Can one reject Christ and everything that he has brought about in the history of mankind? Of course, one can. Man is free. He can say 'no' to God. He can say 'no' to Christ. But the fundamental question remains: Is it legitimate to do this? And what would make it legitimate?"

8. In the modern world there is a tendency to reduce man to his horizontal dimension alone. But without an openness to the Absolute, what does man become? The answer to this question is found in the experience of every individual, but it is also written in the history of humanity with the bloodshed in the name of ideologies or by political regimes which have sought to build a "new humanity" without God.

Moreover, the Second Vatican Council replies to those concerned with safeguarding freedom of conscience: "The human person has a right to religious freedom.... All should have such immunity from coercion by individuals, or by groups, or by any human power, that no one should be forced to act against his conscience in religious matters, nor prevented from acting according to his conscience, whether in private or in public, whether alone or in association with others, within due limits."

Proclaiming Christ and bearing witness to him, when done in a way that respects consciences, does not violate freedom. Faith demands a free adherence on the part of man, but at the same time faith must also be offered to him, because the "multitudes have the right to know the riches of the mystery of Christ-riches in which we believe that the whole of humanity can find, in unsuspected fullness, everything that it is gropingly searching for concerning God, man and his destiny, life and death, and truth.... This is why the Church keeps her missionary spirit alive, and even wishes to intensify it in the moment of history in which we are living." But it must also be stated, again with the Council, that "in accordance with their dignity as persons, equipped with reason and free will and endowed with personal responsibility, all are impelled by their own nature and are bound by a moral obligation to seek truth, above all religious truth. They are further bound to hold to the truth once it is known, and to regulate their whole lives by its demands."

Pope John Paul II goes on to say that there are two truths about this missionary activity that must be relayed to the world -first, that all people can be saved (salvation can be had by all), and yet this salvation comes alone through the Catholic Church. He explains beautifully:

> *9. The first beneficiary of salvation is the Church. Christ won the Church for himself at the price of his own blood and made the Church his co-worker in the salvation of the world. Indeed, Christ dwells within the Church. She is his Bride. It is he who causes her to grow. He carries out his mission through her.*
>
> *The Council makes frequent reference to the Church's role in the salvation of mankind. While acknowledging that God loves all people and grants them the possibility of being saved (cf. 1 Tm 2:4), the Church believes that God has established Christ as the one mediator and that she herself has been established as the universal sacrament of salvation. 16 "To this catholic unity of the people of God, therefore,...all are called, and they belong to it or are ordered to it in various ways, whether they be Catholic faithful or others who believe in Christ or finally all people everywhere who by the grace of God are called to salvation." It is necessary to keep these two truths together, namely, the real possibility of salvation in Christ for all mankind and the necessity of the Church for salvation. Both these truths help us to understand the one mystery of salvation, so that we can come to know God's mercy and our own responsibility. Salvation, which always remains a gift of the Holy Spirit, requires man's cooperation, both to save himself*

and to save others. This is God's will, and this is why he established the Church and made her a part of his plan of salvation. Referring to "this messianic people," the Council says; "It has been set up by Christ as a communion of life, love and truth; by him too it is taken up as the instrument of salvation for all, and sent on a mission to the whole world as the light of the world and the salt of the earth."

Salvation in Christ Is Offered to All

10. The universality of salvation means that it is granted not only to those who explicitly believe in Christ and have entered the Church. Since salvation is offered to all, it must be made concretely available to all. But it is clear that today, as in the past, many people do not have an opportunity to come to know or accept the gospel revelation or to enter the Church. The social and cultural conditions in which they live do not permit this, and frequently they have been brought up in other religious traditions. For such people salvation in Christ is accessible by virtue of a grace which, while having a mysterious relationship to the Church, does not make them formally part of the Church but enlightens them in a way which is accommodated to their spiritual and material situation. This grace comes from Christ; it is the result of his Sacrifice and is communicated by the Holy Spirit. It enables each person to attain salvation through his or her free cooperation.

For this reason, the Council, after affirming the centrality of the Paschal Mystery, went on to declare that "this applies not only to Christians but to all people of good will in whose hearts grace is secretly at work. Since Christ died for everyone, and since the ultimate calling of each of us comes from God and is therefore a universal one, we are obliged to hold that the Holy Spirit offers everyone the possibility of sharing in this Paschal Mystery in a manner known to God."

"We cannot but speak" (Acts 4:20)

11. What then should be said of the objections already mentioned regarding the mission ad gentes? While respecting the beliefs and sensitivities of all, we must first clearly affirm our faith in Christ, the one Savior of mankind, a faith we have received as a gift from on high, not as a result of any merit of our own. We say with Paul, "I am not ashamed of the Gospel: it is the power of God for salvation to everyone who has faith" (Rom 1:16). Christian martyrs of all times - including our own - have given and continue to give their lives in order to bear witness to this faith, in the conviction that every human being needs Jesus Christ, who has conquered sin and death and reconciled mankind to God.

Confirming his words by miracles and by his resurrection from the dead, Christ proclaimed himself to be the Son of God dwelling in intimate union with the Father, and was recognized as such by his disciples. The Church offers mankind the Gospel, that prophetic message which responds to the needs and aspirations of the human heart and always remains

"Good News." The Church cannot fail to proclaim that Jesus came to reveal the face of God and to merit salvation for all humanity by his cross and resurrection.

To the question, "why mission?" we reply with the Church's faith and experience that true liberation consists in opening oneself to the love of Christ. In him, and only in him, are we set free from all alienation and doubt, from slavery to the power of sin and death. Christ is truly "our peace" (Eph 2:14); "the love of Christ impels us" (2 Cor 5:14), giving meaning and joy to our life. Mission is an issue of faith, an accurate indicator of our faith in Christ and his love for us.

The temptation today is to reduce Christianity to merely human wisdom, a pseudo-science of well-being. In our heavily secularized world a "gradual secularization of salvation" has taken place, so that people strive for the good of man, but man who is truncated, reduced to his merely horizontal dimension. We know, however, that Jesus came to bring integral salvation, one which embraces the whole person and all mankind, and opens up the wondrous prospect of divine filiation. Why mission? Because to us, as to St. Paul, "this grace was given, to preach to the Gentiles the unsearchable riches of Christ" (Eph 3:8). Newness of life in him is the "Good News" for men and women of every age: all are called to it and destined for it. Indeed, all people are searching for it, albeit at times in a confused way, and have a right to know the value of this gift and to approach it freely. The Church, and every individual Christian within her, may not keep hidden or monopolize this

> *newness and richness which has been received from God's bounty in order to be communicated to all mankind.*
>
> *This is why the Church's mission derives not only from the Lord's mandate but also from the profound demands of God's life within us. Those who are incorporated in the Catholic Church ought to sense their privilege and for that very reason their greater obligation of bearing witness to the faith and to the Christian life as a service to their brothers and sisters and as a fitting response to God. They should be ever mindful that "they owe their distinguished status not to their own merits but to Christ's special grace; and if they fail to respond to this grace in thought, word and deed, not only will they not be saved, they will be judged more severely."*

In Chapter 2 Pope John Paul II continues showing how Jesus Christ is the Father's answer of Mercy to a fallen world -prepared for in the Old Testament and bringing this prophesized Kingdom of God to an incarnated fulfillment in Himself in the New. He begins this explanation saying:

> *12. "It is 'God, who is rich in mercy' whom Jesus Christ has revealed to us as Father: it is his very Son who, in himself, has manifested him and made him known to us." I wrote this at the beginning of my Encyclical Dives in Misericordia, to show that Christ is the revelation and incarnation of the Father's mercy. Salvation consists in believing and accepting the mystery of the Father and of his love, made manifest and freely*

given in Jesus through the Spirit. In this way the kingdom of God comes to be fulfilled: the kingdom prepared for in the Old Testament, brought about by Christ and in Christ, and proclaimed to all peoples by the Church, which works and prays for its perfect and definitive realization.

Jesus did not come to bring this Kingdom of Heaven simply to the elected few, but to all people of all times and cultures and ages -giving special preference to those who were regularly dismissed and rejected by society, restoring human dignity to all:

> 14. *Jesus gradually reveals the characteristics and demands of the kingdom through his words, his actions and his own person.*
>
> *The kingdom of God is meant for all mankind, and all people are called to become members of it. To emphasize this fact, Jesus drew especially near to those on the margins of society, and showed them special favor in announcing the Good News. At the beginning of his ministry he proclaimed that he was "anointed...to preach good news to the poor" (Lk 4:18). To all who are victims of rejection and contempt Jesus declares: "Blessed are you poor" (Lk 6:20). What is more, he enables such individuals to experience liberation even now, by being close to them, going to eat in their homes (cf. Lk 5:30; 15:2), treating them as equals and friends (cf. Lk 7:34), and making them feel loved by God, thus revealing his tender care for the needy and for sinners (cf. Lk 15:1-32).*

The liberation and salvation brought by the kingdom of God come to the human person both in his physical and spiritual dimensions. Two gestures are characteristic of Jesus' mission: healing and forgiving. Jesus' many healings clearly show his great compassion in the face of human distress, but they also signify that in the kingdom there will no longer be sickness or suffering, and that his mission, from the very beginning, is meant to free people from these evils. In Jesus' eyes, healings are also a sign of spiritual salvation, namely liberation from sin. By performing acts of healing, he invites people to faith, conversion and the desire for forgiveness (cf. Lk 5:24). Once there is faith, healing is an encouragement to go further: it leads to salvation (cf. Lk 18:42-43). The acts of liberation from demonic possession-the supreme evil and symbol of sin and rebellion against God-are signs that indeed "the kingdom of God has come upon you" (Mt 12:28).

15. The kingdom aims at transforming human relationships; it grows gradually as people slowly learn to love, forgive and serve one another. Jesus sums up the whole Law, focusing it on the commandment of love (cf. Mt 22:34-40; Lk 10:25-28). Before leaving his disciples, he gives them a "new commandment": "Love one another; even as I have loved you" (Jn 13:34; cf. 15:12). Jesus' love for the world finds its highest expression in the gift of his life for mankind (cf. Jn 15:13), which manifests the love which the Father has for the world (cf. Jn 3:16). The kingdom's nature, therefore, is one of communion among all human beings-with one another and with God.

> The kingdom is the concern of everyone: individuals, society, and the world. Working for the kingdom means acknowledging and promoting God's activity, which is present in human history and transforms it. Building the kingdom means working for liberation from evil in all its forms. In a word, the kingdom of God is the manifestation and the realization of God's plan of salvation in all its fullness.

The Church is at the service of the Kingdom of God -partaking in Christ's mission first through the gift of preaching, then by establishing communities, spreading 'gospel values' throughout the entire world and finally by her intercession for the salvation of mankind:

> This is seen especially in her preaching, which is a call to conversion. Preaching constitutes the Church's first and fundamental way of serving the coming of the kingdom in individuals and in human society. Eschatological salvation begins even now in newness of life in Christ: "To all who believed in him, who believed in his name, he gave power to become children of God" (Jn 1:12).
>
> The Church, then, serves the kingdom by establishing communities and founding new particular churches, and by guiding them to mature faith and charity in openness toward others, in service to individuals and society, and in understanding and esteem for human institutions.

The Church serves the kingdom by spreading throughout the world the "gospel values" which are an expression of the kingdom and which help people to accept God's plan. It is true that the inchoate reality of the kingdom can also be found beyond the confines of the Church among peoples everywhere, to the extent that they live "gospel values" and are open to the working of the Spirit who breathes when and where he wills (cf. Jn 3:8). But it must immediately be added that this temporal dimension of the kingdom remains incomplete unless it is related to the kingdom of Christ present in the Church and straining towards eschatological fullness.

The many dimensions of the kingdom of God do not weaken the foundations and purposes of missionary activity, but rather strengthen and extend them. The Church is the sacrament of salvation for all mankind, and her activity is not limited only to those who accept her message. She is a dynamic force in mankind's journey toward the eschatological kingdom, and is the sign and promoter of gospel values. The Church contributes to mankind's pilgrimage of conversion to God's plan through her witness and through such activities as dialogue, human promotion, commitment to justice and peace, education and the care of the sick, and aid to the poor and to children. In carrying on these activities, however, she never loses sight of the priority of the transcendent and spiritual realities which are premises of eschatological salvation.

Finally, the Church serves the kingdom by her intercession, since the kingdom by its very nature is God's gift and work, as we are reminded by the gospel parables and by the prayer which Jesus taught us. We must ask for the kingdom, welcome it and make it grow within us; but we must also work together so that it will be welcomed and will grow among all people, until the time when Christ "delivers the kingdom to God the Father" and "God will be everything to everyone" (cf. 1 Cor 15:24, 28).

Like Pope Paul VI, Saint Pope John Paul II in Chapter III strongly emphasizes the fact that it is the Holy Spirit Who is the Principal Agent of Mission, the Director of all Missions and the Formator of the entire Church in their missionary vocations:

CHAPTER III - THE HOLY SPIRIT: THE PRINCIPAL AGENT OF MISSION

21. "At the climax of Jesus' messianic mission, the Holy Spirit becomes present in the Paschal Mystery in all of his divine subjectivity: as the one who is now to continue the salvific work rooted in the sacrifice of the cross. Of course, Jesus entrusts this work to human beings: to the apostles, to the Church. Nevertheless, in and through them the Holy Spirit remains the transcendent and principal agent for the accomplishment of this work in the human spirit and in the history of the world."

The Holy Spirit is indeed the principal agent of the whole of the Church's mission. His action is preeminent in the mission ad gentes, as can clearly be seen in the early Church: in the conversion of Cornelius (cf. Acts 10), in the decisions made about emerging problems (cf. Acts 15) and in the choice of regions and peoples to be evangelized (cf. Acts 16:6ff). The Spirit worked through the apostles, but at the same time he was also at work in those who heard them: "Through his action the Good News takes shape in human minds and hearts and extends through history. In all of this it is the Holy Spirit who gives life."

Sent Forth "to the end of the earth" (Acts 1:8)

22. All the Evangelists, when they describe the risen Christ's meeting with his apostles, conclude with the "missionary mandate": "All authority in heaven and on earth has been given to me. Go therefore and make disciples of all nations,...and lo, I am with you always, to the close of the age" (Mt 28:18-20; cf. Mk 16:15-18; Lk 24:46-49; Jn 20:21-23).

This is a sending forth in the Spirit, as is clearly apparent in the Gospel of John: Christ sends his own into the world, just as the Father has sent him, and to this end he gives them the Spirit. Luke, for his part, closely links the witness the apostles are to give to Christ with the working of the Spirit, who will enable them to fulfill the mandate they have received.

23. The different versions of the "missionary mandate" contain common elements as well as characteristics proper to each. Two elements, however, are found in all the versions. First, there is the universal dimension of the task entrusted to the apostles, who are sent to "all nations" (Mt 28:19); "into all the world and...to the whole creation" (Mk 16:15); to "all nations" (Lk 24:47); "to the end of the earth" (Acts 1:8). Secondly, there is the assurance given to the apostles by the Lord that they will not be alone in the task, but will receive the strength and the means necessary to carry out their mission. The reference here is to the presence and power of the spirit and the help of Jesus himself: "And they went forth and preached everywhere, while the Lord worked with them" (Mk 16:20).

As for the different emphases found in each version, Mark presents mission as proclamation or kerygma: "Preach the Gospel" (Mk 16:15). His aim is to lead his readers to repeat Peter's profession of faith: "You are the Christ" (Mk 8:29), and to say with the Roman centurion who stood before the body of Jesus on the cross: "Truly this man was the Son of God!" (Mk 15:39) In Matthew, the missionary emphasis is placed on the foundation of the Church and on her teaching (cf. Mt 28:19-20; 16:18). According to him, the mandate shows that the proclamation of the Gospel must be completed by a specific ecclesial and sacramental catechesis. In Luke, mission is presented as witness (cf. Lk 24:48; Acts 1:8), centered especially on the resurrection (cf. Acts 1:22). The missionary is invited to believe in the transforming power of the Gospel and to proclaim what Luke presents so well, that is, conversion to God's love and mercy, the experience of a complete liberation which goes to the root of all evil, namely sin.

John is the only Evangelist to speak explicitly of a "mandate," a word equivalent to "mission." He directly links the *mission which Jesus entrusts to his disciples with the mission which he himself has received from the Father: "As the Father has sent me, even so I send you" (Jn 20:21). Addressing the Father, Jesus says: "As you sent me into the world, so I have sent them into the world" (Jn 17:18). The entire missionary sense of John's Gospel is expressed in the "priestly prayer": "This is eternal life, that they know you the only true God, and Jesus Christ whom you have sent" (Jn 17:3). The ultimate purpose of mission is to enable people to share in the communion which exists between the Father and the Son. The disciples are to live in unity with one another, remaining in the Father and the Son, so that the world may know and believe (cf. Jn 17:21-23). This is a very important missionary text. It makes us understand that we are missionaries above all because of what we are as a Church whose innermost life is unity in love, even before we become missionaries in word or deed.*

The four Gospels therefore bear witness to a certain pluralism within the fundamental unity of the same mission, a pluralism which reflects different experiences and situations within the first Christian communities. It is also the result of the driving force of the Spirit himself; it encourages us to pay heed to the variety or missionary charisms and to the diversity of circumstances and peoples. Nevertheless, all the Evangelists stress that the mission of the disciples is to cooperate in the mission of Christ; "Lo, I am with you always, to the close of the age" (Mt 28:20). Mission, then, is based not on human abilities but on the power of the risen Lord.

The Spirit Directs the Church's Mission

24. The mission of the Church, like that of Jesus, is God's work or, as Luke often puts it, the work of the Spirit. After the resurrection and ascension of Jesus, the apostles have a powerful experience which completely transforms them: the experience of Pentecost. The coming of the Holy Spirit makes them witnesses and prophets (cf. Acts 1:8; 2:17-18). It fills them with a serene courage which impels them to pass on to others their experience of Jesus and the hope which motivates them. The Spirit gives them the ability to bear witness to Jesus with "boldness." When the first evangelizers go down from Jerusalem, the Spirit becomes even more of a "guide," helping them to choose both those to whom they are to go and the places to which their missionary journey is to take them. The working of the Spirit is manifested particularly in the impetus given to the mission which, in accordance with Christ's words, spreads out from Jerusalem to all of Judea and Samaria, and to the farthest ends of the earth.

The Acts of the Apostles records six summaries of the "missionary discourses" which were addressed to the Jews during the Church's infancy (cf. Acts 2:22-39; 3:12-26; 4:9-12; 5:29-32; 10:34-43; 13:16-41). These model speeches, delivered by Peter and by Paul, proclaim Jesus and invite those listening to "be converted," that is, to accept Jesus in faith and to let themselves be transformed in him by the Spirit.

Paul and Barnabas are impelled by the Spirit to go to the Gentiles (cf. Acts 13:46-48), a development not without certain tensions and problems. How are these converted Gentiles to live their faith in Jesus? Are they bound by the traditions of Judaism and the law of circumcision? At the first Council, which gathers the members of the different churches together with the apostles in Jerusalem, a decision is taken which is acknowledged as coming from the Spirit: it is not necessary for a Gentile to submit to the Jewish Law in order to become a Christian (cf. Acts 15:5-11, 28). From now on the Church opens her doors and becomes the house which all may enter, and in which all can feel at home, while keeping their own culture and traditions, provided that these are not contrary to the Gospel.

25. The missionaries continued along this path, taking into account people's hopes and expectations, their anguish and sufferings, as well as their culture, in order to proclaim to them salvation in Christ. The speeches in Lystra and Athens (cf. Acts 14:15-17; 17:22-31) are acknowledged as models for the evangelization of the Gentiles. In these speeches Paul enters into "dialogue" with the cultural and religious values of different peoples. To the Lycaonians, who practiced a cosmic religion, he speaks of religious experiences related to the cosmos. With the Greeks he discusses philosophy and quotes their own poets (cf. Acts 17:18, 26-28). The God whom Paul wishes to reveal is already present in their lives; indeed, this God has created them and mysteriously guides nations and history.

But if they are to recognize the true God, they must abandon the false gods which they themselves have made and open themselves to the One whom God has sent to remedy their ignorance and satisfy the longings of their hearts. These are speeches which offer an example of the inculturation of the Gospel.

Under the impulse of the Spirit, the Christian faith is decisively opened to the "nations." Witness to Christ spreads to the most important centers of the eastern Mediterranean and then to Rome and the far regions of the West. It is the Spirit who is the source of the drive to press on, not only geographically but also beyond the frontiers of race and religion, for a truly universal mission.

The Holy Spirit Makes the Whole Church Missionary

26. The Spirit leads the company of believers to "form a community," to be the Church. After Peter's first proclamation on the day of Pentecost and the conversions that followed, the first community takes shape (cf. Acts 2:42-47; 4:32-35).

One of the central purposes of mission is to bring people together in hearing the Gospel, in fraternal communion, in prayer and in the Eucharist. To live in "fraternal communion" (koinonia) means to be "of one heart and soul" (Acts 4:32), establishing fellowship from every point of view: human, spiritual and material. Indeed, a true Christian community is also committed to distributing earthly goods, so that no one is in *want, and all can receive such goods "as they need" (cf. Acts 2:45; 4:35). The first communities, made up of "glad and generous hearts" (Acts 2:46), were open and missionary: they enjoyed "favor with all the people" (Acts 2:47). Even before activity, mission means witness and a way of life that shines out to others.*

27. The Acts of the Apostles indicates that the mission which was directed first to Israel and then to the Gentiles develops on many levels. First and foremost, there is the group of the Twelve which as a single body, led by Peter, proclaims the Good News. Then there is the community of believers, which in its way of life and its activity bears witness to the Lord and converts the Gentiles (cf. Acts 2:46-47). Then there are the special envoys sent out to proclaim the Gospel. Thus, the Christian community at Antioch sends its members forth on mission; having fasted, prayed and celebrated the Eucharist, the community recognizes that the Spirit has chosen Paul and Barnabas to be "sent forth" (cf. Acts 13:1-4). In its origins, then, mission is seen as a community commitment, a responsibility of the local church, which needs "missionaries" in order to push forward toward new frontiers. Side by side with those who had been sent forth, there were also others, who bore spontaneous witness to the newness which had transformed their lives, and who subsequently provided a link between the emerging communities and the Apostolic Church.

Reading the Acts of the Apostles helps us to realize that at the beginning of the Church the mission ad gentes, while it had missionaries dedicated "for life" by a special vocation, was in fact considered the normal outcome of Christian living, to which every believer was committed through the witness of personal conduct and through explicit proclamation whenever possible.

The Spirit Is Present and Active in Every Time and Place

28. The Spirit manifests himself in a special way in the Church and in her members. Nevertheless, his presence and activity are universal, limited neither by space nor time. The Second Vatican Council recalls that the Spirit is at work in the heart of every person, through the "seeds of the Word," to be found in human initiatives-including religious ones-and in mankind's efforts to attain truth, goodness and God himself.

The Spirit offers the human race" the light and strength to respond to its highest calling"; through the Spirit, "mankind attains in faith to the contemplation and savoring of the mystery of God's design"; indeed, "we are obliged to hold that the Holy Spirit offers everyone the possibility of sharing in the Paschal Mystery in a manner known to God." The Church "is aware that humanity is being continually stirred by the Spirit of God and can therefore never be completely indifferent to the problems of religion" and that "people will always...want to know what meaning to give their life, their activity and their death." The Spirit, therefore, is at the very source of man's existential and religious questioning, a questioning which is *occasioned not only by contingent situations but by the very structure of his being.*

The Spirit's presence and activity affect not only the individuals but also society and history, peoples, cultures and religions. Indeed, the Spirit is at the origin of the noble ideals and undertakings which benefit humanity on its journey through history: "The Spirit of God with marvelous foresight directs the course of the ages and renews the face of the earth." The risen Christ "is now at work in human hearts through the strength of his Spirit, not only instilling a desire for the world to come but also thereby animating, purifying and reinforcing the noble aspirations which drive the human family to make its life one that is more human and to direct the whole earth to this end." Again, it is the Spirit who sows the "seeds of the Word" present in various customs and cultures, preparing them for full maturity in Christ.

29. Thus the Spirit, who "blows where he wills" (cf. Jn 3:8), who "was already at work in the world before Christ was glorified," and who "has filled the world,...holds all things together [and] knows what is said" (Wis 1:7), leads us to broaden our vision in order to ponder his activity in every time and place. I have repeatedly called this fact to mind, and it has guided me in my meetings with a wide variety of peoples. The Church's relationship with other religions is dictated by a twofold respect: "Respect for man in his quest for answers to the deepest questions of his life, and respect for the action of the Spirit in man." Excluding any mistaken interpretation, the interreligious meeting held in Assisi was meant to confirm my conviction that "every authentic prayer is prompted by the Holy Spirit, who is mysteriously present in every human heart."

This is the same Spirit who was at work in the Incarnation and in the life, death and resurrection of Jesus, and who is at work in the Church. He is therefore not an alternative to Christ, nor does he fill a sort of void which is sometimes suggested as existing between Christ and the Logos. Whatever the Spirit brings about in human hearts and in the history of peoples, in cultures and religions serves as a preparation for the Gospel and can only be understood in reference to Christ, the Word who took flesh by the power of the Spirit" so that as perfectly human he would save all human beings and sum up all things."

Moreover, the universal activity of the Spirit is not to be separated from his particular activity within the body of Christ, which is the Church. Indeed, it is always the Spirit who is at work, both when he gives life to the Church and impels her to proclaim Christ, and when he implants and develops his gifts in all individuals and peoples, guiding the Church to discover these gifts, to foster them and to receive them through dialogue. Every form of the Spirit's presence is to be welcomed with respect and gratitude, but the discernment of this presence is the responsibility of the Church, to which Christ gave his Spirit in order to guide her into all the truth (cf. Jn 16:13).

Chapter 9: John Paul II's *Redemptoris Missio*

As we continue through Pope John Paul II's encyclical, he emphasizes greatly that the first form of evangelization is witness. He teaches:

42. People today put more trust in witnesses than in teachers, in experience than in teaching, and in life and action than in theories. The witness of a Christian life is the first and irreplaceable form of mission: *Christ, whose mission we continue, is the "witness" par excellence (Rv 1:5; 3:14) and the model of all Christian witness. The Holy Spirit accompanies the Church along her way and associates her with the witness he gives to Christ (cf. Jn 15:26-27).*

The first form of witness is the very life of the missionary, of the Christian family, and of the ecclesial community, which reveal a new way of living. The missionary who, despite all his or her human limitations and defects, lives a simple life, taking Christ as the model, is a sign of God and of transcendent realities. But everyone in the Church, striving to imitate the Divine Master, can and must bear this kind of witness; in many cases it is the only possible way of being a missionary.

The evangelical witness which the world finds most appealing is that of concern for people, and of charity toward the poor, the weak and those who suffer. The complete generosity underlying this attitude and these actions stands in marked contrast to human selfishness. It raises precise questions which lead to God and to the Gospel. A commitment to peace, justice, human rights and human promotion is also a witness to the

Gospel when it is a sign of concern for persons and is directed toward integral human development.

43. Christians and Christian communities are very much a part of the life of their respective nations and can be a sign of the Gospel in their fidelity to their native land, people and national culture, while always preserving the freedom brought by Christ. Christianity is open to universal brotherhood, for all men and women are sons and daughters of the same Father and brothers and sisters in Christ.

The Church is called to bear witness to Christ by taking courageous and prophetic stands in the face of the corruption of political or economic power; by not seeking her own glory and material wealth; by using her resources to serve the poorest of the poor and by imitating Christ's own simplicity of life. The Church and her missionaries must also bear the witness of humility, above all with regard to themselves-a humility which allows them to make a personal and communal examination of conscience in order to correct in their behavior whatever is contrary to the Gospel and disfigures the face of Christ.

After stressing the importance of witness, Saint Pope John Paul II hones in on the central point that proclamation of Christ as Savior is the first and permanent priority of all mission. He says:

44. Proclamation is the permanent priority of mission. The Church cannot elude Christ's explicit mandate, nor deprive men and women of the "Good News" about their being loved and saved by God. "Evangelization will always contain-as the foundation, center and at the same time the summit of its dynamism-a clear proclamation that, in Jesus Christ...salvation is offered to all people, as a gift of God's grace and mercy." All forms of missionary activity are directed to this proclamation, which reveals and gives access to the mystery hidden for ages and made known in Christ (cf. Eph 3:3-9; Col 1:25-29), the mystery which lies at the heart of the Church's mission and life, as the hinge on which all evangelization turns.

In the complex reality of mission, initial proclamation has a central and irreplaceable role, since it introduces man "into the mystery of the love of God, who invites him to enter into a personal relationship with himself in Christ" and opens the way to conversion. Faith is born of preaching, and every ecclesial community draws its origin and life from the personal response of each believer to that preaching. Just as the whole economy of salvation has its center in Christ, so too all missionary activity is directed to the proclamation of his mystery.

The subject of proclamation is Christ who was crucified, died and is risen: through him is accomplished our full and authentic liberation from evil, sin and death; through him God bestows "new life" that is divine and eternal. This is the "Good News" which changes man and his history, and which all peoples have a right to hear. This proclamation is to be made within the context of the lives of the individuals and peoples who receive it. It is to be made with an attitude of love and esteem toward those who hear it, in language which is practical and adapted to the situation. In this proclamation the Spirit is at work and establishes a communion between the missionary and his hearers, a communion which is possible inasmuch as both enter into communion with God the Father through Christ.

45. **Proclamation, because it is made in union with the entire ecclesial community, is never a merely personal act. The missionary is present and carries out his work by virtue of a mandate he has received;** *even if he finds himself alone, he remains joined by invisible but profound bonds to the evangelizing activity of the whole Church. Sooner or later, his hearers come to recognize in him the community which sent him and which supports him.*

Proclamation is inspired by faith, which gives rise to enthusiasm and fervor in the missionary. As already mentioned, the Acts of the Apostles uses the word parrhesia to describe this attitude, a word which means to speak **frankly and with courage.** *This term is found also in St. Paul: "We had courage in our God to declare to you the Gospel of God in the face of great opposition" (1 Th 2:2); "Pray...also for me, that utterance may be given me in opening my mouth boldly to proclaim the mystery of the*

Gospel for which I am an ambassador in chains; that I may declare it boldly, as I ought to speak" (Eph 6:18-20).

In proclaiming Christ to non-Christians, the missionary is convinced that, through the working of the Spirit, there already exists in individuals and peoples an expectation, even if an unconscious one, of knowing the truth about God, about man, and about how we are to be set free from sin and death. The missionary's enthusiasm in proclaiming Christ comes from the conviction that he is responding to that expectation, and so he does not become discouraged or cease his witness even when he is called to manifest his faith in an environment that is hostile or indifferent. He knows that the Spirit of the Father is speaking through him (cf. Mt 10:17-20; Lk 12:11-12) and he can say with the apostles: "We are witnesses to these things, and so is the Holy Spirit" (Acts 5:32). He knows that he is not proclaiming a human truth, but the "word of God," which has an intrinsic and mysterious power of its own (cf. Rom 1:16).

The supreme test is the giving of one's life, to the point of accepting death in order to bear witness to one's faith in Jesus Christ. Throughout Christian history, martyrs, that is, "witnesses," have always been numerous and indispensable to the spread of the Gospel. In our own age, there are many: bishops, priests, men and women religious, lay people-often unknown heroes who give their *lives to bear witness to the faith. They are par excellence the heralds and witnesses of the faith.*

Pope John Paul II then leads the reader into a reflection on how after the initial proclamation of Jesus Christ to a people, conversion, baptism and the formation of local churches should naturally develop. This is the goal of such proclamation. He writes:

> *46. The proclamation of the Word of God has Christian conversion as its aim: a complete and sincere adherence to Christ and his Gospel through faith. Conversion is a gift of God, a work of the Blessed Trinity. It is the Spirit who opens people's hearts so that they can believe in Christ and "confess him" (cf. 1 Cor 12:3); of those who draw near to him through faith Jesus says: "No one can come to me unless the Father who sent me draws him" (Jn 6:44).*
>
> *From the outset, conversion is expressed in faith which is total and radical, and which neither limits nor hinders God's gift. At the same time, it gives rise to a dynamic and lifelong process which demands a continual turning away from "life according to the flesh" to "life according to the Spirit" (cf. Rom 8:3-13). Conversion means accepting, by a personal decision, the saving sovereignty of Christ and becoming his disciple.*
>
> *The Church calls all people to this conversion, following the example of John the Baptist, who prepared the way for Christ by "preaching a baptism of repentance for the forgiveness of sins" (Mk 1:4), as well as the example of Christ*

himself, who "after John was arrested,...came into Galilee preaching the Gospel of God and saying: 'The time is fulfilled, and the kingdom of God is at hand; repent and believe in the Gospel'" (Mk 1:14-15).

Nowadays the call to conversion which missionaries address to non-Christians is put into question or passed over in silence. It is seen as an act of "proselytizing"; it is claimed that it is enough to help people to become more human or more faithful to their own religion, that it is enough to build communities capable of working for justice, freedom, peace and solidarity. What is overlooked is that every person has the right to hear the "Good News" of the God who reveals and gives himself in Christ, so that each one can live out in its fullness his or her proper calling. This lofty reality is expressed in the words of Jesus to the Samaritan woman: "If you knew the gift of God," and in the unconscious but ardent desire of the woman: "Sir, give me this water, that I may not thirst" (Jn 4:10, 15).

47. The apostles, prompted by the Spirit, invited all to change their lives, to be converted and to be baptized. Immediately after the event of Pentecost, Peter spoke convincingly to the crowd: "When they heard this, they were cut to the heart, and said to Peter and the rest of the Apostles, 'Brethren, what shall we do?' And Peter said to them, 'Repent, and be baptized every one of you in the name of Jesus Christ for the forgiveness of your sins; and you shall receive the gift of the Holy Spirit'" (Acts 2:37-38). That very day some three

thousand persons were baptized. And again, after the healing of the lame man, Peter spoke to the crowd and repeated: "Repent therefore, and turn again, that your sins may be blotted out!" (Acts 3:19)

Conversion to Christ is joined to Baptism not only because of the Church's practice, but also by the will of Christ himself, who sent the apostles to make disciples of all nations and to baptize them (cf. Mt 28:19). Conversion is also joined to Baptism because of the intrinsic need to receive the fullness of new life in Christ. As Jesus says to Nicodemus: "Truly, truly, I say to you, unless one is born of water and the Spirit, he cannot enter the kingdom of God" (Jn 3:5). In Baptism, in fact, we are born anew to the life of God's children, united to Jesus Christ and anointed in the Holy Spirit. Baptism is not simply a seal of conversion, and a kind of external sign indicating conversion and attesting to it. Rather, it is the sacrament which signifies and effects rebirth from the Spirit, establishes real and unbreakable bonds with the Blessed Trinity, and makes us members of the Body of Christ, which is the Church.

All this needs to be said, since not a few people, precisely in those areas involved in the mission ad gentes, tend to separate conversion to Christ from Baptism, regarding Baptism as unnecessary. It is true that in some places sociological considerations associated with Baptism obscure its genuine meaning as an act of faith. This is due to a variety of historical and cultural factors which must be removed where they still exist, so that the sacrament of spiritual rebirth can be seen for what it truly is. Local ecclesial communities must devote themselves to this task. It is also true that many profess an interior commitment to Christ and his message yet do not wish to be committed sacramentally, since, owing to prejudice or because of the failings of Christians, they find it difficult to grasp the true nature of the Church as a mystery of faith and love. I wish to encourage such people to be fully open to Christ, and to remind them that, if they feel drawn to Christ, it was he himself who desired that the Church should be the "place" where they would in fact find him. At the same time, I invite the Christian faithful, both individually and as communities, to bear authentic witness to Christ through the new life they have received.

Certainly, every convert is a gift to the Church and represents a serious responsibility for her, not only because converts have to be prepared for Baptism through the catechumenate and then be guided by religious instruction, but also because - especially in the case of adults-such converts bring with them a kind of new energy, an enthusiasm for the faith, and a desire to see the Gospel lived out in the Church. They would be greatly disappointed if, having entered the ecclesial community, they were to find a life lacking fervor and without signs of renewal! We cannot preach conversion unless we ourselves are converted anew every day.

48. Conversion and Baptism give entry into a Church already in existence or require the establishment of new communities which confess Jesus as Savior and Lord. This is part

> *of God's plan, for it pleases him "to call human beings to share in his own life not merely as individuals, without any unifying bond between them, but rather to make them into a people in which his children, who had been widely scattered, might be gathered together in unity."*
>
> *The mission ad gentes has this objective: to found Christian communities and develop churches to their full maturity. This is a central and determining goal of missionary activity, so much so that the mission is not completed until it succeeds in building a new particular church which functions normally in its local setting.*
>
> *49. It is necessary first and foremost to strive to establish Christian communities everywhere, communities which are "a sign of the presence of God in the world" and which grow until they become churches. Notwithstanding the high number of dioceses, there are still very large areas where there are no local churches or where their number is insufficient in relation to the vastness of the territory and the density of the population. There is still much to be done in implanting and developing the Church.*

As the Encyclical continues, the Holy Father makes it very clear that it is important that the Gospel is incarnated into people's culture. And yet there are important guidelines one must follow in doing so to ensure that the deposit of the faith is not changed by the culture -instead that it is simply given a reflection cognizant with the local ways and norms of a given culture. Pope John Paul II writes:

52. As she carries out missionary activity among the nations, the Church encounters different cultures and becomes involved in the process of inculturation. The need for such involvement has marked the Church's pilgrimage throughout her history, but today it is particularly urgent.

The process of the Church's insertion into peoples' cultures is a lengthy one. It is not a matter of purely external adaptation, for inculturation "means the intimate transformation of authentic cultural values through their integration in Christianity and the insertion of Christianity in the various human cultures." The process is thus a profound and all-embracing one, which involves the Christian message and also the Church's reflection and practice. But at the same time it is a difficult process, for it must in no way compromise the distinctiveness and integrity of the Christian faith.

Through inculturation the Church makes the Gospel incarnate in different cultures and at the same time introduces peoples, together with their cultures, into her own community. She transmits to them her own values, at the same time taking the good elements that already exist in them and renewing them from within. Through inculturation the Church, for her part, becomes a more intelligible sign of what she is, and a more effective instrument of mission....

...53. **Missionaries, who come from other churches and countries, must immerse themselves in the cultural milieu of those to whom they are sent, moving beyond their own cultural limitations. Hence they must learn the language of**

the place in which they work, become familiar with the most important expressions of the local culture, and discover its values through direct experience. Only if they have this kind of awareness will they be able to bring to people the knowledge of the hidden mystery (cf. Rom 16:25-27; Eph 3:5) in a credible and fruitful way. It is not of course a matter of missionaries renouncing their own cultural identity, but of understanding, appreciating, fostering and evangelizing the culture of the environment in which they are working, and therefore of equipping themselves to communicate effectively with it, adopting a manner of living which is a sign of gospel witness and of solidarity with the people.

Developing ecclesial communities, inspired by the Gospel, will gradually be able to express their Christian experience in original ways and forms that are consonant with their own cultural traditions, provided that those traditions are in harmony with the objective requirements of the faith itself. To this end, especially in the more delicate areas of inculturation, particular churches of the same region should work in communion with each other and with the whole Church, convinced that only through attention both to the universal Church and to the particular churches will they be capable of translating the treasure of faith into a legitimate variety of expressions. Groups which have been evangelized will thus provide the elements for a "translation" of the gospel message, keeping in mind the positive elements acquired down the centuries from Christianity's contact with different cultures and not *forgetting the dangers of alterations which have sometimes occurred.*

54. In this regard, certain guidelines remain basic. Properly applied, inculturation must be guided by two principles: "compatibility with the gospel and communion with the universal Church." Bishops, as guardians of the "deposit of faith," will take care to ensure fidelity and, in particular, to provide discernment, for which a deeply balanced approach is required. In fact, there is a risk of passing uncritically from a form of alienation from culture to an overestimation of culture. Since culture is a human creation and is therefore marked by sin, it too needs to be "healed, ennobled and perfected."

This kind of process needs to take place gradually, in such a way that it really is an expression of the community's Christian experience. As Pope Paul VI said in Kampala: "It will require an incubation of the Christian 'mystery' in the genius of your people in order that its native voice, more clearly and frankly, may then be raised harmoniously in the chorus of other voices in the universal Church." In effect, inculturation must involve the whole people of God, and not just a few experts, since the people reflect the authentic sensus fidei which must never be lost sight of Inculturation needs to be guided and encouraged, but not forced, lest it give rise to negative reactions among Christians. It must be an expression of the community's life, one which must mature within the community itself, and not be exclusively the result of erudite research.

The safeguarding of traditional values is the work of a mature faith.

It is also important to draw the reader's attention to Saint Pope John Paul II's emphasis that in the Church's mission work, the primary help given to any people is spiritual -a missionary is not supposed to try to change all political or economic problems. The greatest law he is to follow is that of charity and following the way of the Beatitudes. He explains:

> 58.) ....*It is not the Church's mission to work directly on the economic, technical or political levels, or to contribute materially to development. Rather, her mission consists essentially in offering people an opportunity not to "have more" but to "be more," by awakening their consciences through the Gospel. "Authentic human development must be rooted in an ever deeper evangelization."*
>
> *The Church and her missionaries also promote development through schools, hospitals, printing presses, universities and experimental farms. But a people's development does not derive primarily from money, material assistance or technological means, but from the formation of consciences and the gradual maturing of ways of thinking and patterns of behavior. Man is the principal agent of development, not money or technology. The Church forms consciences by revealing to peoples the God whom they seek and do not yet know, the grandeur of man created in God's image and loved by him, the*

equality of all men and women as God's sons and daughters, the mastery of man over nature created by God and placed at man's service, and the obligation to work for the development of the whole person and of all mankind.

59. Through the gospel message, the Church offers a force for liberation which promotes development precisely because it leads to conversion of heart and of ways of thinking, fosters the recognition of each person's dignity, encourages solidarity, commitment and service of one's neighbor, and gives everyone a place in God's plan, which is the building of his kingdom of peace and justice, beginning already in this life. This is the biblical perspective of the "new heavens and a new earth" (cf. Is 65:17; 2 Pt 3:13; Rv 21:1), which has been the stimulus and goal for mankind's advancement in history. Man's development derives from God, and from the model of Jesus - God and man - and must lead back to God. That is why there is a close connection between the proclamation of the Gospel and human promotion.

Charity: Source and Criterion of Mission

60. As I said during my pastoral visit to Brazil: "The Church all over the world wishes to be the Church of the poor....she wishes to draw out all the truth contained in the Beatitudes of Christ, and especially in the first one: 'Blessed are the poor in spirit.' ...She wishes to teach this truth and she wishes to put it into practice, just as Jesus came to do and to teach."

The young churches, which for the most part are to be found among peoples suffering from widespread poverty, often give voice to this concern as an integral part of their mission. The Conference of Latin American Bishops at Puebla, after recalling the example of Jesus, wrote that "the poor deserve preferential attention, whatever their moral or personal situation. They have been made in the image and likeness of God to be his children, but this image has been obscured and even violated. For this reason, God has become their defender and loves them. It follows that the poor are those to whom the mission is first addressed, and their evangelization is par excellence the sign and proof of the mission of Jesus."

In fidelity to the spirit of the Beatitudes, the Church is called to be on the side of those who are poor and oppressed in any way. I therefore exhort the disciples of Christ and all Christian communities - from families to dioceses, from parishes to religious institutes - to carry out a sincere review of their lives regarding their solidarity with the poor. At the same time, I express gratitude to the missionaries who, by their loving presence and humble service to people, are working for the integral development of individuals and of society through schools, health-care centers, leprosaria, homes for the handicapped and the elderly, projects for the promotion of women and other similar apostolates. I thank the priests, religious brothers and sisters, and members of the laity for their

> *dedication, and I also encourage the volunteers from non-governmental organizations who in ever increasing numbers are devoting themselves to works of charity and human promotion.*
>
> *It is in fact these "works of charity" that reveal the soul of all missionary activity: love, which has been and remains the driving force of mission, and is also "the sole criterion for judging what is to be done or not done, changed or not changed. It is the principle which must direct every action, and end to which that action must be directed. When we act with a view to charity, or are inspired by charity, nothing is unseemly and everything is good."*

Saint Pope John Paul II explains at length the various missionary vocations. Although all are called to mission, there are 'special vocations' -both individuals and missionary institutes -who are called to give particular ardent attention to faithfully fulfilling the Lord's missionary command. The Holy Father goes through all of the varying vocations detailing their individual role in the missionary work of the Church:

> *What is involved, therefore, is a "special vocation," patterned on that of the apostles. It is manifested in a total commitment to evangelization, a commitment which involves the missionary's whole person and life, and demands a self-giving without limits of energy or time. Those who have received this vocation, "sent by legitimate authority, go out, in faith and*

obedience, to those who are far from Christ, set aside for the work to which they have been called as ministers of the Gospel." Missionaries must always meditate on the response demanded by the gift they have received, and continually keep their doctrinal and apostolic formation up to date.

DIOCESAN PRIESTS

67. As co-workers of the bishops, priests are called by virtue of the sacrament of Orders to share in concern for the Church's mission: "The spiritual gift that priests have received in ordination prepares them, not for any narrow and limited mission, but for the most universal and all-embracing mission of salvation 'to the end of the earth.' For every priestly ministry shares in the universal scope of the mission that Christ entrusted to his apostles." For this reason, the formation of candidates to the priesthood must aim at giving them "the true Catholic spirit whereby they will learn to transcend the bounds of their own diocese, country or rite, and come to the aid of the whole Church, in readiness to preach the Gospel anywhere." All priests must have the mind and the heart of missionaries - open to the needs of the Church and the world, with concern for those farthest away, and especially for the non-Christian groups in their own area. They should have at heart, in their prayers and particularly at the Eucharistic Sacrifice, the concern of the whole Church for all of humanity.

Especially in those areas where Christians are a minority, priests must be filled with special missionary zeal and commitment. The Lord entrusts to them not only the pastoral care of the Christian community, but also and above all the evangelization of those of their fellow-citizens who do not belong to Christ's flock. Priests will "not fail to make themselves readily available to the Holy Spirit and the bishop, to be sent to preach the Gospel beyond the borders of their country. This will demand of them not only maturity in their vocation, but also an uncommon readiness to detach themselves from their own homeland, culture and family, and a special ability to adapt to other cultures, with understanding and respect for them."

CONTEMPLATIVE AND ACTIVE RELIGIOUS

69. From the inexhaustible and manifold richness of the Spirit come the vocations of the Institutes of Consecrated Life, whose members, "because of the dedication to the service of the Church deriving from their very consecration, have an obligation to play a special part in missionary activity, in a manner appropriate to their Institute." History witnesses to the outstanding service rendered by religious families in the spread of the faith and the formation of new churches: from the ancient monastic institutions, to the medieval Orders, up to the more recent congregations.

(a) Echoing the Council, I invite institutes of contemplative life to establish communities in the young churches, so as

to "bear glorious witness among non-Christians to the majesty and love of God, as well as to unity in Christ." This presence is beneficial throughout the non-Christian world, especially in those areas where religious traditions hold the contemplative life in great esteem for its asceticism and its search for the Absolute.

(b) To institutes of active life, I would recommend the immense opportunities for works of charity, for the proclamation of the Gospel, for Christian education, cultural endeavors and solidarity with the poor and those suffering from discrimination, abandonment and oppression. Whether they pursue a strictly missionary goal or not, such institutes should ask themselves how willing and able they are to broaden their action in order to extend God's kingdom. In recent times many institutes have responded to this request, which I hope will be given even greater consideration and implementation for a more authentic service. The Church needs to make known the great gospel values of which she is the bearer. No one witnesses more effectively to these values than those who profess the consecrated life in chastity, poverty and obedience, in a total gift of self to God and in complete readiness to serve humanity and society after the example of Christ.

70. I extend a special word of appreciation to the missionary religious sisters, in whom virginity for the sake of the kingdom is transformed into a motherhood in the spirit that is rich and fruitful. It is precisely the mission ad gentes that offers them vast scope for "the gift of self with love in a total and undivided manner." The example and activity of women who through virginity are consecrated to love of God and neighbor, especially the very poor, are an indispensable evangelical sign among those peoples and cultures where women still have far to go on the way toward human promotion and liberation. It is my hope that many young Christian women will be attracted to giving themselves generously to Christ, and will draw strength and joy from their consecration in order to bear witness to him among the peoples who do not know him.

LAITY

71. Recent popes have stressed the importance of the role of the laity in missionary activity. In the Exhortation Christifideles Laici, I spoke explicitly of the Church's "permanent mission of bringing the Gospel to the multitudes - the millions and millions of men and women - who as yet do not know Christ the Redeemer of humanity," and of the responsibility of the lay faithful in this regard. The mission ad gentes is incumbent upon the entire People of God. Whereas the foundation of a new church requires the Eucharist and hence the priestly ministry, missionary activity, which is carried out in a wide variety of ways, is the task of all the Christian faithful.

It is clear that from the very origins of Christianity, the laity - as individuals, families, and entire communities - shared in spreading the faith. Pope Pius XII recalled this fact in his first encyclical on the missions, in which he pointed out some instances of lay missions. In modern times, this active participation of lay men and women missionaries has not been lacking. How can we forget the important role played by women: their work in the family, in schools, in political, social and cultural life, and especially their teaching of Christian doctrine? Indeed, it is necessary to recognize - and it is a title of honor - that some churches owe their origins to the activity of lay men and women missionaries.

The Second Vatican Council confirmed this tradition in its description of the missionary character of the entire People of God and of the apostolate of the laity in particular, emphasizing the specific contribution to missionary activity which they are called to make. The need for all the faithful to share in this responsibility is not merely a matter of making the apostolate more effective, it is a right and duty based on their baptismal dignity, whereby "the faithful participate, for their part, in the threefold mission of Christ as Priest, Prophet and King." Therefore, "they are bound by the general obligation and they have the right, whether as individuals or in associations, to strive so that the divine message of salvation may be known and accepted by all people throughout the world. This obligation is all the more insistent in circumstances in which only through them are people able to hear the Gospel and to know Christ." Furthermore, because of their secular character, they especially are called "to seek the kingdom of God by engaging in temporal affairs and ordering these in accordance with the will of God."

72. The sphere in which lay people are present and active as missionaries is very extensive. "Their own field...is the vast and complicated world of politics, society and economics..." on the local, national and international levels. Within the Church, there are various types of services, functions, ministries and ways of promoting the Christian life. I call to mind, as a new development occurring in many churches in recent times, the rapid growth of "ecclesial movements" filled with missionary dynamism. When these movements humbly seek to become part of the life of local churches and are welcomed by bishops and priests within diocesan and parish structures, they represent a true gift of God both for new evangelization and for missionary activity properly so-called. I therefore recommend that they be spread, and that they be used to give fresh energy, especially among young people, to the Christian life and to evangelization, within a pluralistic view of the ways in which Christians can associate and express themselves.

Within missionary activity, the different forms of the lay apostolate should be held in esteem, with respect for their nature and aims. Lay missionary associations, international Christian volunteer organizations, ecclesial movements, groups and solidarities of different kinds - all these should be involved in the mission ad gentes as cooperators with the local churches. In this way the growth of a mature and responsible laity will be fostered, a laity whom the younger churches are recognizing as "an essential and undeniable element in the plantatio Ecclesiae."

The Work of Catechists and the Variety of Ministries

73. Among the laity who become evangelizers, catechists have a place of honor. The Decree on the Missionary Activity of the Church speaks of them as "that army of catechists, both men and women, worthy of praise, to whom missionary work among the nations owes so much. Imbued with the apostolic spirit, they make a singular and absolutely necessary contribution to the spread of the faith and of the Church by their strenuous efforts." It is with good reason that the older and established churches, committed to a new evangelization, have increased the numbers of their catechists and intensified catechetical activity. But "the term 'catechists' belongs above all to the catechists in mission lands.... Churches that are flourishing today would not have been built up without them."

Even with the extension of the services rendered by lay people both within and outside the Church, there is always need for the ministry of catechists, a ministry with its own characteristics. Catechists are specialists, direct witnesses and irreplaceable evangelizers who, as I have often stated and experienced during my missionary journeys, represent the basic strength of Christian communities, especially in the young churches. The new Code of Canon Law acknowledges the tasks, qualities and qualifications of catechists.

However, it must not be forgotten that the work of catechists is becoming more and more difficult and demanding as a result of ecclesial and cultural changes. What the Council

Chapter 9: John Paul II's *Redemptoris Missio*

> *suggested is still valid today: a more careful doctrinal and pedagogical training, continuing spiritual and apostolic renewal, and the need to provide "a decent standard of living and social security." It is also important to make efforts to establish and support schools for catechists, which are to be approved by the Episcopal Conferences and confer diplomas officially recognized by the latter.*
>
> *74. Besides catechists, mention must also be made of other ways of serving the Church and her mission; namely, other Church personnel: leaders of prayer, song and liturgy; leaders of basic ecclesial communities and Bible study groups; those in charge of charitable works; administrators of Church resources; leaders in the various forms of the apostolate; religion teachers in schools. All the members of the laity ought to devote a part of their time to the Church, living their faith authentically.*

In Chapter VII, the encyclical covers the universal call to mission work in the Church and highlights different ways that every member of the faithful can aid in this most important labor:

> *77. Since they are members of the Church by virtue of their Baptism, all Christians share responsibility for missionary activity. "Missionary cooperation" is the expression used to describe the sharing by communities and individual Christians in this right and duty.*

Missionary cooperation is rooted and lived, above all, in personal union with Christ. Only if we are united to him as the branches to the vine (cf. Jn 15:5) can we produce good fruit. Through holiness of life every Christian can become a fruitful part of the Church's mission. The Second Vatican Council invited all "to a profound interior renewal, so that having a lively awareness of their personal responsibility for the spreading of the Gospel, they may play their part in missionary work among the nations."

Sharing in the universal mission therefore is not limited to certain specific activities, but is the sign of maturity in faith and of a Christian life that bears fruit. In this way, individual believers extend the reach of their charity and show concern for those both far and near. They pray for the missions and missionary vocations. They help missionaries and follow their work with interest. And when missionaries return, they welcome them with the same joy with which the first Christian communities heard from the apostles the marvelous things which God had wrought through their preaching (cf. Acts 14:27).

Prayer and Sacrifice for Missionaries

78. Among the forms of sharing, first place goes to spiritual cooperation through prayer, sacrifice and the witness of Christian life. **Prayer should accompany the journey of missionaries so that the proclamation of the word will be effective**

through God's grace. *In his Letters, St. Paul often asks the faithful to pray for him so that he might proclaim the Gospel with confidence and conviction.* ***Prayer needs to be accompanied by sacrifice. The redemptive value of suffering, accepted and offered to God with love, derives from the sacrifice of Christ himself, who calls the members of his Mystical Body to share in his sufferings, to complete them in their own flesh (cf. Col 1:24). The sacrifice of missionaries should be shared and accompanied by the sacrifices of all the faithful.*** *I therefore urge those engaged in the pastoral care of the sick to teach them about the efficacy of suffering, and to encourage them to offer their sufferings to God for missionaries.* ***By making such an offering, the sick themselves become missionaries, as emphasized by a number of movements which have sprung up among them and for them.*** *The solemnity of Pentecost - the beginning of the Church's mission - is celebrated in some communities as a "Day of Suffering for the Missions."*

"Here I am, Lord! I am ready! Send me!" (cf. Is 6:8)

79. *Cooperation is expressed above all by promoting missionary vocations. While acknowledging the validity of various ways of being involved in missionary activity, it is necessary at the same time to reaffirm that a full and lifelong commitment to the work of the missions holds pride of place, especially in missionary institutes and congregations. Promoting such vocations is at the heart of missionary cooperation. Preaching the Gospel requires preachers; the harvest needs*

laborers. The mission is carried out above all by men and women who are consecrated for life to the work of the Gospel and are prepared to go forth into the whole world to bring salvation.

I wish to call to mind and to recommend this concern for missionary vocations. Conscious of the overall responsibility of Christians to contribute to missionary activity and to the development of poorer peoples, we must ask ourselves how it is that in some countries, while monetary contributions are on the increase, missionary vocations, which are the real measure of self-giving to one's brothers and sisters, are in danger of disappearing. Vocations to the priesthood and the consecrated life are a sure sign of the vitality of a church.

80. As I think of this serious problem, I appeal with great confidence and affection to families and to young people. Families, especially parents, should be conscious that they ought to "offer a special contribution to the missionary cause of the Church by fostering missionary vocations among their sons and daughters."

An intense prayer life, a genuine sense of service to one's neighbor and a generous participation in Church activities provide families with conditions that favor vocations among young people. When parents are ready to allow one of their children to leave for the missions, when they have sought this grace from the Lord, he will repay them, in joy, on the day that their son or daughter hears his call.

I ask young people themselves to listen to Christ's words as he says to them what he once said to Simon Peter and to Andrew at the lakeside: "Follow me, and I will make you fishers of men" (Mt 4:19). May they have the courage to reply as Isaiah did: "Here am I, Lord! I am ready! Send me!" (cf. Is 6:8) They will have a wonderful life ahead of them, and they will know the genuine joy of proclaiming the "Good News" to brothers and sisters whom they will lead on the way of salvation.

"It is more blessed to give than to receive" (Acts 20:35)

81. **The material and financial needs of the missions are many: not only to set up the Church with minimal structures (chapels, schools for catechists and seminarians, housing), but also to support works of charity, education and human promotion–a vast field of action especially in poor countries.** The missionary Church gives what she receives, and distributes to the poor the material goods that her materially richer sons and daughters generously put at her disposal. Here I wish to thank all those who make sacrifices and contribute to the work of the missions. Their sacrifices and sharing are indispensable for building up the Church and for showing love.

In the matter of material help, it is important to consider the spirit in which donations are made. For this we should reassess our own way of living: the missions ask not only for a contribution but for a sharing in the work of preaching and charity toward the poor. All that we have received from God -

life itself as well as material goods - does not belong to us but is given to us for our use. Generosity in giving must always be enlightened and inspired by faith: then we will truly be more blessed in giving than in receiving.

World Mission Day, which seeks to heighten awareness of the missions, as well as to collect funds for them, is an important date in the life of the Church, because it teaches how to give: as an offering made to God, in the Eucharistic celebration and for all the missions of the world.

Saint Pope John Paul II's final and incredibly beautiful chapter of this Encyclical is about the missionary spirituality that all missionaries are called to follow -and how truly each and every missionary is actually called to be a saint:

CHAPTER VIII - MISSIONARY SPIRITUALITY

87. Missionary activity demands a specific spirituality, which applies in particular to all those whom God has called to be missionaries.

Being Led by the Spirit

This spirituality is expressed first of all by a life of complete **docility to the Spirit***. It commits us to being molded from within by the Spirit, so that we may become ever more like Christ. It is not possible to bear witness to Christ without* *reflecting his image, which is made alive in us by grace and the power of the Spirit. This docility then commits us to receive the gifts of fortitude and discernment, which are essential elements of missionary spirituality.*

An example of this is found with the apostles during the Master's public life. Despite their love for him and their generous response to his call, they proved to be incapable of understanding his words and reluctant to follow him along the path of suffering and humiliation. The Spirit transformed them into courageous witnesses to Christ and enlightened heralds of his word. It was the Spirit himself who guided them along the difficult and new paths of mission.

Today, as in the past, that mission is difficult and complex, and demands the courage and light of the Spirit. We often experience the dramatic situation of the first Christian community which witnessed unbelieving and hostile forces "gathered together against the Lord and his Anointed" (Acts 4:26). Now, as then, we must pray that God will grant us boldness in preaching the Gospel; we must ponder the mysterious ways of the Spirit and allow ourselves to be led by him into all the truth (cf. Jn 16:13).

<u>Living the Mystery of Christ, "the One who was sent"</u>

*88. An essential characteristic of missionary spirituality is **intimate communion with Christ**. We cannot understand or carry out the mission unless we refer it to Christ as the one* *who was sent to evangelize. St. Paul describes Christ's attitude: "Have this mind among yourselves, which is yours in Christ Jesus, who, though he was in the form of God, did not count equality with God a thing to be grasped, but emptied himself, taking the form of a servant, being born in the likeness of men. And being found in human form he humbled himself and became obedient unto death, even death on a cross" (Phil 2:5-8).*

The mystery of the Incarnation and Redemption is thus described as a total self-emptying which leads Christ to experience fully the human condition and to accept totally the Father's plan. This is an emptying of self which is permeated by love and expresses love. The mission follows this same path and leads to the foot of the cross.

The missionary is required to "renounce himself and everything that up to this point he considered as his own, and to make himself everything to everyone." This he does by a poverty which sets him free for the Gospel, overcoming attachment to the people and things about him, so that he may become a brother to those to whom he is sent and thus bring them Christ the Savior. This is the goal of missionary spirituality: "To the weak I became weak...; I have become all things to all men, that I might by all means save some. I do it all for the sake of the Gospel..." (1 Cor 9:22-23).

It is precisely because he is "sent" that the missionary experiences the consoling presence of Christ, who is with him at every moment of life - "Do not be afraid...for I am with you"

Chapter 9: John Paul II's *Redemptoris Missio*

(Acts 18:9-10) - and who awaits him in the heart of every person.

Loving the Church and Humanity As Jesus Did

89. Missionary spirituality is also marked by apostolic charity, the charity of Christ who came "to gather into one the children of God who are scattered abroad" (Jn 11:52), of the Good Shepherd who knows his sheep, who searches them out and offers his life for them (cf. Jn 10). Those who have the missionary spirit feel Christ's burning love for souls, and love the Church as Christ did.

The missionary is urged on by "zeal for souls," a zeal inspired by Christ's own charity, which takes the form of concern, tenderness, compassion, openness, availability and interest in people's problems. Jesus' love is very deep: he who "knew what was in man" (Jn 2:25) loved everyone by offering them redemption and suffered when it was rejected.

The missionary is a person of charity. In order to proclaim to all his brothers and sisters that they are loved by God and are capable of loving, he must show love toward all, giving his life for his neighbor. The missionary is the "universal brother," bearing in himself the Church's spirit, her openness to and interest in all peoples and individuals, especially the least and poorest of his brethren. As such, he overcomes barriers and divisions of race, cast or ideology. He is a sign of God's love in the world - a love without exclusion or partiality.

Finally, like Christ he must love the Church: "Christ loved the Church and gave himself up for her" (Eph 5:25). This love, even to the point of giving one's life, is a focal point for him. Only profound love for the Church can sustain the missionary's zeal. His daily pressure, as St. Paul says, is "anxiety for all the churches" (2 Cor 11:28). For every missionary "fidelity to Christ cannot be separated from fidelity to the Church."

The True Missionary Is the Saint

90. The call to mission derives, of its nature, from the call to holiness. **A missionary is really such only if he commits himself to the way of holiness:** *"Holiness must be called a fundamental presupposition and an irreplaceable condition for everyone in fulfilling the mission of salvation in the Church."*

The universal call to holiness is closely linked to the universal call to mission. **Every member of the faithful is called to holiness and to mission.** *This was the earnest desire of the Council, which hoped to be able "to enlighten all people with the brightness of Christ, which gleams over the face of the Church, by preaching the Gospel to every creature." The Church's missionary spirituality is a journey toward holiness.*

The renewed impulse to the mission ad gentes demands holy missionaries. *It is not enough to update pastoral techniques, organize and coordinate ecclesial resources, or delve more deeply into the biblical and theological foundations of faith. What is needed is the encouragement of a new "ardor* *for holiness" among missionaries and throughout the Christian community, especially among those who work most closely with missionaries.*

Dear brothers and sisters: let us remember the missionary enthusiasm of the first Christian communities. Despite the limited means of travel and communication in those times, the proclamation of the Gospel quickly reached the ends of the earth. And this was the religion of a man who had died on a cross, "a stumbling block to Jews and folly to Gentiles"! (1 Cor 1:23) Underlying this missionary dynamism was the holiness of the first Christians and the first communities.

91. I therefore address myself to the recently baptized members of the young communities and young churches. Today, you are the hope of this two-thousand-year-old Church of ours: being young in faith, you must be like the first Christians and radiate enthusiasm and courage, in generous devotion to God and neighbor. In a word, you must set yourselves on the path of holiness. Only thus can you be a sign of God in the world and re-live in your own countries the missionary epic of the early Church. You will also be a leaven of missionary spirit for the older churches.

For their part, missionaries should reflect on the duty of holiness required of them by the gift of their vocation, renew themselves in spirit day by day, and strive to update their doctrinal and pastoral formation. **The missionary must be a "contemplative in action."** *He finds answers to problems in the light of God's word and in personal and community* *prayer. My contact with representatives of the non-Christian spiritual traditions, particularly those of Asia, has confirmed me in the view that the future of mission depends to a great extent on contemplation.* **Unless the missionary is a contemplative he cannot proclaim Christ in a credible way.** *He is a witness to the experience of God, and must be able to say with the apostles: "that which we have looked upon...concerning the word of life,...we proclaim also to you" (1 Jn 1:1-3).*

The missionary is a person of the Beatitudes. *Before sending out the Twelve to evangelize, Jesus, in his "missionary discourse" (cf. Mt 10), teaches them the paths of mission: poverty, meekness, acceptance of suffering and persecution, the desire for justice and peace, charity - in other words, the Beatitudes, lived out in the apostolic life (cf. Mt 5:1-12). By living the Beatitudes, the missionary experiences and shows concretely that the kingdom of God has already come, and that he has accepted it.* **The characteristic of every authentic missionary life is the inner joy that comes from faith.** *In a world tormented and oppressed by so many problems, a world tempted to pessimism, the one who proclaims the "Good News" must be a person who has found true hope in Christ.*

Conclusion

92. Today, as never before, the Church has the opportunity of bringing the Gospel, by witness and word, to all people and nations. I see the dawning of a new missionary age, which will become a radiant day bearing an abundant harvest, if all Christians, and missionaries and young churches in particular, respond with generosity and holiness to the calls and challenges of our time.

Like the apostles after Christ's Ascension, the Church must gather in the Upper Room "together with Mary, the Mother of Jesus" (Acts 1:14), in order to pray for the Spirit and to gain strength and courage to carry out the missionary mandate. We too, like the apostles, need to be transformed and guided by the Spirit.

On the eve of the third millennium the whole Church is invited to live more intensely the mystery of Christ by gratefully cooperating in the work of salvation. **The Church does this together with Mary and following the example of Mary, the Church's Mother and model: Mary is the model of that maternal love which should inspire all who cooperate in the Church's apostolic mission for the rebirth of humanity.** *Therefore, "strengthened by the presence of Christ, the Church journeys through time toward the consummation of the ages and goes to meet the Lord who comes. But on this journey ...she proceeds along the path already trodden by the Virgin Mary."*

To "Mary's mediation, wholly oriented toward Christ and tending to the revelation of his salvific power," I entrust the Church and, in particular, those who commit themselves to carrying out the missionary mandate in today's world. As Christ sent forth his apostles in the name of the Father and of the Son and of the Holy Spirit, so too, renewing that same mandate, I extend to all of you my apostolic blessing, in the name of the same Most Holy Trinity. Amen.

Given in Rome, at St. Peter's, on December 7, the twenty-fifth anniversary of the Conciliar Decree Ad Gentes, in the year 1990, the thirteenth of my Pontificate.

Chapter 10

Mission in My Own Life

At first glance this book might seem only apropos for one called to a radical mission in a faraway country. And yet, this book -and the missionary call in general -is for all people who are baptized. Christ's command to *'Go into the whole world and preach the Gospel'* (Mark 16:15) was not meant only for a few disciples present with Him when He first spoke those words. Instead, it is the command given to each soul at the moment of their Baptism -to go into the world and to preach the Gospel first and foremost by holy lives lived according to the precepts of the Church -and then also as megaphones proclaiming the love of God for His children in the midst of a world that has fallen into a deep paganism. And how does one do this?

Hanging on the kitchen walls of several of my siblings' homes is a quote by Mother Teresa that says: **'Do you want to change the world? Go home and love your family.'** It is not difficult to live Jesus' missionary mandate -the young and the old, the rich and the poor, the educated and the uneducated can all follow His missionary example by simply first and foremost loving the people God places around them. For the majority of people this constitutes their immediate (and then extended) family. The family is not only the first mission field that a child will encounter, but also the school where they will learn to live authentic love, Gospel values and a life of service. (If a child is born and placed in an orphanage, this orphanage becomes their family.) Children are not born perfectly virtuous. They are born with the effects of original sin -which are taken away from them in Baptism -and yet, they are raised in a fallen world by fallen people. And for this reason, children need to be concretely taught virtue. They need to hear people explain virtue ("Family shares and you are in a family so you have to share your toys." "We should be thankful for a gift regardless if it's what you really wanted because it was given in love by someone who was trying to make you happy." "Lying is always wrong." "God gave you a body to serve people -what can you do today to use your body to help someone else?"). They also need to see and hear virtue (examples of patience, forgiveness, sacrifice, hard-work, generosity, respect, modesty, etc.,) lived by those around them. This all first and foremost happens in a family. If children are raised in an atmosphere of love, holiness and virtue, then the soil of their hearts is fertile and ready for God to call them into a life of missionary service.

 The bed where my own missionary vocation was born was that of my family. My parents had 12 children of their own and then we began to take in foster babies. My youngest brother was our last foster child who we adopted. My second oldest sister ran Catholic Charities in our city and several times we had teenage moms with their children who would live with us for a while. We had immigrants and college kids without housing stay for periods of time in our home. Our doors were open to all because my parents followed Jesus' words *'Whatsoever you do to the least of my little ones you do unto Me.'* (Mt 25:40) From a young age my Mom exposed me to books about real-life missionaries and my entire family fed me a hunger for God. When people ask me when did I decide to become

Chapter 10: Mission in My Own Life

a missionary, I do not actually remember. It seems as if this part of my life -this desire and a 'knowledge' that God would use me in this way -was always written in my heart. I did not have a clear understanding of how it would unfold. I thought I would be married with many children, but I also thought we would be a missionary family. It was only many years down the line when the Lord showed me that such an intense desire to love and help the entire world was only possible to fulfill with Him as my Husband. I had to live completely single-heartedly united with Him in everything.

Already in grade school my heart was burning to help the poorest of the poor all over the world. I saw in the newspaper advertisements to sponsor poor children by sending a donation once a month. My Mom was not ready to do this for me because she couldn't afford to do it for all of my siblings. But my older brother Bobby was at Notre Dame at the time and he decided to nurture my desire to help the poor. He pulled me aside one day and told me that we together would sponsor a child. I would pay $1 a month (which I would 'earn' by asking my Mom for extra chores or the like -I do not actually remember how I earned this monthly dollar because my parents did not believe in allowances) and he would pay the remaining $9. He took the photo of the child we were supporting and hung it in his dorm room with a sign asking for donations. It was actually he along with his friends who would come up with $9 a month to help me sponsor a child. I was thrilled.

In middle school I remember the city bought a new house to be used as a Women's Shelter and they were looking for volunteers to help fix it up. My Mom, sisters and I spent a few nights scrubbing the floors and I remember imagining what it would be like to meet the abused women who would come there and how I longed to help them (or at least their children). In Junior High I also volunteered at Catholic Charities with my sister -I remember helping her deliver food baskets to the projects at Christmas -and even babysitting children while their parents met with her for counseling. In high school I wanted to do more so I contacted the local Child Abuse Prevention Organization and offered to volunteer watching children. They put me in charge of the 2-and-under children during 'parenting classes' and not long after they offered me a paid position to work there -especially with small children. That is where I learned how to watch multiple small children at the same time. Sometimes there were 10 or 15 children for just me and a couple other volunteers/workers.

And then it happened. My Junior year in high school I met missionary sisters from Slovakia who worked in Russia and they invited me on a mission trip. If you are interested in this work I did in Russia in 1994 -when I was 17 -you will have to read my book *A Heart Frozen in the Wilderness: Reflections of a Siberian Missionary*. That summer was a 'baptism by fire' (truly by the Fire of the Holy Spirit) as to what mission life was all about and through that experience, I found my vocation. In a village house without water and electricity I fell in love with Jesus and a life dedicated totally to Him in service to the poorest of the poor. I remember thinking, *"All I want to do the rest of my life is to pray and work serving these suffering souls. Work and prayer. Poverty and love. This is true Joy."* When I returned home for my Senior year in High School the trajectory of my life had taken a totally new direction. My goal was to be a poor, foreign missionary the rest of my life.

Chapter 10: Mission in My Own Life

With this aim in mind, I studied Russian and Italian at Notre Dame, praying I could quickly find my way somehow back to the mission in Russia after graduation. By a series of miraculous events, a wealthy family friend offered to pay my way through the University (being the 9th child, my Dad did not have the money to pay for me even though I was accepted to study there). While at Notre Dame Jesus very clearly became the center of my life. I would spend hours daily in adoration in all of the many chapels on campus -with a broken heart that He was present and yet so often left alone. And as I drew closer to Jesus, He convicted me that I was not just 'getting through Notre Dame' so that afterwards I could find my real vocation in the missions. Instead, He had called me (vocated me) to the 'mission of Notre Dame.' If He provided for someone to pay my way, it was not for fun and games. Such a magnanimous gift came with the responsibility to give everything back to Jesus. He brought me there as a mission field. And I saw this clearly. I helped start Eucharistic Adoration at Notre Dame -meeting weekly with the Head of Campus Ministry to report how it was going. I was personally in charge of signing people up for the needed hours and arranging for the priests to expose and repose Jesus. This work weighed heavily on my back (I was told if anything went wrong they would rescind their permission) and there was great spiritual warfare surrounding this. I also was very involved in the Children of Mary and Knights of Immaculata prayer groups on campus, along with starting a women's prayer and reflection group that met once a week. My entire life was Jesus and so my Junior year I changed my major to Theology so that I could focus more on Him.

During my time at Notre Dame a hermit priest visited campus and held a retreat (off campus) for several of the Children of Mary members. It was a small retreat -but he insisted that in littleness we could be sure God was working -for He always starts with that which is small. (*"Our Lady said...'He has lifted up the lowly.'"* Luke 1:52) At this retreat he encouraged all of us after graduation to take a time of retreat (or service) -a time given directly to the Lord where we could listen to Him and discern His will for our lives. He said that so often people jump into life with their own plans (that are often misguided) and end up disillusioned and frustrated (sometimes even at God Who they never asked for help in the first place). Instead, this priest suggested that young people should take a year of intense prayer and/or service dedicated to listening to God's plan for their lives. In this way they would truly be happier.

I was already strongly attracted to prayer -spending 5 or more hours in front of the Blessed Sacrament daily praying -and I immediately desired to visit these hermits in south Texas after graduation and to spend a year of discernment with them. I only ended up staying 6 months -afterwards I spent another 3 months living a retired life in Bosnia much like a hermit -and during the course of this time I strongly heard the Lord calling me back to Russia. Providentially I also was told of a seminarian who had served with me in Russia when I was in High School who was now a priest planning to go back to Eastern Siberia to found a Catholic mission there and I was given his number. He spoke to his superiors, as well as the founder of his order, about me and all agreed that God wanted me to join his team. They invited me back to Texas to volunteer teach in one of their schools while at the same time going through formation in their religious community as a lay missionary and planning out with this priest and religious sister what our mission would entail.

And then in the summer of 2001 I left for Eastern Siberia -not knowing if I would be martyred in this country newly freed from Communism, but still run by Mafia giants of corruption -and definitely hostile to the Catholic Church. My two years in Krasnoyarsk were years that stripped me of everything I had and who I was to the core -teaching me prayer, humility, authentic sacrifice, and teaching me missionary values and wisdom. After two years our mission closed (in 2003) and the Lord took me on a path of wild love with Him all over the world. I spent the next 8 years (2003-2011) traveling all over the world as a missionary -going wherever Jesus called and made a path for me and working always with the local churches, priests, bishops and religious of the area. This time of mission life was divided between intense service in faraway cultures and places and times of intense solitude and prayer living the life of a hermit and giving Jesus lots of time to further form and guide my heart. The greatest gift He gave me was in making me all His. Because of how He worked with me during these formative years, my heart began to truly dwell in His Hands and wherever He took it, I followed with my 'Fiat.'

During these years I served in Europe, the Philippines, several countries in Africa, Israel and Mexico. My 'work' varied greatly. When I was in Russia I served with 'SOLT -the Society of Our Lady of the Most Holy Trinity' and their charism is to serve the poorest of the poor in areas of deepest apostolic need. This spirituality stayed with me -and no matter where I went, I ended up serving the outcasts, the forgotten, those who had no hope. This took concrete shape in running a baby room in an orphanage in Tanzania where I at times was left to care for 30 infants alone, to consoling 100 year old homeless babushkas on the streets of Russia who were experiencing flashbacks of being taken from their family as a child and sent to concentration camps, to exorcism ministry with teenagers who had fallen into the occult, to teaching catechesis at parishes, running AA groups, visiting those who lived in trash dumps, working alongside Mother Teresa's sisters, and simply sitting in a chapel in Northern Nigeria praying for the diocese where volatile attacks from the Muslims were a daily occurrence. What the Lord taught me in this was a complete flexibility -a total detachment from everyone and everything but Him. These days were the days before cell phones and internet (at least these poor missions had no internet). I had to give up the family I loved to serve the family of God entrusted to me. I had to be indifferent to whether I had only hot water, cold water, dirty water or no water to bath with at night. I had to be okay with sleeping on concrete floors, dirt floors, mice-infested floors -whatever was offered (which I never knew ahead of time what to expect) I had to receive graciously in thanksgiving trusting God Himself had gone ahead to prepare the way. I spent years not being able to speak to people around me because I had not yet mastered their language -sitting at dinner tables while people spoke about me laughing through a meal while I simply was called to be a child and smile and trust God. I learned these years the power of Love -it was my only weapon, my only defense, my only strength, my only comfort, my only guide. I was always free to love in any situation, with any people, in any problem and that love meant the world to my God.

Chapter 10: Mission in My Own Life

People often asked me which country or people was my favorite -but to me that was like asking a mother who was their favorite child. I loved all of them. For they all belonged to my Husband Jesus. Every place and people had a cross that was difficult for me to bear and yet also a blessing. Russia was so full of evil, wounds and suffering -and yet the people were hungry, the people were deep, the people were naturally spiritual. Africa was physically poor -one bucket of water was brought to me a day to use for washing, brushing my teeth, etc., -and yet the joy on the faces of those people was something inspiring! The people who lived in 'Smokey Mountain' (the trash dump) in Manila, Philippines endured squalor -and yet their generosity and childlike heart was infectious. I felt very 'at home' among my own people in Poland (I was born in the US but am 100% Polish) and yet my suffering there was similar to Christ in His homeland -very often He came to His Own people *'but His people did not accept Him.'* (John 1:11)

In 2 Corinthians 11:18, 21-30 St. Paul writes:

"So many others have been boasting of their worldly achievements, that I will boast myself. But if anyone wants some brazen speaking – I am still talking as a fool – then I can be as brazen as any of them, and about the same things. Hebrews, are they? So am I. Israelites? So am I. Descendants of Abraham? So am I. The servants of Christ? I must be mad to say this, but so am I, and more than they: more, because I have worked harder, I have been sent to prison more often, and whipped many times more, often almost to death. Five times I had the thirty-nine lashes from the Jews; three times I have

been beaten with sticks; once I was stoned; three times I have been shipwrecked and once adrift in the open sea for a night and a day. Constantly travelling, I have been in danger from rivers and in danger from brigands, in danger from my own people and in danger from pagans; in danger in the towns, in danger in the open country, danger at sea and danger from so-called brothers. I have worked and labored, often without sleep; I have been hungry and thirsty and often starving; I have been in the cold without clothes. And, to leave out much more, there is my daily preoccupation: my anxiety for all the churches. When any man has had scruples, I have had scruples with him; when any man is made to fall, I am tortured. If I am to boast, then let me boast of my own feebleness."

I also feel like the greatest gift that I can offer to Jesus from my years in the missions is a pile of my seeming failures, persecutions, weakness and sufferings. It was precisely through these, that He has born the greatest fruit -and He continues to bear fruit through them even now (20 years later). I could write a long list of various sufferings I endured in the missions -and yet I also will say that my list of graces and blessings would be longer. Often it was through the suffering that He blessed me. I remember when I returned home one summer for a short visit and I went to Mass at our local parish one Sunday, they sang the song '*Be Not Afraid*' and I was blown away by the fact that I had literally lived every line of that song in the missions:

Chapter 10: Mission in My Own Life

You shall cross the barren desert
But you shall not die of thirst
(I lived and served in many deserts throughout the world -where water was scarce
-as well as in spiritual deserts where I was truly left 'alone.')

You shall wander far in safety
Though you do not know the way
(I lived in many places where I had no idea where to go or what to do -but God guided me.
I lived among Mafia, KGB, satanists, radical Muslims, etc., -but always kept safe by the Lord.)

You shall speak your words to foreign men
And they will understand
(Countless times in the missions, people heard me speak their language when I did not know it
-or I was able to speak and understand a language that I did not know.)

You shall see the face of God and live
(The Eucharist is the same everywhere.)

Be not afraid
I go before you always
Come, follow me and I will give you rest

If you pass through raging waters in the sea

You shall not drown
(At times I had to wade through torrential waters filled with poisonous snakes
and alligators to get to safety -but God protected me.)

If you walk amid the burning flames
You shall not be harmed
(In Africa we had to walk and drive on roads with 12-foot-high flames on either side
-trusting God would keep us from catching fire and getting burned.)

If you stand before the power of hell
And death is at your side
Know that I am with you through it all
(Many times, I stood before satan in the eyes of a possessed man or woman and God protected me.
Many times, I faced death -said my Act of Contrition -not seeing any way out -and God saved me.)

Be not afraid
I go before you always
Come, follow me and I will give you rest

(And, of course, if you are a missionary, you must live these Beatitudes to the full!)
And blessed are your poor
For the kingdom shall be theirs

Chapter 10: Mission in My Own Life

> *Blest are you that weep and mourn*
> *For one day you shall laugh*
> *And if wicked men insult and hate you*
> *All because of me*
> *Blessed, blessed are you*
> *Be not afraid*
> *I go before you always*
> *Come, follow me and I will give you rest.*

After spending over a decade in the foreign missions the Lord called me deep into His Own Heart to live a permanent state of eremitical prayer. I lived for three years as a Diocesan Hermit with vows under a Bishop -offering my intense life of prayer, fasting, silence and solitude *for the world* who I felt had become my family through my missionary work. After my vows expired, I continued to live a hermit life for another three years until the lack of support prevented me from continuing. These six years of intense prayer and sacrifice offered to the Lord hiddenly watered the souls I had encountered years before -as well as prepared the ground for the future work that God was preparing me for (although I had no idea at the time). Without financial donations and sufficient support from the church to continue this vocation of solitude, I became a night nanny to newborn triplets in the wealthiest neighborhood of Chicago. This year of caring for these babies was very contemplative -nights spent in prayer as I changed, fed and rocked the little ones. And although I served the wealthy, my own apartment was poor and I found myself sleeping once more on a hard floor. But I was happy. I continued to work as a nanny to the wealthy whose children are in the same need of Christ's love as the orphans I cared for years earlier -and I began publishing books -this present book being my eighth. Simultaneously, I began a weekly podcast on the spiritual life *("The Heart of Fiat Crucified Love")* and a daily Facebook rosary that reached 100,000 people daily for some time. And then God began to lead the persecuted Church to me. I began to be contacted by persecuted Christians all over the world and we began to translate my books into their languages -raising funds to print them for free to be used by the local church. This ministry with my books grew so large I started the *Fiat Foundation* to process the donations -and we began *Children of the Cross* prayer groups throughout the Middle East and Africa -these are prayer groups of children who meet either weekly or monthly to pray for priests and persecuted Christians. Today I continue to work as a nanny for the wealthy while writing, painting icons (used as the covers of my books), doing podcasts and interviews and running missions in over 25 countries. Here while I thought my missionary activity would cease, being replaced by a life of contemplation offered to the Lord, Jesus has led me step by step into a missionary ministry larger than anything I thought I could ever be part of. God writes straight with crooked lines -and when we follow God -day in and day out -He can do things beyond our imagination that fulfill the deepest longings of our hearts. The longing for a contemplative life remains -and I keep my Hermit Rule (that I had to write for the Bishop the years I lived vows under him) hung on the wall of my house (a new center for this ministry) praying daily that the Lord will send donors to help me pay for my daily needs (and this house -which is central to our work), as well as the needs of our missions all over the world -so I can once again live a life totally consumed in prayer and service to Him.

The words I write in this book are not words I thought up in my head by reading theological tracts on missionary life. Such words would be true, but empty of the love with which I write. I am speaking all that is within these last 10 chapters personally to each one of you who picks up this book from my heart -a heart that has learned throughout my lifetime as a missionary, that has learned through experience, suffering, intense prayer, and from saintly men and women who I have met all over the world what it means to be a missionary after the Heart of Christ the Perfect Missionary. From the time I was young He alone was held up to me as a model -and it is His Heart from which I try to pattern my own missionary heart. It is Jesus and Mary who have stood on my right and left since my childhood -but most profoundly the past 30 years that I have spent pouring myself out for the foreign missions. Jesus said, *"Amen, amen, I say to you, unless a grain of wheat falls to the ground and dies, it remains just a grain of wheat; but if it dies, it produces much fruit. Whoever loves his life loses it, and whoever hates his life in this world will preserve it for eternal life. Whoever serves me must follow me, and where I am, there also will my servant be."* (John 12:24-26) Each Christian is called to empty himself and 'die' to the world in order to allow God to fill Him completely and bear fruit through him. But all the more a missionary is called to a radical self-abnegation -often finding himself 'dying' in the mission field day after day, moment by moment –*'hating his life in this world'* so as to *'preserve it in the next'*. A true missionary must follow the footprints of Christ that lead up Calvary -and it is from stepping in His bloody footprints of light that one finds himself running swiftly into the arms of the Father in Heaven.

The last word I want to leave for you all here is the word 'Love.' St. John of the Cross said, **'At the end of life we will solely be judged on love.'**

It doesn't matter how much seemingly incredible work you do in the missions -how many people you reach -how many programs you build -how many places you go -if you do not do it with Jesus Christ, for Jesus Christ, because Jesus Christ asked you to do it and with the Love of Jesus Christ burning in your heart. **Love alone changes the world.**

"So be imitators of God, as beloved children, and **live in love***, as Christ loved us and handed himself over for us as a sacrificial offering to God for a fragrant aroma…" (Ephesians 5:1-2)*

"If I speak in human and angelic tongues but do not have love, I am a resounding gong or a clashing cymbal. And if I have the gift of prophecy and comprehend all mysteries and all knowledge; if I have all faith so as to move mountains but do not have love, I am nothing. If I give away everything I own, and if I hand my body over so that I may boast but do not have love, I gain nothing. Love is patient, love is kind. It is not jealous, [love] is not pompous, it is not inflated, it is not rude, it does not seek its own interests, it is not quick-tempered, it does not brood over injury, it does not rejoice over wrongdoing but rejoices with the truth. It bears all things, believes all things, hopes all things, endures all things.

Love never fails. If there are prophecies, they will be brought to nothing; if tongues, they will cease; if knowledge, it will be brought to nothing. For we know partially and we prophesy partially, but when the perfect comes, the partial will pass away. When I was a child, I used to talk as a child, think as a child, reason as a child; when I became a man, I put aside childish things. At present we see indistinctly, as in a mirror, but then face to face. At present I know partially; then I shall know fully, as I am fully known. So faith, hope, love remain, these three; but the greatest of these is love. **Pursue love***...* " (1 Corinthians 13:1-1 Corinthians 14:1)

Mary Kloska's Vocation

For more information about Mary Kloska's vocation, books, icons (Artist Shop), music, podcasts, prayer ministry or to become a monthly donor to support her missionary work, please see:

www.marykloskafiat.com

Blog: http://fiatlove.blogspot.com

Books:

The Holiness of Womanhood:
https://enroutebooksandmedia.com/holinessofwomanhood/

Out of the Darkness:
https://enroutebooksandmedia.com/outofthedarkness/

In Our Lady's Shadow:
The Spirituality of Praying for Priests:
https://enroutebooksandmedia.com/shadow/

A Heart Frozen in the Wilderness:
Reflections of a Siberian Missionary:
https://enroutebooksandmedia.com/frozen/

Mornings With Mary: A Rosary Prayer Book:

https://enroutebooksandmedia.com/morningswithmary/

Raising Children of the Cross:
The Spiritual Formation of Children
https://enroutebooksandmedia.com/childrenofthecross/

House of Gold: Maria Bambina – Morning Star, Mystical Rose
A Marian Consecration to the Immaculate and Sorrowful Infant Heart of Mary
https://enroutebooksandmedia.com/houseofgold/

La Santidad de La Mujer:
https://enroutebooksandmedia.com/lasantidaddelamujer/

Swietosc Kobiecosci:
https://enroutebooksandmedia.com/swietosckobiecosci/

Z Ciemnosci:
Z ciemności… | En Route Books and Media

Fuera de las Tinieblas:
https://enroutebooksandmedia.com/fueradelastinieblas/

Radio Podcasts: https://wcatradio.com/heartoffiatcrucifiedlove/

YouTube VIDEO Podcasts Playlist: http://www.tinyurl.com/marykloska

Artist Shop (Icon prints and other items for sale): http://marykloskafiat.threadless.com
Music CD "FIAT" is also available on all music platforms.

Please consider supporting Mary's Vocation and Ministry by becoming a monthly donor:
Patreon: www.patreon.com/marykloskafiat

OR

Please consider making a donation to the **FIAT Foundation** (a 501 (c) 3 tax-deductible foundation) to help in the printing and distribution of her books for free among the poorest of the poor –with a special emphasis on helping persecuted Christians throughout the world. Please contact Mary through her website (www.marykloskafiat.com) for more information about the FIAT Foundation.

To read about Mary Kloska's work specifically in Pakistan and Afghanistan, please see:
Memoir of Grace
written by her Pakistani Urdu translator Aqif Shahzad
https://enroutebooksandmedia.com/memoirofgrace/

www.ingramcontent.com/pod-product-compliance
Lightning Source LLC
Chambersburg PA
CBHW050850160426
43194CB00011B/2103